SPEAKING TO LEAD

HOW TO MAKE SPEECHES
THAT MAKE A DIFFERENCE

DR JOHN SHOSKY lives in Virginia, where he is the president and CEO of Roncalli Communications, a communications consultancy which he founded in 1993. He was a speechwriter in three US presidential administrations, working at various times in the Executive Office of the President, White House Public Affairs, the Department of Health and Human Services, the Department of Education and the Department of Housing and Urban Development. He has conducted more than 200 workshops on public speaking in North America, Europe, Asia and Africa. In addition, Dr Shosky writes a monthly column on political communication for *Total Politics* magazine. He is currently a visiting senior member of Linacre College, Oxford.

SPEAKING TO LEAD

HOW TO MAKE SPEECHES
THAT MAKE A DIFFERENCE

JOHN SHOSKY

First published in Great Britain in 2010 by

Biteback Publishing Ltd

Heal House

375 Kennington Lane

London

SE11 5QY

ISBN 978-1-84954-013-1

10 9 8 7 6 5 4 3 2 1

A CIP catalogue record for this book is available from the British Library.

Set in Constantia, Frutiger and Trade Gothic

Printed and bound in Great Britain by TJ International Ltd, Padstow

To Michael Anderson

CONTENTS

ACKNOWLEDGEMENTS

I was a debater in high school and college, then a professional speechwriter and university lecturer. I worked in a number of manual labour, blue-collar jobs too, but the kind of jobs where you had to constantly interact with co-workers. That adds up to about forty years of thinking and working in communication. Now, I think about language and its uses every waking moment, and that's no exaggeration. I have developed something the late, great, great, great actor Richard Burton called 'a love of language', a love as deep and passionate, with the same kind of total commitment and proud partnership, that one would have for another person. I study language constantly, verbal and non-verbal, looking for what works and what doesn't. For me, some words are jewels, absorbing in their cut and brilliance, and mystifying in their potential. I also have the great privilege of sharing that work with clients and students in the United States and around the world. This study of language is not limited to one setting or culture. Over the years I have worked with clients in politics, education and business. My work has enabled me to be part of three presidential administrations, and taken me to Europe, Asia and Africa. I've had clients who are executives in Fortune 500 companies. And there have been clients trying to win everything from election to the local council all the way to the presidency of a country.

I often think about those who started me on this path and helped me along the way. So many people have given me the gift of knowledge, or maybe the better word is 'awareness', of different aspects of communication.

Of course, one learns a lot from good speakers such as Abraham Lincoln, Teddy Roosevelt, John and Robert Kennedy, Benjamin Elijah Mays, Martin Luther King, Jr, Ronald Reagan, Margaret Thatcher, Otis Bowen, Don Newman, Louis W. Sullivan, Jesse Jackson, Antonia Novello, Mario Cuomo, Daniel Patrick Moynihan, Tony Blair, William Hague, Nelson Mandela, Azarias Ruberwa Manywa, Diana DeGette, Alphonso Jackson, Roy Bernardi, Dan Hannan and Barack Obama, among others.

I have been extremely fortunate, fabulously lucky, to have worked with some amazing speechwriters. A great writer named Bill Nixon taught me the importance of dedication to language and the dignity of good prose. He also explained what to look for in Hemingway, which led to a new way of reading fiction. Bob Siegrist, who was an original scriptwriter for the *Lone Ranger* radio programme, taught me the importance of oral communication, urging me to listen to radio as a way of learning speechwriting. That was a very valuable lesson, showing me the way to create a world through words in the imagination. Roger Woodworth was a role model for two things: passionate commitment to excellence and learning the journalist's eye for soundbites that explain the story. And he never, ever threw away a newspaper. Bob Longood hated everything I wrote, absolutely everything, and didn't like me much either. He made me a better writer as a result. He also showed me there are words in whisky, and that a gathering in his office on Friday afternoons should not be missed. Tim Pagel taught me how to write through writer's block. Campbell Gardett taught me a reverence for good writing, that the right words had a grace and sanctity that transcended politics and process. Richard Teske, who became my friend and linguistic blood brother, put it all together, showing me how to strive for excellence in every dimension of speechwriting and delivery. He loves words and their history. Ann Molinari and Sarah Carter showed me a great deal about literate discourse and subtle style. From afar, from a distance I would have never attempted to bridge, but from inside a common political effort because I was a lowly novice in a cabinet agency or a second-level writer in White House public affairs, I learned about effectiveness and persuasive discourse from some of President Reagan's amazing speechwriters. For me, that means Peggy Noonan (a speechwriting goddess), David Gergen, Pat Buchanan and Peter Robinson. I really don't know any of them. But they were teachers, nonetheless. Frankly, Reagan himself was a constant teacher for everyone who worked for him, as Noonan and Robinson have documented so capably. So was Mrs Reagan, whom I admire enormously. From earlier on, Ted Sorensen, Arthur Schlesinger, Jr and Richard Goodwin had been top-level teachers of the craft through their speeches and their books. Kathleen Hall Jamieson's scholarship has been formative and expansive with each one of her valuable publications. Recently, working for George W. Bush, Mike Gerson put on a clinic in good speechwriting, especially in the year after 9/11.

There were also some inspiring teachers who gave me an education that worked well for speechwriting. Brother Peter Loehr, Brother Al Blume, Homer Bisel, Ruth Bisel and Father Richard O'Shaunessey at Roncalli High School gave me a solid foundation for debate and public speaking, and O'Shaunessey made poetry and Shakespeare a part of my life. How can one adequately thank teachers who enrich your life in such lasting ways? Tom DeYarman later taught me an enormous amount about economics and audience analysis, which, strangely, had a lot to do with each other. I still talk to him, learning with every conversation. In college, the legendary Jed Richardson patiently taught me about the nature and structure of arguments, and about the history of argumentation. As we drove to debate tournaments or talked in his office, he literally spent hundreds of hours teaching me about Plato, Aristotle, Demosthenes, Isocrates and Cicero. I can hear him now: 'Ooh, Shosky, the Greeks showed that examples are a superior form of proof. They have impact on the brain.' Or: 'Ooh, you know Aristotle, he talked about how to channel thinking, the stuff on enthymemes. That's how to say more with less.' Or: 'Ooh, Socrates knew the power of the right question. Those questions are killers. . . destroyed his opponents.' It was an honour to be his student. I especially loved those late-night asides as we were driving through the Southwestern Desert or the Rocky Mountains: 'John, those guys were smarter than we are' or 'There are great speeches in the Bible' or 'Tell your opponent what he must do. . . define his obligations.' Jed gave every one of us priceless treasures of knowledge and insight. He showed me that speechwriting in ancient Athens and Rome was more advanced and effective than speechwriting today, unlocking a library of ancient wisdom and craftsmanship that provides endless insights. Jed has been a unique person in my life, virtually a father figure in teaching me about how to live life and what to value. Following Jed, Al Johnson's prudential judgement was a source of wonder to me, showing me how rational people make decisions. I have relied on his decision-making ever since. And James J. Unger taught me about strategy, winning arguments and calculated logic. I should add that Aristotle has been a constant teacher throughout all of my time in debate, public speaking and speechwriting. Over the distance of two millennia, he has become a contemporary friend, teacher and mentor.

Speaking of philosophy, I learned an appreciation of language and real sensitivity to the power of words and the logical structure of language, from John Locke, Bertrand Russell, Ludwig Wittgenstein, A. J. Ayer, J. L. Austin, Gilbert Ryle, Pavel Materna, Karel Berka, Peter Strawson, Steven Toulmin and Willard van Orman Quine. In fact, Austin's 'Plea for Excuses' drew me into philosophy for good, forcing me to give up communication theory as my course of study in graduate school and put in my lot with the philosophers, starting almost from scratch. I owe a special debt of gratitude to Antony Flew. He became my friend in graduate school and over the years instilled in me a careful examination of arguments. He created for me an 'ethics of argumentation', especially with his book *Thinking Straight*. He also gave me more confidence, which took years of conversation and hundreds of letters. I learned more about being a teacher from him than from anyone else, because he was so giving of his time. I also learned from him not to give a damn when criticised for my loyalties and my friendships. I love him for being such a good man. In the last decade and a half, I have been guided and challenged by Rom Harré, also my friend and mentor. I love him too, for being such a constant and comprehensive source of knowledge and inspiration. He is a scholar's scholar, with first class work in philosophy, psychology, history of science, linguistics, logic and history. He gave me a powerful and profound gift, a desire to develop a knowledge base in several disciplines and to remain a life-long student. He shared my interests in so many areas: classical music, detective fiction, Spanish wine, the uses of language, the history of logic, politics, New Zealand and Oxford. In fact, in 1997, Rom made it possible for me to become a visiting senior member of Linacre College in Oxford, the single best thing that has ever happened to me. I have been at Linacre during golden years under the wise administration of the principal, Paul Slack. It is a unique college, with a wonderful atmosphere of family, friends and scholarship. I am proud of any association with this great institution.

I want to thank Shane Greer and Iain Dale for suggesting I write this book. I also thank Jonathan Wadman and Biteback Publishing for editing and encouragement. I have been helped with proofreading by Nicky Noble and Lisa Anderson. And I have to mention Matt Richardson, although I'm not sure why. . . probably for legal protection beyond my comprehension. Thanks to Bertram, Kylie and Winston Shosky.

My life has been enriched by many great speakers and friends: Mark Carmel, Shannon Hogan, Carla Proctor, Cliff Henke, Mac Haddow, Gar Dennett, Cheryl Wilson, Cherie Harding, Diana DeGette, David Askman, Lee Christian, Darold Kilmer, Don Newman, Nick Medina, Matt Peterson, Bob Barnard and Tim Childers.

Finally (and thanks for reading all of this), the book is dedicated to the best speaker I've ever heard, Mike Anderson. Mike and I were born on the same day to mothers who were best friends. I'm a few hours older. I've known him as long as I've known anything. And I remember the day, riding on the bus to school, when he suggested that I try out for the debate team. Good idea. . . a fateful decision. Mike has been there for every part of my life, like a second self. We debated together in team competition and I had the best seat in the room, listening to him give hundreds of speeches, with a style that was a cross between Jimmy Stewart and Mr Spock, a relentless logic pleasantly and conversationally shared with the audience, leading to an inevitable, winning conclusion. I've been very lucky indeed to have his friendship.

Winston Churchill (Time & Life Pictures/Getty Images)

INTRODUCTION

This is a book about language, persuasion and action. It is about the art of public speaking, and the science. It is also about the humanity of people relating to each other, trusting each other, believing in each other and learning how to read each other. It is not an 'introduction to public speaking' text. There are plenty of those. Rather, this is a book with a more specialised purpose. It is designed to produce top-quality speeches. . . speeches that make a difference, speeches that change our lives, speeches that produce positive results, speeches that we will never forget. It is a book for those who want to give speeches that do something: touch hearts, change attitudes, initiate policies, inform people, unite audiences, stimulate positive behaviour and channel thinking. Provided the reader is open and 'coachable', this book will make a profound difference in the preparation, composition, performance and impact of public speeches.

There is a demand for the highest level of performance. There are thousands of speeches given every day, in places as far flung as London and Laramie, Prague and Perth, Singapore and Santiago. These speeches may be given in the halls of power or in the waysides of the bush, in high-tech hotel ballrooms or dilapidated colonial classrooms. Some speeches are made in stadiums and from the porches of palaces. Others are spoken on street corners or from flatbed trucks. These speeches may be heard by millions on CNN or by a handful of people far from global telecommunications. Wherever they happen, each speech is a chance to make a difference, to remake the world. These opportunities are virtually sacred moments when a speaker and audience come together to talk and listen for a common purpose. So each speech has a task, a job, a purpose and mission.

Sadly, most speeches do nothing at all. Most speeches are pretty bad, really a waste of time. They fill space with words, but nothing changes. Those speeches are failed opportunities, stolen moments, when the speaker just goes through the motions, mouthing the words, and the audience sits politely (or not) waiting for the end, which doesn't come soon enough. Sadly, many speakers don't care enough to provide a good speech. They just show up, perform and leave, checking the event off the day's schedule and proceeding to the next item of duty. There is no quality control. . . little thought of quality at all. Instantly, the speech is forgotten, if it was actually heard.

In my view, 99 out of 100 speeches fall into the category of 'failed, did nothing'.

If that sounds like pessimism, it is. I sit through too many awful speeches each year. And there is usually too much on the line. Each speech has to be good. An audience travels to a speech, sometimes with inconvenience and expense, in a world where we are increasingly pushed to get the most out of each day, to listen to a speaker. The audience expects the speaker to deliver. It is virtually an act of faith, an unwritten contract, that the speaker will provide the information and motivation necessary for the audience. And most speeches fail to do that, becoming a new form of torture as the audience assesses the possibility of death before the speech is ended. . . their death or the speaker's. By the way, there have been speeches where members of the audience have died during the event, but the death certificates did not read 'Cause: Boredom'. I wonder. . .

However, some speeches, a rare few, transform the world, becoming landmarks in our lives. Those speeches touch the heart and inspire us to greatness. They make our lives richer, nobler and better. We remember large portions of those speeches, often years after they were given. Our internal DNA is restructured. These speeches have what is called 'impact' by speechwriters because they enter the brain, become part of memory, settle in and continue to persuade the listener after the speech is over. They become a part of us, and become part of a shared experience for all of us. Such speeches, like Winston Churchill's 'Blood, Toil, Tears and Sweat' or Dr Martin Luther King, Jr's 'I Have a Dream' have a kind of immortality. Their impact reaches out over time and circumstance to continue their inspirational persuasion. They have an immediacy that makes them relevant again and again, now, right now!

Consider this example. In 1978, the great writer and dissident Alexander Solzhenitsyn spoke at Harvard. The audience expected a denunciation of the Soviet Union. Instead, Solzhenitsyn spoke of the weakness of the West, the failures of capitalism, the complacency of modern life and a cultural decline. He said: 'The Western way of life is less and less likely to become the leading model.' The speech was shocking, dramatic, provocative, disturbing. And, now, decades later, it still gives rise to serious thought about the direction of policy and culture. Sometimes this speech is called 'The Warning to the West'. The words of warning are still powerful, still doing their job.

That is what happens, or, at least, could happen, with every speech! Their shelf life could be decades, or even centuries.

Great speeches may be given in a variety of settings: protest rallies, political campaigns, policy explanations, business meetings with colleagues, union gatherings, weddings, funerals, graduations, commemorations, religious services, or any event in which public words are requested. Anyone could potentially give a memorable speech. Almost everyone is called upon to give a speech at some point, and some people give a speech a day, sometimes even more than that.

If you want to give a great speech, a speech that is authentically and personally your own, with a powerful message for a listening audience, this book may be just what you need. If you care about speeches, and want to learn the 'traits of the greats', this book explores every aspect of public speaking. If you don't want to bore the audience or waste their time, there are techniques to enliven and enhance your public speaking. If you love language, as I do, then we will look at words and their jobs.

There are heroes and villains in these pages. The heroes are speakers or writers who care enough to use language well. The villains are those who arrogantly don't care about quality or performance. The vast majority of readers would fall between these extremes, wanting to get better, hoping to produce a good speech, searching for unification with the audience. As you read these pages, we will journey through a number of ideas and practices that could improve your speeches.

You will learn a lot about yourself. You will also see how language constructs and frames our world. I hope you will indulge the view that, ultimately, those two tasks become the same.

So, this book is a combination of front-line reporting, analysis of the speech process, stories and experiences, how-to manual, anxiety therapy and explication of practices that work. It is grounded in a theory that a speech is always a persuasive argument. . . always. . . and that the speaker strives to be the 'voice of collective assent' and tries to bring the listening audience to 'a point of collective agreement'. There is a firm belief that a speech is audience oriented, that it is always, always, always about the audience. So, in that sense, the book is also a plea for a certain approach to speeches that will make the speaker more effective.

In other words, this book will help produce speeches that change the world. Your speeches!

Azarias Ruberwa Manywa (Michel Euler/AP/PA)

1. THE LANGUAGE OF LEADERSHIP

There are many ways to give a speech. Every day thousands of people stand up and speak. They display idiosyncratic styles. Some speakers are very good; most are not.

Theories about public speaking abound. Some of them are helpful; some are misleading. For example, there are a number of self-help approaches to public speaking that mask the depth and difficulty of the task. You've seen them: 'Public Speaking Made Ridiculously Easy' or 'Blood, Toil, Tears and Sweat-Free Public Speaking'. These books sound hopeful. Maybe they are helpful. But I just don't think the task is easy. Public speaking requires mastery of many skills. If it was easy, then everybody would be good and there would be more top-notch speakers. In fact, if asked to name ten great speakers in the world, few of us could come up with that number (Barack Obama, Tony Blair, Nelson Mandela, William Hague and Nick Clegg should be on anyone's list, and I would easily add David

Cameron, Dan Hannan, Václav Havel, Azarias Ruberwa Manywa and Neil Kinnock). Good speaking is a life-long effort. Public speaking comprises a set of skills that requires comprehension and mastery, much like learning the game of golf. There is a constant need for self-assessment and better performance. No speaker is perfect, no speaker beyond improvement.

The ancient Greeks and Romans recognised this fact. Writers and speakers like Demosthenes and Isocrates, Cicero and Quintilian were students of speaking, just as some people are acutely knowledgeable about football or keen observers of horse racing. They made it a point to know as much as possible and to keep searching for more information, because they found that public speaking was about character, reasoning, persuasion, public appearance, crowd management, politics, business, psychology and science. There was also an element of luck, risk-taking with new approaches or a challenge to fortune by entering unknown rhetorical territory. They knew that rhetoric was a subject matter of infinite depth and complexity. So they made it an area of scholarship, a subject of refined and detailed study. They realised that it involved self-understanding and self-control. It also involved understanding the thinking process and motivation of those who would hear a particular message delivered in a fluid, hopefully manageable context.

Everyone who cares about public speaking looks for patterns, characteristics, elements, categorisations, or pathways to persuasion. And, like football and horse racing, there are numerous competing theories about what works and what doesn't. Speech scholarship doesn't require a PhD or an academic position, although it doesn't exclude them either. Instead, like in Greece and Rome, the general public can be just as aware as professional scholars, and often even more so. And those who speak gain much detailed knowledge from the experience of performance.

This book is my own view about what works. It is actually more than that. It is a set of ideas about what makes a speech effective. I am very interested in what works for an audience. For me, every speech is audience oriented. So I want to know what messages and techniques will persuade a group of people. Over time I have had to experiment with different approaches to public speaking, rejecting ideas that fail to persuade and constructing a foundational process for speeches that work well. A speech must do something. It is extremely frustrating to listen to speeches that are unpersuasive or make little effort to do anything at all. Many speeches are self-indulgent words designed to tell the audience about the speaker or the government, with little effort to meet the needs of the listening audience. Madness! Waste! Self-glorification! Ego!

Now, let me introduce a word that is important to this book: methodology. There are many methodologies for public speaking. David Lloyd George was spontaneous in his approach to public speaking, a sort of inspirational preacher, Winston Churchill very methodical and prepared, relying on patriotism and cold logic. Likewise, there are different ways of doing speeches. I have a few methodological thoughts, some ideas that should govern the composition and delivery of a speech. So in this chapter I will lay out a set of ideas that will explain the development of the rest of the book. Many of these ideas will reappear along the way. You will read repeatedly about the need to persuade, that every speech is about the audience, that every speech must establish a vision, and that speeches should unify an audience with the speaker and with each other. I make no apologies for this repetition; it is a necessary element of explanation. The weaving and re-weaving of ideas acts to bind the book into an eventual coherent viewpoint, or at least that is what I hope will happen. Like many things in life, this may be a mere delusion on my part. But I've noticed that the emergence and re-emergence of certain ideas and themes demonstrates that they are necessary for effective public speaking. And I've noticed that their employment helps create and sustain great speakers who have made a profound difference with their words.

I don't claim this book is the final word on public speaking. That book will never, ever be written. But I hope it is a guide to better speaking for those who care enough to want improvement, for those who recognise the potential power that the right words unleash on history. It would be an honour if this book ignited your own personal interest in the art, science and humanity of public speaking. I expect there will be disagreement with some of what is said. And I might be wrong in some of the boldness of my assertions. But I do know, from experience, that the ideas and approaches that form the content of this book work well. Thoughtful application and steadfast commitment to their use will make a positive difference in almost anyone's public speaking performance.

Unique rhetorical persona

Let's start with a discussion about the speaker. The good news is that you already have some of the traits you need to be a great speaker. The bad news is that you probably are not aware of them. Most speakers haven't developed their rhetorical persona. Each person has one, a singular presence, style and voice. But the persona has not been identified, shaped, branded and fine tuned. Instead, there is a roughness that remains unshaped, a dimness that is unpolished.

I've discovered that most speakers emphasise the wrong traits. So the key is to change the mix, bringing more effective traits to the fore and pushing some others into the background. Winston Churchill is a good case in point. He had a lisp and a grating voice. He spoke in a halting and sometimes hesitant manner. Recognising this, he pushed his voice into the background, allowing his magnificent prose to move to the forefront. He used action verbs, often with Anglo-Saxon lineage, to give his speeches more direct power. He then built a cadence into his words, constructing the speech phrase by phrase, with a light rhythm. His voice could then gain a staccato delivery that made the phrases move and dart like a rapier thrust (Churchill was a fencer in his early life). This allowed his delivery to become more effective and his voice more distinctive. It created a unique rhetorical persona.

Churchill worked hard to develop this persona. And he kept at it throughout his life, never settling for what he had, always striving to make a speech better. I should also mention his great attention to word choice in each sentence, making sure that he had the right word for the job. His calibration of words, choosing the right one for maximum effect, is a great lesson in speech composition.

But you can't be Churchill. No one can. He is a singular figure. But he couldn't have been you either. You are unique in your own way. I find it strange when people say 'I want to speak like David Cameron or Nick Clegg'. My reply is 'You can't'. That is the wrong approach. There are lessons to be learned from great speakers, and even from bad speakers, who can be fascinating in their own self-destructive way. But modelling oneself after a great speaker from the past is usually futile and frustrating for all involved: speaker, staff and audience. Rather, there must be a candid, thorough assessment of each speaker's strengths and weaknesses. Then, the work must centre on making the person the best possible speaker. Each speaker must find his or her unique rhetorical persona. Sometimes this will take years; some people never find it. But it is there, awaiting discovery and shaping.

So let's look for it. Take the following questionnaire. Answer each question in as much depth as possible.

Self-assessment questionnaire
1. What are my strengths as a public speaker?
2. What are my weaknesses?
3. How do I usually prepare for a speech?
4. What can I do to improve?
5. What do I look for in an audience?
6. Is there one idea that sets the course of my life?
7. Is there a way of saying what positions or issues I embody?
8. How does the audience perceive me?
9. For the audience, who am I?
10. For the audience, what do I symbolise?
11. What policies do they think I support?

12. How do I usually dress?
13. What does the audience see when they look at me?
14. What message(s) do my clothes send?
15. What non-verbal gestures do I use?
16. Do I enjoy public speaking? Why or why not?

You can see that some of the questions cluster together. Some of them, like numbers 1 and 2, are about direct self-examination. Numbers 3 and 4 are about speech construction and the way you generally write the speech and what you can do to get better at composition. Number 5 is an attempt to shift your thinking a bit to become more audience oriented. Then, numbers 6 to 11 examine what the audience thinks about you and how they see you. These questions are very helpful because you begin to see the ways that your life story and accomplishments frame the way the audience sees and hears you. Numbers 12 to 15 attract your attention to the extremely powerful messages that are transmitted non-verbally, messages that may overwhelm or complement the verbal message. Finally, number 16 is about your comfort level and enjoyment. The answers should signify improvement over time, although comfort level is not the primary goal, if the speech is audience oriented. As you become more familiar with public speaking and more capable as a speaker, the answer to number 16 should become more positive.

Based on these answers we can begin to identify strengths and weaknesses in both speechwriting and delivery. Adjustments can be made. Further adjustments are inevitable. But when the core parts come together, you will have a voice and style all of your own. This is how you develop your unique rhetorical persona.

Voice of collective assent

In reading one of the books by the great scholar Kathleen Hall Jamieson I came across a phrase I liked. She said the speaker is the 'voice of collective assent'. I tried to work with that phrase, exploring what it meant and how the phrase could describe the communication process of message and feedback, delivered through certain channels and contexts, overcoming barriers and interference. I'm not sure she meant it this way, but I felt that the phrase described the purpose, role and position of the speaker.

One of my high school friends is currently a member of the American Congress. Her name is Diana DeGette, and she is a dynamic, yet low-key, conversational speaker. In my mind she embodies the 'voice of collective assent', even though her political stance is often left of centre and therefore a source of disagreement for those who have a different viewpoint. Her pleasant personality and sincere conviction often win over the most ardent opponents. Effective speeches do that. They build bridges.

Speakers and audiences have roles. The audience is there to listen to the speaker, evaluate both speaker and message, and make a decision about the future. The job of the audience is to listen, to analyse and to think. Clapping and other forms of approval are part of the dynamic. Heckling and hostility may also be a part of the speech (see Chapter 5). The speaker also has a role: to become the voice of collective assent. This means that the speaker is 'the speaker' because this person can deliver a persuasive message to the audience that will unite them in joint action, and will also unite them with the speaker. The person who speaks must have the ability to give voice to the hopes, aspirations and dreams of the listening audience. The speaker must have the ability to present a clear and compelling message that will inspire the audience and begin a process of unification. The speaker becomes a leader because of an ability to represent the best interests and the needs of the listening audience, and to suggest a credible and motivating set of actions that will create a path forward for the audience. The speaker is a unique figure because he or she has the ability to do all of this. That is the role, the position, of the speaker. Anyone who cannot do this will create confusion, division and dissatisfaction within the audience. A person who cannot perform the job of speaker has no business being given that role.

So speaker selection is an art, an appreciation of the powers and requirements of a speaker. Someone should be invited to speak because of what they can and will do.

Perhaps some of the problems with contemporary speeches arise from the fact that the wrong people are asked to talk. Perhaps position, celebrity or friendship govern invitations for conferences or other events more than they should. Perhaps a better criterion for selection of a speaker is audience outcome.

Persuasion

Years ago I had a professor, Philip Emmert, who taught a simple thesis: every speech is a persuasive speech. We fought with him in class about this for an entire semester. But through the disagreements I became a convert to his viewpoint. For him, every speaking opportunity is a chance to persuade. He said that we would soon realise the truth of his view. But he also said that the depth of this realisation would reveal itself over time and begin to haunt us.

I think he is right about all of that. He is certainly right that speeches in politics and business are all about persuasion. Yes, they are!

Typically, in a book about public speaking, there is the claim that speeches come in two varieties, informative and persuasive. An informative speech is supposed to be composed primarily of information, stating a position on an issue or explaining how to do something, like fix a problem or assemble a piece of furniture. The informative speech is recognised by the focus on the information, rather than an attempt to ask the audience to do something. Because when you ask the audience for action or behaviour change, you have then entered the zone of the persuasive speech, which moves beyond information to advocate something: a change of attitude, adoption of an action, a request for a vote, acceptance of a contract bid, or anything else that would alter the current course of events and change the direction of the future.

Emmert's argument was that even information demands an exercise in persuasion. The audience has to believe the information is correct, that it is true, that the speaker is knowledgeable and trustworthy, that the speaker is an expert on the subject and that any decisions based on this information will be better than deciding in ignorance.

So, if Emmert is right, and I think he is, then every speech is an act of persuasion. That persuasion extends to all messages in the speech, verbal and non-verbal. There is no such thing as a purely informative speech. There is no value-free or persuasively neutral speaking situation.

Point of collective agreement

So, what is the speaker trying to persuade the audience to do? The answer is to change. The speaker wants the audience to adopt an attitude, change a belief, initiate an action or do anything else that an audience can. The speaker effects this by bringing the audience to a point of collective agreement with a persuasive argument.

I like that phrase, 'point of collective agreement'. It is an imaginary point for the speaker's reference. It represents a position where the audience is unified with the speaker and in agreement that something, whatever it is, must be done. Not everyone in the audience has to get to this point, and in almost every speech there will be people who will oppose joining the speaker or the audience in collective agreement about a problem or issue. But this ideal is a goal to which the speaker will attract as many people as possible. Some speakers have little trouble generating collective agreement, people of goodwill like Desmond Tutu or the Dalai Lama.

Sometimes an audience needs little to move them to the point of collective agreement. Here is an example of unification. At the time of writing Poland is in mourning for its President, Lech Kaczyński, and other government and national leaders who died in a plane crash on 10 April 2010. Speaking on the day of the President's funeral, the speaker of the Polish parliament, Bronisław Komorowski, said: 'There are certain moments in the life of a nation, when we know we are together, that our feelings and our emotions are one. The catastrophe of that aeroplane was one of them.' The audience is already one, unified in grief and sadness.

On the other hand, some speeches are controversial and never achieve complete consensus, and perhaps generate more disagreement. On the day of President Kaczyński's funeral, 18 April 2010, Pope Benedict XVI met eight victims of sexual abuse in Malta. The problem of child abuse in the Catholic Church is horrifying and terrible, a genuine crisis of faith. The Pope spoke about his efforts to address child abuse within the Church. Surely this was a painful meeting, and one that was difficult for the immediate audience and for a larger world audience. It may not have generated much unification with the speaker, the Pope, who faces an ocean of doubt and disappointment. The *Washington Post* reported on 19 April the comments of Peter Isely, spokesperson for the Survivors' Network of Those Abused by Priests (SNAP). He said: 'It's easy to promise; it's hard to deliver, especially in a rigid, ancient, secretive all-male monarchy. Not a single adult should feel relieved until strong steps are actually taken, not promised, that will prevent future child sex crimes and cover-ups.' For Mr Isely, it will take more than one speech, however well crafted, before the Pope can unify his audience. Perhaps it can never be done. But even in the swirling demands that the Church cooperate more with civilian authorities, expose child molesters for prosecution and implement better safeguards to protect young people from paedophiles, at least one person was led to a point of collective agreement by the Pope's words. There are small victories, changes of attitude, however humble. Lawrence Grech, who had been victimised as a child, said: 'I lost my faith in the last twenty years. I told [the Pope]: "You can fill up the emptiness, fill up what the priests took from me when I was young." This experience is going to change my life. Now I can go to my daughter and say: "I believe."'

Now, how to get the audience to the point of collective agreement? Well, the speaker will use every credible and appropriate technique in the speech. However, as a paradigm of the process, I believe the speech starts out by presenting a thesis and then developing an argument to channel the thinking of an audience. The point of collective agreement is where the flow of the speech takes the audience. It is at this point, when the audience is there, that the action step is proposed. Because the audience is in agreement that something must be done, the next question is this: 'OK, so do what?' That is how you know you've reached the point of collective agreement. The audience has joined together in believing that there is a problem and it must be addressed. That is the point of collective agreement. . . that is what they are in agreement about. So now the action step of proposed solutions follows. Then the conclusion ends the speech with a motivating sense of urgency.

Make a difference

Each speech has the potential to make a difference. That is the allure of a speech. . . it can be a landmark moment that changes the world forever. Speakers can do a tremendous amount of good for the audience and the community at large.

There is also an impact on the speaker. Sometimes successful speakers talk about the feedback they receive at the podium. As the audience comes together internally and also joins with the speaker, there is measurable, forceful feedback. It is a mixture of acceptance, agreement, affirmation and action. There is appreciation for the speaker and the event. The audience is prepared to follow and to act. They are ready to make a difference. Sometimes speakers talk about holding the audience 'in their hands' and for 'feeling one with them'. That does happen. And it is a tangible experience. The speaker can feel the growing force of the positive feedback, and can feel it slowly slip away as the audience lets go after the speech. And at that moment, the moment of departure, the speaker understands the experience of joining together with a group of people in common purpose.

It takes a great amount of courage to try to make a difference. I discovered this during the presidential election in the Democratic Republic of the Congo in 2006. There, candidates took their lives in their hands, risking death for good governance, an end to corruption and the establishment of the rule of law. One man I came to greatly admire is Azarias Ruberwa Manywa, who was one of four vice presidents of DR Congo at that time. His speeches often took him to refugee camps. On one occasion, where rival armies had slain unarmed civilians fleeing the violence on both sides of the Congo–Rwanda border, he spoke with the coffins laid out in front of the podium, hundreds of them. His very presence was a provocation to the armed rebels. But he brought comfort and solace with his soothing words. He laid his life on the line to give his speech because he understood the power of the right words in a time of armed conflict, especially within a failed state.

Ruberwa's speeches highlight the great power and the vast danger of public speaking. If you are effective, you are a threat to someone. There are so many great speakers who have been silenced with a bullet: Mahatma Gandhi, John Kennedy, Martin Luther King, Jr, Robert Kennedy, Yitzhak Rabin and Benazir Bhutto, to name a few. You have to admire those who have the fortitude to enter the public arena. I know I do. But we also cannot let danger stop positive change. That is a lesson to learn from their courage and sacrifice.

The traits of the greats

Most speeches, the vast majority, are instantly forgettable. But some speeches really do change the world. They endure, inspiring new generations of speakers and thinkers.

How? Well, in a number of ways. Great speeches may capture a moment in time. Some visionary comments move a debate or a nation forward. Landmark speeches articulate important ideas.

And some great speeches touch the heart with authentic humanity, often expressing appropriate joy or grief. These speeches stand apart. They are worthy of comment and acute examination. Great speeches have historical value, becoming a referential benchmark.

Great speeches are examples of what can be done when the right words are expressed at a crucial moment. So I applaud those who remind us of the power of public speaking. For example, over a two-week period in July 2007, the *Guardian* generously offered fourteen of the greatest speeches of the twentieth century in booklet form. These speeches are now online at www.guardian.co.uk/ theguardian/series/greatspeeches. In July 2008, the *Daily Telegraph* ranked the twenty-five greatest political speeches of all time, and these too are available online, at www.telegraph.co.uk/ news/newstopics/uselection2008/barackobama/2446608/Top-25-political-speeches-of-all-time.html.

These rankings reproduce the words themselves and offer short biographical backgrounds of the speakers and the history behind the events. But we should do more to examine the techniques or traits that made the speeches memorable. Great speeches achieve a sort of immortality because they change the course of history. We can see how they do this through identification of common elements – 'traits of the greats'. Here are a few.

1. Vision

Great speeches almost always have a vision of the future. They compare a known present with a possible future. Those that persuasively articulate a better future help people visualise, then actualise, change. One of the most famous examples is Ronald Reagan's continual reference to the 'shining city on the hill', a future where America remains a beacon of hope for the world. Dr Martin Luther King, Jr had a dream he shared with others: 'With this faith we will be able to transform the jangling discords of our nation into a beautiful symphony of brotherhood.' Margaret Thatcher spoke at Brighton in 1975 of freedom, of choice and personal fulfilment: 'Let me give you my vision: a man's right to work as he will, to spend what he earns, to own property, to have the state as servant and not as master – these are the British inheritance.' When George H. W. Bush was criticised for not having a vision, the 'vision thing' became more than an issue. Its absence was fatal.

2. Conviction
Great speakers believe in their vision. President Kennedy said: 'We will pay any price, bear any burden, meet any hardship, support any friend, oppose any foe, in order to assure the survival and the success of liberty.' That is conviction. Prime Minister Thatcher said: 'The lady's not for turning.' That is what conviction sounds like. There is no doubt, just confident articulation of direction and purpose. Conviction is not to be confused with stubbornness or short-sightedness.

3. Hope
President Reagan instructed his speechwriters to make his words uplifting, to give people hope, to help them believe that the future could be better. Time and again, audiences identify with those who offer a positive message of hope. One of the most stunning examples was offered by Pope John Paul II in 1983 in the Polish town of Częstochowa, home to the Jasna Góra monastery. He spoke to the large audience in a kind of code, comparing Our Lady of Jasna Góra to Poland itself: 'You who have been given to us by Providence for the defence of the Polish nation, accept this evening this call of the Polish youth together with this Polish Pope, and help us to persevere in hope!' Remember also the idealistic hope offered by Woodrow Wilson in fighting for America's involvement in the League of Nations. Tony Blair spoke with a strong emphasis on hope and empowerment in his speeches. So did Barack Obama in his presidential campaign.

4. Unity
Great speeches heal division. Great speeches unite. They use the power of speech as action. Speeches that fragment the audience

with the words of class warfare or the use of economic or ethnic division, or inflame an audience with vile hatred are dangerous and ultimately self-defeating. Such an approach does not win elections any more in American politics and it is certainly not sustainable in 21st-century Britain. Nelson Mandela understood this when he said in his inaugural address in 1994 that 'we must therefore act together as a united people, for national reconciliation, for nation-building, for the birth of a new world'. That language contains the inclusion and respect that flows from unifying words. In my mind, the template for healing division is a phrase once used by the Oxford philosopher Derek Parfit: 'what we together do'. Every great speech is about what we could do together – all of us. No one can be expendable. No one can, or should, be left out.

5. Collective assent

Great speeches make the speaker the 'voice of collective assent'. This means that the speaker gives voice to the hopes, aspirations and dreams of the audience, becoming the oracle of the words that others would say, if they could. I believe this is the underlying greatness of Pericles's Funeral Oration, Abraham Lincoln's Gettysburg Address or President Mandela's wonderful inaugural address. Collective assent can happen even with a hostile crowd. If you listen to a tape of Neil Kinnock's remarks at Bournemouth in 1985, you can actually hear the audience's affirmation when he says: 'You can't play politics with people's jobs and with people's services or with their homes.' He becomes one with the audience, in his own words: 'The voice of the real people with real needs.' In the dark hours of May 1940, Winston Churchill did become the voice of the people in the 'Blood, Toil, Tears and Sweat' speech, as he did later in June of that year, when he rallied the nation for the Battle of Britain, predicting this would be 'their finest hour'.

6. Principle

Great speeches advocate equality, dignity and respect. They stand for moral purpose and embody moral clarity. There is a feeling expressed among certain historians that a great speech can emerge from even the most difficult situations, if the remarks are grounded in universal principles. Time and circumstance change, but the principles remain. A profound, moving example of this use of morality and articulation of rights is the speech Václav Havel gave on New Year's Day in 1990. Contrasting the climate of lies and violence under communism in Czechoslovakia with the expectations of a society ruled by law and respect for human rights, Havel spoke of the need for truth in speech, of the need to create a 'moral atmosphere', of a country that emphasised responsibility, freedom and democracy. And that speech had a unifying theme of moral conduct, overtly referencing two great figures in Czech history: Tomáš Masaryk and Comenius.

7. Action

Great speeches inspire action. Probably none did this more effectively than those of Theodore Roosevelt. His speeches about 'The Strenuous Life' or 'The Man in the Arena' are models of personal responsibility and political participation. Roosevelt argued that each person could make a difference, but he or she had to try, to take a risk, to enter the arena and work for the betterment of others. That action can be non-violence, as articulated by Mahatma Gandhi, the educator and theologian Dr Benjamin Elijah Mays or his Morehouse College student Dr Martin Luther King, Jr. The power of action is part of Robert Kennedy's moving speech at the University of Cape Town in 1966:

> Each time a man stands up for an ideal, or acts to improve the lot of others, or strikes out against injustice, he sends forth a tiny ripple of hope, and crossing each other from a million different centres of energy and daring, those ripples build a current which can sweep down the mightiest walls of oppression and resistance.

8. Compressing the message

All great speeches are known by a phrase that condenses the message and the entire argument of the speech. In 1953, Kwame Nkrumah spoke of Ghana's liberation as 'the motion of destiny'. John Kennedy's *'Ich bin ein Berliner'* is a fantastic display of one sentence expressing the whole point of the speech. Earl Spencer's comment about Princess Diana as 'the most hunted person of the modern age' abbreviates the speech in a haunting sentence. And we can't forget Reagan's demand in 1987: 'Mr Gorbachev, tear down this wall!'

These elements of great speeches deserve notice. They are an important part of what makes a speech memorable. While they have a sort of immortality, great speeches are human creations, the product of the speakers and their writers, a skilful triumph over cliché and dreary prose. We remember them because they will not let us forget. Great speeches demand to be heard. And, as current interest in these speeches demonstrates, we still seem to be listening.

Robert Kennedy (Getty Images)

2. AUDIENCE ANALYSIS

A speech is human interaction, one to one, between the speaker and every member of the audience. Great speakers know this. They count on it. The speaker and audience reach out to each other, often with great courage: Anwar Sadat before the Knesset, Ronald Reagan speaking to students at Moscow State University, Nelson Mandela at his inauguration or Benazir Bhutto that fateful day in Rawalpindi. A speaker asks for faith, trust and belief. The audience evaluates the speaker for character, honesty and commitment. In this interaction, one side is more important than the other. Every speech is always, always, always about the audience. A great speech is not about the speaker showing up and settling in, their comfort level, ego, CV, position of power or celebrity status. A speech must never be simply and solely about the speaker. The audience is sitting there, asking this question: 'What's in it for me?' If the speaker is not answering that question, then something is horribly wrong.

Of course, not every speaker realises this. Sadly, disappointingly, disastrously, many see a speaking opportunity as a chance to fill the air with worldly wisdom, exposing the audience to a disappointing display of narcissism. Many speakers love to hear themselves talk (often you can tell the narcissism level by the length of sentences – clause after clause, the speaker stretching out the lifespan to the last adjective or adverb, unable to let a sentence go. . . no assisted sentencide). Some spoil the event by boring the audience, who may feel left out or even ignored by the speaker. You've seen it – the audience might just as well have stayed at home (many of them will wish they had). Some speakers tell an audience what they already know, failing to make the speech interesting while also failing to move the debate forward into new territory. Some speakers elaborately say nothing at all. There is a memorable moment when Socrates is asked to evaluate just such a speech and this is his verdict: 'Words, words, words.' They were words that did nothing. . . just pretty phrases and clever quips that evaporated immediately from memory. And audiences can become alienated by conceited, thoughtless, inconsiderate, empty or dull speakers, actually loathing them, turning against speaker and message, and avoiding future encounters. The audience is actually persuaded to dislike the speaker. . . by the speaker!

For the audience, the common trait of all these problems is irrelevance – irrelevance of the message to them. Effective speeches that make a difference are always judged by their impact on the audience. Effective speeches are intended to engage the audience, make them think, weigh alternatives and feel emotions. Every effective speech is a persuasive enterprise, hoping to motivate attitude change and/or action. In an effective speech, the division between speaker and audience disappears; the speaker becomes the voice of collective assent, representing the hopes, aspirations and dreams of the audience. And great speeches are remembered long after the event, with phrases and whole paragraphs still in the mind, working away, doing the job, months and years later. Effective speeches unite an audience with the speaker, joining in common cause to make a difference. Perhaps the worst possible evaluation of a speech is this: 'I don't really remember what was said.' And the best possible evaluation is this: 'She's right. Let's take action.'

So, if persuasion is the goal and the audience the target, then the purpose of every speech is to use every available, credible, authentic and effective means to skilfully bring the audience to a point of collective agreement with the speaker, which means that the audience is willing to do what the speakers asks, and do it right away. . . right now. . . immediately.

Therefore, every speech must be the product of two factors: the speaker's message and audience analysis. The message must be framed to motivate the audience. And that doesn't happen by chance. It happens because the speaker carefully weighs the impact of each word, each gesture for its persuasive appeal to the audience.

From the speaker's perspective

It is shocking how little time is spent by most speakers and speechwriters on audience analysis. Yes, the speechwriter usually asks a few questions or looks up some information (although that sometimes doesn't happen, because many speeches are prepared and given absolutely blind to the needs of the audience). The standard questions – Who will introduce the speaker? How many people are in the audience? Where are they from? What is the purpose or mission of the organisation? What are they interested in? What do they want from us? – are just the beginning of a process of information-gathering and message formation, not its completion. A successful speech demands a thorough, comprehensive understanding of the audience that is virtually limitless, bordering on paranoia. The speaker must know everything about everybody, which is impossible. But the more you know, the better the speech can be crafted to do the job.

Here are some things to keep in mind.

1. Identify the real target audience

Who is the real audience? Are they the people in the room, or the people watching on C-Span, CNN or the BBC? Is the press the intended audience? A speech must be targeted to specific audiences, ideally just one audience so the message construction can be completely consistent, coherent and successful without redirection, contradiction or confusion. Yet, in our global media age, identifying one target audience is not so simple. When Gordon Brown spoke to a joint session of Congress in America on 4 March 2009, who was the intended audience? Was it the members of Congress? The Obama administration? The American people? The British people? The world community? If the answer is 'yes' in varying strengths to all of these possibilities, which I am sure must be right, then Brown's speech might have a multiplicity of inter-related and layered messages, each directed to a specific audience. Constructing such a speech is a difficult task. But whether one audience or many, every word, every argument, every policy proposal must be there to persuade the targeted audience, whoever that may be. That means having a clear idea about the targeted audience, even if that audience shifts and is not the same one throughout the entire speech.

2. Demographics

The more we know about the audience, the better. Demographic information is important, vitally so. We must know about age range, education, gender, background, ethnicity, income levels, class identification and more, much more. This information should help you understand the values, concerns and hopes of the audience. A thorough approach requires getting beyond classifications that are basic and often fallacious. Dig, dig, dig! Never stop until the speech is given!

3. Build on shared beliefs

Too often, a speech is really a resume: 'I voted this way,' 'I met with your CEO,' 'I authored this legislation.' Often we hear speeches like this: talking points about personal accomplishments that are nothing but pandering to the audience. This often happens when staff prepare speeches on specific topics for single-issue audiences ('You are speaking to military veterans. Here are some talking points on your record on defence spending'). The audience should already know that stuff. They are often insulted that the speaker has to go over the old facts and the historical background, prominently featuring votes or press releases. If the audience doesn't know the basics, then it is the job of the introductory speaker to make all this clear. The job of the main speaker is to go quickly beyond the resume, showing solidarity with the audience through word choice, references and shared values. Push into new territory. Expand the frontiers of knowledge. Look to the future. It is not the resume that counts now; it is the way things are said, the word choices, the new ideas and the values embraced by the speaker. Show commitment and knowledge by the examples cited, the reports referenced and the steps to be taken in the months ahead. Value-sharing should be organic, not grafted on. An effective speech unites the audience to move forward. If you have to spend the speech selling yourself to the audience, then you are auditioning, not leading. Leaders find common ground and then go from there. In Margaret Thatcher's 'The Lady's Not for Turning' speech in 1980, there is a powerful section about the 'instincts' of the British people, the values they prize: freedom, family, pride, hard work, safety, participating in the building and history of a great nation. She has a haunting line: 'If we cannot trust the deepest instincts of our people we should not be in politics.' That speech identified shared values and used them to persuade a nation to change direction and policy.

4. Reach out to opinion leaders
Every audience has leaders who help form the attitudes and beliefs of those in attendance. Find out who they are. Know where they are seated. Use them in the speech. Perhaps even mention them by name. When one of these opinion leaders nods in agreement,

hundreds of members in the audience may take a cue. By proxy, the opinion leaders can help you persuade the listening audience. Their credibility and standing are useful tools to help persuade the audience. Opinion leaders can help you do your job. Speaking of Lady Thatcher, in December 2002, she received the Clare Boothe Luce Award from the Heritage Foundation, a Washington think tank. Standing behind her as she gave her speech of acceptance were the then Vice President, Dick Cheney, and the foundation's president, Ed Feulner. The cameras often panned the audience for their reaction. As either Cheney or Feulner agreed with Thatcher, you could see a split second later hundreds of heads nodding. It was like a wave of agreement, starting at the front of the room and moving outward.

5. Mention names

Sometimes it is good to mention people in the audience, to openly use the affection or esteem of those in the audience to underscore a point or to stand as an example to support your message. If the audience loves them, they may share the love with the speaker, too. In one of history's most famous speeches, Socrates mentions names at his trial both of those in attendance who confirm his words and those who shamefully told the lies that led to his conviction. You can bet that Plato and other supporters were nodding their heads.

6. Test the message

While constructing the speech, talk to people who are similar to the audience. Run the message by them. Get input on word choice or policy reference. Even construct informal focus groups to examine the power and impact of the speech. Get feedback before the speech. Ask the organisation contacts very specific questions about the content: 'Ideally, in the best of all possible worlds, what exactly would you like the speaker to say?' Then run drafts by trusted members of the organisation and audience, gauging their reaction. Do this repeatedly to make sure the message will work well.

7. Adjust to feedback during the speech

The audience analysis continues during the speech. The speaker should be finely tuned to the reactions of the audience. Every person, every face, tells a story. Emphasis and eye contact must be adjusted throughout. You should search out those who are persuadable, yet are still not there. Too often the speaker looks for a friendly face, a face in agreement, and finds comfort there. He or she remains fixed on those won over, rather than working the audience for more converts. You should not waste much time on those in agreement – they are at the point of collective agreement already. Just do enough to keep them there. The search must be for those who have yet to decide. Talk to them. Give them more time and attention. Work it! Win them over!

These are just a few ideas about audience analysis. Each speech has its own set of needs and demands. Audiences are unique. So matching the message with the audience is always a challenge, and never the same one twice. That's why every good speech is hard work. The audience can never be taken for granted.

One of the best examples of audience analysis was John Kennedy's speech at the Berlin Wall in 1963. He started by mentioning the popular mayor, Willy Brandt, and the Chancellor, Konrad Adenauer. He then joined with the audience, became the voice of collective assent, with the words '*Ich bin ein Berliner*'. This was a speech all about the audience there and the audience over the wall. Near the end, he said:

> So let me ask you . . . to lift your eyes beyond the dangers of today, to the hopes of tomorrow, beyond the freedom merely of this city of Berlin, or your country of Germany, to the advance of freedom everywhere, beyond the wall to the day of peace with justice, beyond yourself and ourselves to all mankind.

He was persuasive. The audience did more than that. At the

conclusion of the speech, thousands of people rushed the Berlin Wall and tried to destroy it with their fingers. The riot squad had to be called out. And that speech resonated over the years, until finally sledgehammers and bulldozers accomplished what fingers and anger could not. Kennedy understood his audience. That speech shows how it is done.

From the audience's perspective

Again, every speech is always, always, always about the audience. So, what is it that the audience wants? What is an audience hoping to obtain by listening to a speech? Many speakers ignore such questions, allowing their speeches to become exhibitions of indulgent self-gratification, even barely disguised self-glorification. Why should an audience put up with a speech that is more posing and performance than unification and leadership? Given the constant, overwhelming demands on our time and the difficulties in attending a speech, or even listening to one through media transmission, why would anyone pay attention to a speech or a speaker? Each member of the audience is asking: 'What's in it for me?' The answers to these questions tell us about audience expectations. . . expectations that must be met for the speech to be a success. And a speech is successful only if it meets the expectations of the audience.

For example, when New York Senator Robert Kennedy travelled to South Africa and spoke at the University of Cape Town on 7 June 1966, there was a large audience of 18,000 people. There were high expectations, considerable buzz. There were also warnings, official discouragement and worse. Kennedy was told that the speech would lead to support for radicals, leftists, freedom fighters, even international communist movements. He might instigate violence with horrifying consequences.

Kennedy responded with a deeply moving, profoundly inspirational speech urging individual empowerment and social action to end government oppression, disenfranchisement, poverty and violence. He unified the audience by appealing to their humanity, courage and aspirations. This speech resonated then, and still commands attention in our time.

But the audience didn't know all that before the speech. So, why did they come, especially given the dangers of travel, the possibility of violence and the possible repercussions of retribution?

1. Speaker assessment

Robert Kennedy had star power long before Bono and Barack. Even though he was at the beginning of middle age, his attitude and idealism appealed to those much younger. His mere presence was a draw for students in those tense times. Some people came because the speech was an event, a political statement. Showing up sent a message to the government and supporters of apartheid. But many came because they wanted to examine and gauge Kennedy's message and the man giving it. Why? Well, Aristotle said one of the major reasons for attending a speech is to assess the character of the speaker. A speech is more than art or science; it is a human interaction. The audience wants to understand the speaker and his motives. Each person in the audience wants to know if the speaker is honest, trustworthy, credible and believable. Each person wants to know if they can have faith in the promises and commitment of the speaker. Many in Senator Kennedy's audience probably worried beforehand that he had come to Cape Town for his own personal benefit, perhaps for political gain, or for top-of-the-hour publicity. The audience needed to know that his advocacy was genuine and sincere, reflecting a dedication to liberty and freedom for all people. And they wanted to decide whether or not to heed *his* call to action, whether to recognise him as an opinion leader and to follow that lead. They wanted hope that apartheid would end, that each person would be granted the full rights of citizenship.

The philosopher John Locke once spoke of the 'politics of trust'. That is a great phrase for describing democracy and commitment to constitutional government. But is also a good description of the human bonding between an audience and a speaker. The presence of both speaker and audience was an exercise of mutual trust, with mutual risk.

2. Unification with the speaker
The audience wants to join with the speaker, to become one. So, the audience must accept the speaker as an equal, as a friend, and allow the speaker to become their spokesperson, giving voice to the needs, demands and aspirations of the audience.

Senator Kennedy did this immediately. He started the speech with these words: 'We stand here in the name of freedom.' Note the pronoun and the collective purpose. He assumed the role of speaker for the audience, becoming the voice of those 18,000 people, and of everyone who agreed with his next words:

> At the heart of that Western freedom and democracy is the belief that the individual man, the child of God, is the touchstone of value and all society, groups, the state, exist for his benefit. Therefore the enlargement of liberty for individual human beings must be the supreme goal and the abiding practice of any Western society.

3. Respect
Unification is an act of respect, maybe the ultimate act of solidarity. Each speech must reflect an inner Aretha Franklin: 'R-E-S-P-E-C-T'. That respect must be shown in approach and style. Modern audiences want a conversation between the speaker and the audience. The members of the audience do not want false flattery, pandering, patronising, lecturing, hectoring, sermonising or self-indulgence from the speaker. Each person wants to believe that the speaker recognises their importance, equality, worth and uniqueness.

Senator Kennedy had a conversation with his audience. After discussing the need to recognise the human rights of each person in each country, he spoke of the different 'evils' in various countries, and said that the commonality in each case was to recognise that the troubles are man made. Therefore he appealed to the audience of students and activists to join with other young people everywhere 'to wipe away the unnecessary sufferings of our fellow human beings at home and particularly around the world'. I would draw attention to the last prepositional phrase. Even if South Africa ended apartheid, the work would not be done across the globe. Where suffering still exists, 'particularly around the world', then we must transcend our nationality and circumstances and act to help anyone in need. This language bridged any division between those in attendance and those unable to come. The message was global. So was the solution: international citizenship and compassionate action.

4. *Information*

Respect also means sharing information. The speaker is invited because of his or her expertise and experience. By 1966, Kennedy was a civil rights leader, an advocate for the poor and disenfranchised. His wealth and background created doubts about his commitment. But his personality, sincerity and message overcame those doubts. I should also add that he had a strange humility that is noticeable throughout this speech. He doesn't come across as a powerful and influential figure. He just talks to the audience in a very personal and direct way, friend to friend.

Audiences don't want to be told what they already know, unless the speech is just an exercise in energising true believers, nor do they want a list of problems. Rather, audiences want to learn and grow. They want the speaker to tell them something new, to move the debate on issues forward. They are looking for new viewpoints, data, positions, policies or proposals. They want to see the world afresh. This creates a tricky problem for speakers, because there is the temptation to try to 'educate' and lecture the audience. That might become preachy or professorial. Rather, the conversational aspect of the speech must be maintained. The tone must be one of sharing insights and vision, not assuming the role of the 'pencil-neck know-it-all.'

Kennedy shared his perspective of the international situation. He spoke of 'the danger of futility; the belief there is nothing one man or one woman can do against the enormous array of the world's ills – against misery and ignorance, injustice and violence'. In his view, there were ample examples of one person making a difference. He also spoke of the 'danger . . . of practicality', of compromise between principle and necessity. He argued that there was no inconsistency between idealism and realism. And he spoke of a third danger: 'timidity'. He said each person must have the moral courage to do that which is right and just.

5. Solutions

The audience wants solutions. They don't want cheap talk. The audience wants plausible, credible and workable answers. This audience knew that any action could be deadly. So it was time for serious talk about realistic actions.

Kennedy offered a solution that was direct and confrontational: personal action against injustice. He said:

> One answer is the world's hope; it is to rely on youth . . . It demands the qualities of youth: not a time of life but a state of mind, a temper of the will, a quality of the imagination, a predominance of courage over timidity, of the appetite for adventure over the love of ease.

He told the audience that the choice was theirs. But it was young people who would make the difference in the generations to come. He added:

> As I have seen, and as I have said – in Europe, in Asia, in Latin America and now in South Africa – it is the revolutionary world we live in; and thus, I have said in Latin America, in Asia, in Europe and in the United States, it is the young people who must take the lead.

So, what must they do? Have moral courage. Stand up against oppression – not once or twice, but always, everywhere. No other action would be as effective. And Kennedy was with them. Claiming it a 'privilege' to be part of 'the world's largest younger generation', he stressed that the work lay ahead to build a better future. Quoting his late brother, he said: 'The energy, the faith, the devotion which we bring to this endeavour will light our country and all who serve it – and the glow from that fire will truly light the world.'

6. Hope

Such comments inspire and empower. They provide direction and focus. They also meet another need. Audiences want to know that the future will be better than the past. They want hope. They want to know that their actions will make a difference.

Kennedy understood this and, in one of the most famous and exciting passages in speechmaking, he said:

> Each time a man stands up for an ideal, or acts to improve the lot of others, or strikes out against injustice, he sends forth a tiny ripple of hope, and crossing each other from a million different centres of energy and daring, those ripples build a current that can sweep down the mightiest walls of oppression and resistance.

7. Preparation

None of this happens if the speaker is unprepared. Some people, especially some politicians and celebrities, believe that '90 per cent is just showing up'. Wrong! The audience wants preparation, professionalism and serious effort. The audience wants respect and regard. One way of showing respect is the speaker's commitment to an understandable, concise, thoughtful, well-crafted and well-delivered message. Lack of clarity is sloppy and confusing. And no one wants to waste time. If the speaker wastes the time of the audience he shows disregard and arrogance. Frankly, lack of preparation is deeply insulting. Members of the audience will perceive the insult. A person who is invited to speak assumes a role of voice and leadership. A lack of preparation works against the speaker, almost in direct proportion to the number of minutes wasted or confusing words mangled in tortured sentences. Over the course of the speech the audience becomes more and more offended by the lack of professionalism and commitment to the event.

Kennedy could have just 'shown up'. But instead he thought about the needs of the audience and met them. He understood that each speech is an opportunity to change the world, especially when that speech is made in a time and place that crushed freedom for the majority of a country's people. Kennedy sent forth a ripple of hope. The words are still working more than forty years later, their echo heard throughout the world, lately across Africa and America, and in Iran, Burma and China. It is a model speech, both in terms of delivery and content, a masterpiece of oral prose and inspirational vision. In my view, it is in the top division of speeches, sharing the same virtues as the Sermon on the Mount, Abraham Lincoln's remarks at Gettysburg, Mahatma Gandhi's statement at the trial in Ahmadabad, Winston Churchill's 'Blood, Toil, Tears and Sweat' or 'Fight Them on the Beaches' speeches, Dr. Martin Luther King's 'I Have a Dream' or the inaugural addresses by John Kennedy, Ronald Reagan and Nelson Mandela. It should be on anyone's list of effective political speeches.

Theodore Roosevelt (Getty Images)

3. CONSTRUCTING THE MESSAGE

Sometimes books *demand* to be heard. In April 2010 I was visiting a secondhand bookshop in New York City. This place had a wonderful ancient history section. Sitting on the shelf was the Loeb edition of Cicero's *De Oratore*. I felt a kindred sympathy. For me, that volume of Cicero has the same intention as this book. Cicero is trying to explain the importance of good public speaking to his audience, which includes the powerful political and business leaders of Rome during the time of Julius Caesar and Augustus Caesar. Cicero tried to make the case for good speaking as a part of a good civic community.

I bought the book and opened it at random. These words were underlined on page 25:

> For the one point in which we have our greatest advantage
> over the brute creation is that we hold converse one with

another, and can produce our thought in word . . . To come
. . . to the highest achievements of eloquence, what other
power could have been strong enough either to gather
scattered humanity into one place, or to lead it out of
its brutish existence in the wilderness up to our present
condition of civilisation as men and as citizens, or after the
establishment of social communities, to give shape to the
laws, tribunals and civic rights?

Good question. Cicero understood the power of words, the way
that the right words, spoken at the appropriate time, can change a
culture or redirect history. He knew that every speaking opportunity
– every single one – has the potential to transform a moment into a
milestone, to enable language to become a landmark. He understood
this potential as an obligation of the speaker to the audience. He
continued to say that 'the wise counsel of the complete orator is
that which chiefly upholds not only his own dignity, but the safety
of countless individuals and of the entire state'.

The orator has a stewardship over language and over the polity.
He or she is a trustee of the welfare of the community. A great speech
can be a source of tremendous good for our friends, neighbours,
family, loved ones and even people we don't know. And the orator
has a duty to give a great speech, as the voice of the audience, the
voice of collective assent.

Sadly, most speeches are instantly forgettable. They are the
equivalent of sound and fury, signifying absolutely nothing at all.
They fill the air with words and take up space and time. Yet they
move no one, only demanding the patience and loyalty of party.

But some speeches transcend the moment, remain in the
memory, becoming part of history. They may be given in a great
hall or a humble classroom, heard by millions around the world or
by an audience counted in single digits. They do something.

Every great speech fulfils the task of persuasion. In fact, that is
how a speech may be judged, by its persuasive effectiveness. Did
it convince the audience to vote in a certain way, or to adopt a new

attitude on taxes or government services? Did it make an audience support a piece of legislation or initiate an action? A great speech must do more than energise the base or reinforce previous beliefs. A great speech changes the audience; it changes the world.

So a great speech is more than an essay or collection of words. It is language in action, language as action. It shows that the speaker is a leader and an authority on the subject. It also advances the debate on the issues discussed. And a great speech unites an audience around a point of collective agreement.

It does this by presenting a persuasive argument, making a case for a person, belief, philosophy or action. As an argument, it requires proof and reasoning, leading to a conclusion. So it does not conform to the standard plot of a speech learned in communication courses: tell them what you will say, say it, and then tell them what you said, winning virtue with circularity. Rather, it is more direct and economical, starting the persuasive enterprise with the first sentences, stating a thesis, developing that thesis as an argument, and then inspiring the audience with a conclusion that demands immediate results. The goal is to channel the thinking of the listening audience to a point of agreement with the action steps proposed later in the speech. The speech development increasingly narrows the scope of thinking to the point of the action steps.

Learning to use the power of a speech is a sign of maturity in thinking and in purpose. It is an obligation that is inherent in the task itself, the mission of sharing ideas and inspiring action. Cicero urged his audience to master every aspect of public speaking. He said: 'Go forward . . . and bend your energies to that study which engages you, so that it may be in your power to become a glory to yourselves, a source of service to your friends, and profitable members of the Republic.'

We can follow his lead by beginning to study the construction of the message of the speech. Then in the next chapter, we will look at delivery.

Starting the speech

Let's discuss how to start a speech. I've heard some veteran speechwriters say that the introduction of a speech is the hardest part to write, that the rest flows once you figure out how to start.

A great speech starts quickly with few acknowledgements and restrained appreciation. By using principle, historical context, great thoughts or a statement of purpose, a political speech wastes no time. It gets right to the point. It has to do this because an audience wants content and involvement right away, not the slow and crunching list of thanks and names that takes away momentum and interest.

In fact, the best speeches in our time are front loaded. Studies show that audiences make quick decisions about the character, likeability and credibility of a speaker within seconds (studies range from eight to twenty seconds). That means the audience decides if they like you and if you are a person of character right at the start of a speech. Audiences also lose interest within seconds. Studies show that an audience gives you only about thirty seconds of attentive listening before you start to lose people. In other words, the audience will listen carefully to what you have to say for about a half minute, then with each second more people start to fade away. Within two minutes the audience is usually not listening carefully, thinking about other things, or nothing, unless you have given them a good reason to listen for another thirty seconds. Education level is strongly correlated with listening attentively. Doctors, lawyers and others who have gone to graduate school rank highest in listening longevity, according to the studies I've seen.

So a smart strategy is to give the audience a reason to listen for thirty seconds, then give them another reason thirty seconds later, and keep up that pace of measuring audience interest throughout the speech. Perhaps the best way to approach a speech is to ask these questions: what do I have to say? And how can I get the audience to follow my thinking?

The beginning of a speech channels thinking. With each

sentence a speech frames and directs the audience to see a problem a particular way or to think about an issue along certain lines. In a good introduction, each sentence narrows that channel of thinking, bringing an audience very quickly to a point of collective agreement on a topic. An introduction should establish a pattern of listening, initiating habits that help the audience. This is part of the channelling process, signposting to help the audience understand the progression of an argument or using phrases to show them how to hear the words and understand the ideas, such as the repetitive phrase '*Ich bin ein Berliner*'.

There is even more to consider. An introduction can be used to help the speaker build a relationship with the audience, become one with the audience. When this happens, the speaker becomes the voice of collective assent, giving voice to the concerns and aspirations of the audience. A good introduction shows the human side of the speaker, giving the audience an opportunity to develop trust and faith with the speaker.

An introduction sets the tone, creates an atmosphere. It is hard to move from three jokes to a serious topic. That approach often makes the audience uncomfortable. You can actually hear them sigh and slide in their chairs because you are shifting the tone after they became used to the initial approach of stand-up comedy.

A good introduction should immediately direct thinking to a pre-determined end with clarity and force. For instance, in May 1940, when a German attack on Great Britain seemed inevitable, Winston Churchill started a radio address with these words: 'Our task is not only to win the battle – but to win the war.' Right at the start . . . the end he wanted!

That is why I applaud any speech that starts with the heart of the matter, gets right to it, such as Boris Yeltsin's speech at the burial of Tsar Nicholas II's family in St Petersburg in 1998: 'It's an historic day for Russia. Eighty years have passed since the slaying of the last Russian emperor and his family. We have long been silent about this monstrous crime. We must say the truth: the Yekaterinburg massacre has become one of the most shameful pages of our history.' Now, that is the way to start: bold, direct, concise, clear and quotable. In an age where audiences have a very short attention span, you have to get right to the point. No dawdling, no setting the stage, no easing in and getting comfortable, no joke and jive prelude – right to the point!

I know, I know. . . what about all the 'thank you' requirements and acknowledgements? Frankly, the 'thank you' laundry list is overdone and usually bores the audience. I would keep all that to a minimum, and then mention individual people and accomplishments in the body of the speech, giving each person a separate spotlight, using their story as proof for your argument. Such an approach scores a two-for-one: acknowledgement and proof in the same words with the same few seconds of time. You still acknowledge everyone, only gaining greater impact and showing the love with more effect. The only difference is placement in the speech.

Yes, there are some who ardently believe that an introduction must begin with a comprehensive list of thanks and acknowledgements. Here's an example of starting that way. On 21 October 2008, President George W. Bush delivered a major address at the White House Summit on International Development. He started with a litany of names, spending a good three minutes thanking, among the eight people recognised, President Ellen Johnson of Liberia and Bob Geldof of Live Aid fame. These were heavy hitters who needed recognition. But any and all of the people mentioned could have been spotlighted within the text, which discussed the programmes and efforts underway. Instead, the precious seconds of the start of the speech were wasted on stroking VIPs rather than forcefully catching the audience's attention with a strong, compelling message. When he finally got to the point, President Bush said: 'You know, we meet today in the middle of a global crisis.' In my view, that is what should have been said in the first second of the speech, not 181 seconds later when much of the audience was no longer paying attention. Also, in the long speech that followed, he could have used a good story about President Johnson or Mr Geldof to liven things up, segue into praise for their work, and reclaim the interest of the audience. Placement, placement, placement. . .

If a speech is constructed to get right to the point, then there are a number of ways to do that. Let me suggest a few, although the following is by no means a complete or comprehensive list.

1. Get to it

Show why the event is important. At his inauguration, John Kennedy began: 'We observe today not a victory of a party but a celebration of freedom – symbolising an end as well as a beginning – signifying renewal as well as change.' Tony Blair didn't dawdle with his Brighton speech after obtaining government in 1997: 'It has been a very long time waiting for this moment and all I can tell you is that after eighteen long years of opposition, I am deeply proud – privileged – to stand before you as the new Labour Prime Minister of our country.' This is how the speaker establishes the importance of the moment.

2. Reach out to history

Abraham Lincoln offers stunning simplicity with 'Four score and seven years ago' to give his speech at Gettysburg historical context and to reach back to the vision of the Founding Fathers. Ronald Reagan, speaking on the Normandy beach in 1984, looked across forty years to say: 'We're here to mark that day in history when the Allied people joined in battle to reclaim this continent to liberty.' This is my favourite way to begin a speech because it sets a context and quickly embraces the historical event to help the audience understand the importance and message of the speech.

3. Make history

Show how your speech is an historical benchmark. Nelson Mandela did this in his inauguration in 1990: 'Today all of us do, by our presence here, and by our celebrations in other parts of the country and the world, confer glory and hope to newborn liberty.' Speaking by video tape to the Fourth World Conference on Women in 1995, the Nobel laureate Aung San Suu Kyi told the delegates: 'It is a wonderful but daunting task that has fallen on me to say a few words by way of opening this forum, the greatest concourse of women – joined by a few brave men – that has ever gathered on our planet.' The speeches start by acknowledging their historical importance, which sets a serious tone and imposes gravitas on the speaker.

4. Statement of principle
Use the principle to define yourself and to guide the development of the speech. In the Ahmadabad trial in 1922, Mahatma Gandhi started with these words: 'Non-violence is the first article of my faith. It is the last article of my faith.' Neil Kinnock, in his memorable speech at Bournemouth in 1985, said: 'If socialism is to be successful in this country, it must relate to the practical needs and the mental and moral traditions of the men and women of this country.' You align yourself with the principle and use it as the guiding theme of the speech.

5. Statement of a problem
Alexander Solzhenitsyn told a graduation audience at Harvard in 1978 that 'a decline in courage may be the most striking feature which an outside observer notices in the West today'. A different problem concerned Michael Portillo at Blackpool in 1997: 'Let us begin by recognising the scale of our defeat and of our problem.' By the way, there are many studies that show that the statement of the problem is a good way to get the attention of an audience, which will then want to know what you plan to do about it. This gives you a good avenue to talk about your solutions.

6. Statement of qualifications
Show why you are the one who must give this speech. In 1995, at the fiftieth anniversary of the liberation of Auschwitz, former prisoner Elie Wiesel started his speech with these chilling words: 'I speak to you as a man who fifty years and nine days ago had no name, no

hope, no future and was known only by his number, A 70713.' No one could be more qualified to talk of Auschwitz than a survivor. Years earlier, speaking to the Israeli Knesset in 1977, Anwar Sadat said near the beginning of his remarks: 'I come to you today on solid ground to shape a new life and to establish peace. We all love this land, the land of God; we all, Muslims, Christians, Jews, all worship God.' His qualification was his political authority and his vision of peace.

7. *Statement of vision*

Begin with your vision, the place you want to take the audience, the distant horizon that is reached through unity and commitment. Prince Charles, in his famous 'monstrous carbuncle' speech in 1984, gives his vision straightaway: 'At last people are beginning to see that it is possible, and important in human terms, to respect old buildings, street plans and traditional scales and at the same time not feel guilty about a preference for façades, ornaments and soft materials.' Eighty-five years earlier, Theodore Roosevelt began his inspiring 'strenuous life' speech with a vision in contrast:

> I wish to preach not the doctrine of ignoble ease but the doctrine of the strenuous life; the life of toil and effort; of labour and strife; to preach that highest form of success which comes not to the man who desires mere easy peace but to the man who does not shrink from danger, from hardship or from bitter toil, and who out of these wins the splendid ultimate triumph.

Speaking of Roosevelt, no discussion of introductions could possibly ignore one of the most dramatic and singular, that of his 'Bull Moose' speech in 1912. While getting into a car for a campaign speech in Milwaukee, Wisconsin, Roosevelt was shot in the chest by John Shrank, who had been stalking him for days. The .32 calibre bullet was slowed down by a thick sheet of paper in Roosevelt's pocket – his speech manuscript. Rather than go to the hospital, Roosevelt insisted on giving the speech. He started this way, according to those in attendance:

> Friends, I shall ask you to be as quiet as possible. I don't know whether you fully understand that I have just been shot; but it takes more than that to kill a bull moose. But fortunately, I had my manuscript, so you see I was going to make a long speech, and there is a bullet – there is where the bullet went through – and it probably saved me from it going into my heart. The bullet is in me now, so that I cannot make a very long speech, but I will try my best.

He later opened his coat to show the blood stains!

Roosevelt was known for his drama and flair. And he just couldn't pass this one up. He was right. . . it is memorable, that introduction. But I hope you don't have to start a speech in similar circumstances.

Developing the argument

Now, let's think about how to move past the beginning. A speech is an argument designed to persuade the audience to do something. It has a thesis or point. The thesis is proven during the speech. In fact, the development of the argument for the speech flows out of the thesis. The speech flows toward the steps you want the audience to take, followed by a conclusion that persuades the audience to take that action now, right now! Then the speech is over.

As I noted earlier, a great speech is always audience centred. The audience is sitting there thinking 'What's in it for me?' The speech has to answer that question. It cannot be about posturing for the speaker or self-absorbed comments about the speaker's life or pleasures. The speech must be about the audience, showing a concern for each member of the audience that demonstrates respect, regard and concern, without pandering or begging. A political speech starts to become effective and successful by framing the content in terms of the audience. A political speech is always, always, always about the audience. Therefore, audience analysis is vital. The speech will be constructed based on information about the demographics, beliefs and needs of the audience.

So, before anything else takes place, find out everything possible about the audience. That is 'Job One'. What does the audience want? How can the speech meet their expectations? Those questions must be answered. Understanding the 'psychology' of the audience is vital to the persuasive element of the speech. In fact, persuasion cannot take place without some knowledge of the way the audience thinks.

Once key information is obtained about the audience the speechwriting process can begin.

Here is a progressive checklist that can be used to construct the speech.

1. Acknowledge key people and sponsors
Limit this list. If a number of people need to be mentioned, generalise if possible.

2. Tell the audience the purpose of the speech
This should happen at the start of the speech, within the first thirty seconds. This thesis statement is the thread running through the speech, enabling the audience to understand the speech, even if something is missed or the audience periodically loses interest. The thesis statement should be a clear, short, memorable declarative sentence, usually no more than six or seven words, such as 'We must lower taxes' or 'The National Health Service must be fixed'.

The thesis statement is indispensable. Many speakers are so wrapped up in themselves that they forget the power of simplicity for an audience, the people who are trying to follow along without a script, for whom the speech is a new experience, revealed at that moment, sentence by sentence. A short thesis statement vastly increases the ability of the audience to understand and follow the speech as it unfolds. This must happen at the start of the speech.

The thesis statement then frames the speech, which now will flow out of it. That's right. . . a great political speech flows like a river, gaining point and purpose as the words and ideas spread out of the thesis statement, channelled and directed by the development of the argument proving the thesis.

3. Develop the speech as a persuasive argument

This gives point and purpose to every paragraph, every sentence and even every word. Each paragraph further develops the argument of the speech. That is why the paragraph is there, to do that very thing. Each new paragraph takes the argument further, expanding and extending the original thesis statement. Such an approach gives unity and cohesion to a speech, linking paragraphs together and moving ideas forward. Such an approach also allows for an expedient decision rule: if the paragraph doesn't develop the argument, cut it. If the sentence within the paragraph doesn't help develop the argument, cut it. If the word is not doing a job that helps persuasively to develop the argument, cut it.

In the development of the argument, let simplicity govern the construction. The speech should contain short, clear sentences, usually with one-syllable words. A quick look at the most famous speeches, such as Jesus' Sermon on the Mount, Abraham Lincoln's Gettysburg Address, or Churchill's 'Blood, Toil, Tears and Sweat' remarks, would show simple speeches, with short sentences or short phrases, with simple, one- or two-syllable words. John Kennedy's masterful, compelling and quotable speeches are models of the strength of simplicity. His inaugural address shows this: 70 per cent of the words are one syllable. Yet that speech embodies one of the most complex and inspiring arguments every made.

4. Choose vocabulary carefully

The word choices in a speech demand special attention, especially the pronouns. Great political speeches unite and heal, they don't tear apart. That means there must be use of inclusive language, such as the pronouns 'we' and 'us'. This unifying language is how the speaker becomes the voice of collective assent, joining with the audience, making the speech an act of union. Divisive language, especially language divisive along the lines of nationality, gender, race, class or income, creates an 'us v. them' environment, which is dangerous in an election and deadly for governance after an election. Great political speeches are language in action, and should be used to bring people together, not drive them apart.

Word choices can do more than develop an argument; they can capture it. Great political speeches have organic soundbites, places where the message is condensed and stated in a way that compresses the entire speech. Kwame Nkrumah spoke of Ghana's liberation as 'the motion of destiny'. John Kennedy's *Ich bin ein Berliner* is a fantastic display of one sentence expressing the whole point of the speech. Earl Spencer's comment about Princess Diana as 'the most hunted person of the modern age' abbreviates the speech in a haunting sentence.

5. Use examples
Examples help. They humanise the abstract. Use of a good example becomes a way of telling a story or offering an instance that proves a point. Audiences relate well to examples, often thinking 'Oh, I know someone who did that' or 'There, but for the grace of God, go I'.

6. Explain the vision
One of the iconic examples is Ronald Reagan's many references to 'the shining city on the hill', a future where America remains a beacon of freedom and hope for the world. I mentioned earlier that Dr Martin Luther King, Jr's speech on the Washington Mall talked about transforming 'the jangling discords of our nation into a beautiful symphony of brotherhood'. That is an inspiring vision. Margaret Thatcher stated hers upfront, leaving the audience in no doubt: 'Let me give you my vision: a man's right to work as he will, to spend what he earns, to own property, to have the state

as servant and not master – these are the British inheritance.' I honestly believe that when George H. W. Bush could not produce a vision it contributed to his political doom. The absence of a vision is often fatal, disastrous. Vision is more than platitudes. It gives the audience hope and points a way forward to a better future.

7. Bring the audience to the point of collective agreement

After developing the argument of the speech, after the audience has been brought to a point of collective agreement that something should be done, then the speaker must explain the solution in clear, workable steps. The speaker must outline the action that must take place, explaining what each member of the audience must do, what the audience must do together. The speaker should show why these action steps or attitude changes are practical, advantageous and desirable.

8. Construct a conclusion with a purpose

The point of the conclusion is to develop a sense of urgency (see the 'In conclusion' section later in this chapter). So it should follow right after the explanation of the action steps. The conclusion answers the question 'When should we do all this?' The answer: right now, immediately, urgently. Delay is fatal. The conclusion is the place to ramp up the enthusiasm, providing a powerful, inspiring, motivational ending to the speech.

What should be the length of a speech? Be brief – shorter is a lot better. Time is valuable. Audiences have short attention spans. This is another set of reasons for a speech as argument, a condensed and simple message that flows, rather than a ponderous and puffy speech that is fattened prose. A speech is not a movie or a concert, although some politicians now want to make speeches into 'events', like a hippie happening. A serious and credible political speech should be no longer than fifteen minutes, twenty on the outside. Then open it up for questions. Don't ever keep an audience for more than an hour. Again, shorter is better, so a speaker should not waste time. Keep the event moving! It is better for the audience to leave a bit unsatisfied, wanting more, than for them to be sitting there hoping the speaker will shut up.

A great speech should be bold, within reason. Qualifications, hedging and hesitancy all take the life out of speech prose. They kill a speech, draining it of its life force. A speech must be bold to change the world!

A great speech is more than an essay. It is writing for oral delivery. Speechwriting is 'for the mind's ear'. The evaluation of speechwriting is how the words will sound with the voice, not necessarily how they look to the eye. That is why speechwriting is a unique form of writing, judged by its own standards. A successful speech must be effective. It must be persuasive. It must unify. A great speech must demonstrate leadership and vision. And if it can do all this, then a speech can make a difference, become part of the current discussion of issues and become a part of history. A great speech moves the audience and stays with them, achieving a kind of immortality.

Proof

Now a few comments about the nature of proof in a speech. If a speech is an argument, then the content of the speech is a persuasive development of the support for the argument. In other words, a speech makes the case for the thesis that it contains.

There are many kinds of proof. Notoriously, the ancient rhetorical handbooks argue that bad reasoning is an acceptable form of proof if it persuades the audience. That is why public speaking books still cover fallacies like *ad hominem* (attack on the person) or *ad ignorantium* (trying to prove a positive from a negative). I'm not going to advocate bad reasoning, even if it works. In my view, that violates the ethics of argumentation. But you see the effective use of bad reasoning every day, virtually as the common currency of political and media discourse ('He's a liar, so don't believe him' or 'They've never had a good fiscal policy and they never will').

Words themselves are a form of proof. Words have jobs. Audiences are partial to certain words, attracted by them. And those same audiences are repelled by other words, hating anyone or anything associated with those words. The right words have a persuasive appeal; the wrong ones dissuade. Competent use of good words can significantly enhance the persuasiveness of a speech.

There are some aspects of proof that demand a more pronounced discussion.

1. Beliefs

Jed Richardson, a communications and debate expert, used to say that there were three levels of proof. The first level was a statement of belief, such as 'The state of the pound is unsound'. That is a statement of someone's personal opinion. Now we all have opinions, some more factually based than others. Many of us form our beliefs based on our experience and reasoned judgement. That is good and reflects a commitment to open-minded inquiry, which is the basis for a successful democracy. However, some people view the opinions of others with suspicion, which may be a healthy form of scepticism and certainly is prudent, given the possibility of error in each and every statement of judgement.

Judgements may also be far from reasoned. Some people just drink the propaganda 'kool-aid', getting their opinions from congenial or like-minded sources, such as political commentators or economists who say the things that person loves to hear. When someone listens only to information sources that reinforce prior opinion, in effect a source that does the thinking for the listener, the situation is called 'feeding time at the zoo'. The listeners are fed the red meat they want. Unfortunately, these sorts of judgements don't prove much, although given to like-minded audiences such opinions may be very persuasive.

Judgements may be more than words. They can be action. There are some people who are primary sources of information, such as a foreign minister or head of government. Their opinions matter because they are more than a belief; they are policy. When a head of government says that a new embassy will be opened in a neighbouring country, that is more than an opinion. The statement is action. When a foreign minister outlines a country's policy towards the United Nations, that is more than words; that is action. These judgements are a powerful form of proof.

Experts are often asked for their opinions. So such a judgement is based on a specialised scholarship or set of experiences. The opinion of an expert can be relevant, even decisive in some cases. But the problem is that experts disagree, and some so-called 'experts' are not qualified. Certain political pundits come to mind.

2. *Examples*

So, if opinions disagree, or more proof is needed, Richardson said that the second level of proof was an example. An example was a superior form of proof because it showed an actual event, an occurrence in the real world, not just a hypothetical or imagined event in the mind of some expert. It demonstrated something. It gave an instance. It showed that the belief is based on some fact.

Examples are so important that they are discussed in the following section. They do more than prove. They humanise the abstract and have a central function in the process of persuasion. So we will take up examples again in more detail.

3. *Statistics*

Richardson claimed that an even better form of proof was a good, reliable and valid statistic that was properly used in a relevant context. A statistic should answer the question 'How many times has this example occurred?'

In the February–March 2010 issue of *Policy Review*, Sally Satel wrote about bioethics. She started with an example about Paul Wagner, who gave Gail Tomas, a stranger, his left kidney. That was a gift of life because there are 83,000 people waiting for a kidney transplant in the United States and thirteen people die each day because not enough kidneys are donated.

That is a good example followed by a good statistic. The example shows that donation is possible and that it can save a life. Then it is contrasted with the number of people who need such a donation.

In other words, the answer to the question 'How many people are not Gail Tomas?' is this: not enough. And the statistics tell us how few are lucky enough to receive a donation.

Of course, we have to be on guard against the manipulation or fabrication of statistics. The humorist Will Rogers once said that 'there are lies, damn lies and statistics'. It was a joke. . . but with a warning about the misuse of statistics. He was asserting a progression of misleading moves. A lie is an untruth. But a lie may not be intentional. A 'damn lie' is an intentional lie, an untruth that the speaker knows is untrue but says anyway to intentionally mislead an audience. That is worse than a mere lie, because of the conscious intention to deceive. A 'statistic', in the progression, is a damn lie that wraps itself up in the credibility of science and the precision of mathematics. In Rogers's view, offered as a joke with a point, he is claiming that a statistic is worse than a damn lie, because it takes the hard-won success of science and uses it to make the deception much more persuasive, it takes the strength of science and misappropriates it.

Now Rogers was making a point and using humour to do it. However, statistics are excellent forms of proof provided that they are well acquired and carefully documented. The statistic must come from a sufficient sample size. It must be the product of a fair question asked with neutral bias. It must be appropriate for the argument. It must not be twisted or misused, even if obtained through reliable and valid information-gathering.

Used well, a statistic can be a powerful form of proof. Note this use of statistics from a recent article in the *Economist* (17 April 2010) about the Democratic Republic of the Congo: 'During its civil war from 1998 to 2003, five million Congolese may have died as a result of violence, disease and starvation.' That is a statistic that makes the reader take notice. This shows what a good statistic can do. It can give the scope and dimension of a problem. Here is another from the same article: 'Corruption is rife, the courts rotten. The UN reckons that 70 per cent of the country's prisoners, most of them kept in vile conditions, have yet to be tried.' That shows that DR Congo is a failed state, one in which corruption and lawlessness rule, that the country is a nation in name only. The statistic makes the case, proves the point. It satisfies the need for substantiation.

Now, if the statistic is good and appropriate, it should be used after an example. The example shows that something has actually happened. The statistic shows that the example is not isolated, that it has happened often. It should flow something like this: 'Karen Froslid is an alumna donor to her university. Thirty per cent of alumni donate.' The statistic shows how many of Karen's colleagues are like her. That is a persuasive use of a statistic, which was Richardson's point about statistics as the best form of proof.

Let's consider examples and statistics in more detail.

Examples

Sadly, many great speeches lack the use of an example. But virtually every speech is improved by having one or two. Examples humanise the abstract. They give weight to a discussion. They linger in the mind, often long after a speech is given. Members of the audience relate to examples and personalise them. Examples help involve the audience. They make a speech more interesting and understandable. Examples are a means of persuasion, much better than assertive prose. As Aristotle said, they are a superior form of proof. If you claim that something has happened, an example proves it so. If you argue that change is possible, an example shows how.

Here's what I mean. Suppose you are giving a speech about homelessness. In the audience are programme directors and staff from non-profit organisations that assist the homeless. You want to persuade them to do even more, to make every possible effort to help the homeless, to undertake new actions and think outside the box. These are highly motivated people who already make profound efforts. The question is 'How can your speech further motivate them?' So, as you make your abstract persuasive case, your words must penetrate beyond delivering a message, they must leave an ingrained example in the mind. You are more convincing when you add in the following example, which was published in the *Fort Worth Star Telegram* newspaper on 20 September 2008.

> I'd like to tell you about Ken Stephens and his son, Thomas, who were homeless on the streets of Fort Worth and were desperate for assistance. Ken's seventeen-year-old son was developmentally disabled and has cerebral palsy. Ken's intense care-giving had cost him his job, his marriage and his savings. And he needed more than shelter; he needed long-term help.
>
> Ken was fortunate to find the Cornerstone Comprehensive Care Program which takes families living in shelters and puts them into rental housing for up to two years. The program pays for their rent and utilities. It also helps the homeless work toward financial empowerment, gradually replacing the program's financial assistance with earned income as residents find employment, eventually helping people like Ken achieve self-sufficiency.
>
> In Ken's case, Cornerstone also helped him go back to school to repair computers. He now has the flexibility to provide care and to work. His son is also now in school. This program works: 85 per cent of those who have completed the program remain in permanent housing for at least six months. When I talk about going the extra mile, making an extraordinary effort to help the homeless, programs like Cornerstone are what I have in mind.

This example shows what is possible. And it adds a human dimension to the discussion. The audience will now start to think about using rental housing and career training as part of their approach to helping the homeless. The example both demonstrates and motivates.

In my view, every important policy speech should have at least one example. There are many ways to use an example in a speech. Here are a few ideas.

1. Use an example to start a speech

César Chávez, the civil rights leader who fought for humane working conditions for farm workers, often began his speeches with an example. This helped him by providing a human context to the speech right from the beginning.

In 1984, speaking at the Commonwealth Club in San Francisco, he began by mentioning thirty-two Bracero farm workers who had lost their lives in a tragic traffic accident. They had come from Mexico ('been imported'), travelling in an unsafe, uninspected bus that was actually a converted flatbed truck. Their employer had not cared enough to provide safer transportation and the driver had vision impairment. After the accident, Chávez said: 'Most of the bodies lay unidentified for days. No one, including the grower who employed the workers, even knew their names.'

He tied this example to the general conditions of immigrant workers on farms and then went further: 'All Hispanics – urban and rural, young and old – are connected to the farm workers' experience.' Upon hearing that story, the audience knows something must be done, and immediately learns that the problem is not limited to farm workers, but to attitudes about minorities in the United States. That is a powerful way to begin a speech.

2. Offer a generalised example to illustrate a problem

You don't mention names, just a situation. Suffragette Emily Pankhurst did this in 1908, discussing the unequal status of women under the law. She offered up a generalised example:

> Take the case of a woman who has been earning a good income. She is told that she ought to give up her employment when she becomes a wife and mother. What does she get in return? All that a married man is obliged by law to do for his wife is to provide for her shelter of some kind, food of some kind and clothing of some kind . . . She has no legal claim upon any definite portion of his income. If he is a good man, a conscientious man, he does the right thing. If he is not, if he chooses almost to starve his wife, she has no remedy. What he thinks sufficient is what she has to be content with.

This type of example helps the audience see the problem. But it does more: it sends a warning that every woman in the audience may face economic enslavement, and that every married woman runs the risk of poverty and helplessness. The example persuades; this situation is not fair. The example demands change; such inequality under the law is unacceptable.

3. Use a personal example to make a broader point
Neil Kinnock did this in his famous Llandudno remarks in 1987. He used a personal situation to demonstrate a broader problem:

> Why am I the first Kinnock in a thousand generations to be able to get to university? Why is Glenys [his wife] the first woman in her family in a thousand generations to be able to get to university? . . . It was because there was no platform upon which they could stand; no arrangement for their neighbours to subscribe to their welfare; no method by which the communities could translate their desires for those individuals into provision for those individuals.

Kinnock shows that his example illustrates the need for collective action. Without it, he would have been in the same circumstances as his ancestors. So would many people in the audience. And note the power of the personal example. This is one of the most memorable sections of a great speech. That is no accident. The speech remains in our memory more than twenty years later. That is how a good example works. It has weight and credibility. The more you think about it, the more persuasive it becomes. So the example keeps churning around in your mind, days after the speech, because it has settled in and continues to do its job.

4. Use an example to report from the streets
This happens twice in Enoch Powell's controversial 'River of Blood' speech in 1968. Has there ever been a speech in British history that has generated more fire and heat, passion and light, than this one? Misunderstood or not, factual or reactionary, interpreted or reinterpreted, attacked or defended, the speech remains unforgettable, even though it is also radioactive, because some people fear even to touch upon it in public. Forty-two years on, the mere mention of the speech draws a forceful response, pro and con.

Two examples are used in the speech to make it so memorable, even dangerous: at the beginning the middle-aged constituent who wants to leave the country and later on the woman in Wolverhampton who won't rent to immigrants. Those examples make the argument of the speech more powerful and disturbing. They are hard to forget.

5. Use multiple examples to create a climate of opinion
One example may not be enough. Perhaps a cluster bomb of examples would be more persuasive. In 1984, at the Democratic National Convention, the then New York governor, Mario Cuomo, was the keynote speaker. Ten days earlier, at his party's gathering, Ronald Reagan argued that America was in the midst of prosperity ('the shining city on a hill'). Cuomo disagreed: not all Americans were doing well. He used several examples to deny Reagan's assertion:

> Maybe if you visited more places, Mr President, you'd understand. Maybe if you went to Appalachia, where

some people still live in sheds; and to Lackawanna, where thousands of unemployed steel workers wonder why we subsidise foreign steel while we surrender their dignity to unemployment and to welfare cheques; maybe if you stepped into a shelter in Chicago and talked with some of the homeless there; maybe, Mr President, if you asked a woman who had been denied the help she needs to feed her children because you say we need the money to give a tax break for a millionaire or to build a missile we can't even afford to use.

After those examples it is hard to argue that everyone is doing well. That is how to use examples to create a climate of opinion. One example may not decisively prove a point; a number of them show counter-examples are widespread. The examples add up. So it becomes difficult to dismiss them. How can we say everything is fine when there are cases like these? Frankly, in this case, they are so persuasive that they demand disproof, and Cuomo says this is not possible. It is, in his words, 'A Tale of Two Cities'.

6. Use an historical example to prove a modern point
History is part of a culture's collective identity. The right historical examples have a powerful appeal.

Speaking to the Polish Senate in 1991, Margaret Thatcher understood this. She urged Poland to act in concert with other European nations. She reminded the senators that 'there is a long tradition of [Polish] regional cooperation – going back, I understand, all the way to the time when the sons of your fifteenth-century King Kazimierz were simultaneously on the Polish, Lithuanian and Hungarian thrones'.

This example is really masterful. It illustrates her point well. The historical comparison was persuasive and contributory to cooperation. Poles are proud of this moment in their history. That pride can be persuasive. The historical example shows Polish importance in Europe and European affairs. Poland can help shape Europe's future, just as it did in the past. The example accomplishes so much at once. It shows what the right example can do in a speech.

7. Speak to the example
Use an example as a proxy for the audience, thereby speaking to the audience through the example.

Tony Blair did this in 1999 at the Labour Party conference in some unforgettable passages. Here is just one: 'To the 45-year-old who came to my surgery a few months ago, scared he'll never work again, I say: you didn't become useless at forty-five. You deserve the chance to start afresh and we will set your potential free.' The man stands proxy for the audience and the nation. If he is set free, then others can be set free too. The message to him is the message to everyone who hears the speech.

8. Use an example for contrast
One of the greatest speeches of the last century was by Ronald Reagan at Pointe du Hoc in 1984. The occasion was the fortieth anniversary of the Normandy landings on D-Day.

With the sea behind him, standing on the beach looking at the cliffs, he vividly described the struggle to land, cross the beach and climb the cliff face under a hail of deadly gunfire. The audience could imagine the difficulty for the young soldiers, the enormity of the moment, seeing in their mind's eye the terror, determination, courage, blood and carnage. But then Reagan pointed to a group of older men in the audience and said: 'These are the boys of Pointe du Hoc. These are the men who took the cliffs. These are the champions who helped free a continent. These are the heroes who helped end a war.'

The contrast is staggering. This is one of the great passages in public speaking precisely because the contrast works so well. These older men (Reagan later said they looked like 'businessmen'), wrinkled, some frail, world-weary, bent by the years, were once those young soldiers. How did they survive? How did they climb those cliffs? Their present age only highlights the difficulty of their task in 1944. The contrast provides needed perspective. It also gives that human dimension, making the picture in the mind's eye more realistic and startling, with greater audience understanding and empathy.

This list is far from comprehensive. These are just some of the many ways that examples can be part of a speech. Of course, some people think examples are staged and 'cheesy'. Well, that can be true. The answer is to make them an authentic and organic part of the speech. Some people worry that examples about real people can be potentially harmful if those same people turn on the speaker and deny the story. That means any real-world example has to be well researched and carefully vetted.

Aristotle said that an example is a look at the past to see the future. He also said that examples make the speaker sound like he is acting as a witness, reporting to the audience. I think he means this: examples are a kind of storytelling. So every speech is a morality tale, with heroes and villains, the need for fellowship between speaker and audience to undertake an epic quest which will encounter difficulties and barriers, but can ultimately lead to a happy ending if the fellowship remains united and true to its purpose.

Years ago, a Hollywood producer was talking about public speaking. He said that speakers should remember the power of storytelling. For him, an example is like a story, a condensed instance of storytelling, a shorter form of a movie. This producer is absolutely right. You remember a good movie because of the example or examples. A great speech is no different from a good movie. Examples add a much-needed human dimension to a speech. They have a profound and powerful persuasive appeal. They help the audience visualise the argument of the speech and relate to it. They are stories within a larger story, a way to tell the tale.

Orwell's advice

Political speech matters. The language we use creates and shapes our world. Words are our world. Every word has a job and our decision to employ one word over another is based on our purpose and mission, what we want to accomplish and what we want others to do. And those words become the way we see the world, the way we understand the world.

Political words convey ideas, beliefs, word choices, expressions, thinking and persuasion. Speechwriters know the power of words, the power of the right words, what I call 'the good words', those with the best emotive, value-laden meaning that will channel thought and persuade the audience to undertake an action or adopt a particular belief. These words help an audience think along pre-determined lines to a desired conclusion.

Thus, George Orwell's 'Politics and the English Language', published in 1946, is required reading for anyone who cares about ethical political persuasion, good governance and the welfare of the nation. The article stands as a warning against those who prize power over the public good and manipulation over choice. Orwell argues for truthful, clear political speech. He also argues for a high level of responsibility from those who use political language.

Orwell is a hero and a demon, for both the left and the right, depending on the argument and mood of the moment. He is a giant, and a pest, along the entire political spectrum. He reveals the tricks and cynicism of those in power, and documents the plight and poverty of those without means or hope. Students read him; most politicians fear him. His fiction is fact. It documents and editorialises, offers reports that are combative, writing that enlightens and stories that enable us to stand watch against the misuse of power. His best books, *Animal Farm* and *Nineteen Eighty-Four*, are part of our intellectual education. His non-fiction is just as important and includes books we should know well, such as *Homage to Catalonia*, *Down and Out in Paris and London* or *The Road to Wigan Pier*.

The article 'Politics and the English Language' is a distillation of his experiences in Great Britain, Burma, Spain and Russia, as well as the epic struggle of the Second World War. Orwell was weary of the linguistic twists and turns, perversions and manipulations of people in power, as a result of which the English language was in decline. Language, Orwell said, reflects thought and action. So as we set a low bar for linguistic expression and accuracy in our practical reasoning, language fails to communicate. It 'becomes ugly and inaccurate not because our thoughts are foolish, but the slovenliness of our language makes it easier for us to have foolish thoughts'. So we descend in a spiralling free fall, with bad language reinforcing fallacious thinking, and poor thinking acting as a strong gravitational pull on our linguistic expression.

But the decline is reversible. That is his hopeful message. And he shows us how to do it.

1. Avoid staleness of expression

Clichés are really a substitute for thought. We learn filler expressions to fill rhetorical space. So we 'can't see the forest for the trees' or 'what goes around comes around' are over-used, vacuous ways of talking. You can see this sort of hackneyed speech in bad sports reporting ('He's a special football player' or 'He's the spark that ignites this team'). And it seems to be part of much political speechmaking ('He's part of the problem in Washington' or 'It's time for change'). In the end, nothing is actually said, no ideas exchanged or proven. Clichés should be avoided at all costs. Say what you really mean. Don't revert to this sort of fast-food, pre-processed, ready-to-order verbal 'McSpeak' (I have just violated Orwell's warning).

2. Avoid imprecision

Strive for precisely the right meaning and the right word. It won't be easy. Work harder to find the right words. For example, in a recent collection of essays, *The War against Cliché*, Martin Amis repeatedly compliments Vladimir Nabokov for always finding the right word, for demonstrating a precision that helps convey exactly the right meaning to the reader (for example, look at Nabokov's autobiography, *Speak, Memory*). That is high praise. It is also about integrity in writing and a responsibility to the reader or listener. This precision is what can make politics noble, not propaganda.

3. Overcome vagueness

Many politicians love vagueness. It is the answer to an absence of ideas or policy. It is useful. Vague ideas can mean anything to any member of the listening audience. Vague speech allows a member of the audience to project his or her own meaning to what they hear or read, thus making the words anything the audience wants them to be. This allows the speaker to become all things to all people, broadening the base and enlarging the tent (to use some more stale speech). This is rhetorical trickery, verbal sleight of hand. And it is disingenuous. It is a lie. That is why it is objectionable. Political speech is about important ideas, policies and programmes. The audience is trying to become informed. Their current well-being and future prosperity are at stake. Democracy needs the free flow of clear and accurate information. Honesty requires clarity. Vagueness gives the illusion of ideas or policy. And when an audience is deceived by the illusion, some politicians think that shows skill and ability. I've heard leaders and their spokespeople say things like 'Can you believe they bought that?' or 'I can't believe we got away with that answer!' In my view, intentional vagueness, disguised imprecision, sadly reveals something about character.

4. Use simple language

Simple words and short sentences are best. They convey meaning with greater clarity. The audience has a better chance of understanding exactly what is said. So Orwell warns us against long words and rambling sentences. He asks for crisp, precise and clear language. He warns us against metaphors which may mislead through the comparison, especially 'dying metaphors' ('no axe to grind'). We must avoid 'operators of false verbal limbs' (words that pack extra syllables to give the appearance of symmetry, thereby avoiding precision and appropriateness in noun and verb usage, phrases such as 'render inoperative' or 'make itself felt'). We must also avoid mixed metaphors ('the Fascist octopus has sung its swansong'). They clash and blur meaning. He says that simple verbs are the best, verbs such as 'break' or 'stop'. He also asks that politicians avoid pretentious diction. This extends to efforts to make political speech sound objective and scientific, when it isn't, or dignified when not.

5. Avoid non-English words

Orwell especially thinks the use of non-English words is pointless in political speech, merely there for display, to create an impression, not for information or understanding. It is pretentious too. So we should close our French and Latin dictionaries and put them back on the shelf. *D'accord!*

6. Avoid jargon

I wish Orwell could comment on our current 'techno-talk', that cutting-edge, mission-driven, programme-sensitive downloading that offlines the words that impact us and grow our economy. Government types that speak in wonk-talk or jargon-jive would have been his deadly enemies.

Orwell issued strong warnings about acronyms. In *Nineteen Eighty-Four*, he discusses the pattern of turning organisational names into one word with the smallest number of syllables. He noted:

> Even in the early decades of the twentieth century, telescoped words and phrases had been one of the characteristic features of political language; and it had been most marked in totalitarian countries and totalitarian organisations . . . In the beginning the practice had been adopted as it were instinctively, but in Newspeak it was used with a conscious purpose. It was perceived that in

thus abbreviating a name one narrowed and subtly altered its meaning, by cutting out most of the associations that would otherwise cling to it.

And virtually every book on good writing asks for avoidance of acronyms. So why do we still use them? Some would answer that they simplify speech. Orwell would respond that they usually replace thought, offering a way for us to avoid thinking. And he would have hated text-messaging English (I M RT U NO). I am not sure how he would have felt about Spanglish or Ebonics, but I think he would have worried that they might be a new form of jargon. They also might be a more precise way of speaking. It would be revealing to have a debate on new forms of English from the Orwellian point of view. Let the debate begin. . .

7. Avoid meaningless words

There are organisations that give awards for the worst writing in a particular field, such as literature or the social sciences. 'Winners' usually display long strings of words that have no meaning at all, or one that is so convoluted or tortured that the reader cannot follow it. So we can talk of the 'atmospheric qualities of political diatribes that soar from the Olympian heights to the denizen of Hades, recalling rapturous melodies of consequence to forge a Wagnerian response to the metamorphosis of mythology'. I just wrote that. . . I have no idea what it means. But it sounds thoughtful and even academic. Again, it fills rhetorical space but doesn't really say anything. Orwell thinks 'the whole tendency of modern prose is away from concreteness'. I think he is right, and this is bad. He worries that these meaningless words are used in a 'consciously dishonest way'. I worry that he is right.

8. Avoid doublespeak

Doublespeak takes place when the meanings of words are twisted and perverted to become their opposites. So 'War is Peace', 'Freedom is Slavery' and 'Ignorance is Strength' are all famously found in *Nineteen Eighty-Four*. There is a very good example of doublespeak to be found in Aldous Huxley's *Eyeless in Gaza*: 'But if you want to be free, you've got to be a prisoner. It is the condition of freedom – true freedom.'

One reason for the existence of doublespeak is to try to take some positive, emotive words like 'freedom' or 'democracy' and use that powerful positive emotional association to disguise practices that are objectionable or suspicious, like slavery or dictatorship. C. L. Stevenson has given this practice another name, 'persuasive definition', in his book *Ethics and Language*. Stevenson shows how the practice relies on trying to pass off an argument as a definition, or, in other words, how the doublespeaker uses words like 'real' and 'true' to make his argument into the paradigm of the definition. You can see it in Huxley: 'true freedom' is imprisonment. The passage looks like a definition of the best meaning of freedom. It is actually an unproven argument, doublespeak in action. There is the appearance of a descriptive definition, but in reality it is the misuse of an emotive word, trying to use the emotional value to delusional advantage.

9. Avoid ideological talk
Beware the conformist political dialect and its language. Orwell said: 'Orthodoxy of whatever colour seems to demand a lifeless, imitative style.' Indeed, Orwell thought ideological talk was another substitute for speech. In *Nineteen Eighty-Four*, he said:

> The intention was to make speech, and especially speech on any subject not ideologically neutral, as nearly as possible independent of consciousness. For the purposes of everyday life it was no doubt necessary, or sometimes necessary, to reflect before speaking, but a Party member called upon to make a political or ethical judgement should be able to spray forth the correct opinions as automatically as a machine gun spraying forth bullets.

It would be better to think for oneself and be wary of ideological answers, both as a speaker and as a listener.

10. *Be honest and sincere*

Good language is a sign of good faith. Orwell noted that 'in our time, political speech and writing are largely the defence of the indefensible'. It is difficult to draw a bright blue line between political speech and non-political speech. He argued: 'In our age there is no such thing as "keeping out of politics". All issues are political issues, and politics itself is a mass of lies, evasions, folly, hatred and schizophrenia. When the general atmosphere is bad, language must suffer.'

But we can make a difference, one word, one conversation, one speech at a time. That is the hope behind the following well-known passage, from 'Politics and the English Language':

> Political language – and with variations this is true of all political parties, from Conservatives to Anarchists – is designed to make lies sound truthful and murder respectable, and to give an appearance of solidity to pure wind. One cannot change this all in a moment, but one can at least change one's own habits, and from time to time one can even, if one jeers loudly enough, send some worn-out and useless phrase – some *jackboot, Achilles' heel, hotbed, melting pot, acid test, veritable inferno* or other lump of verbal refuse – into the dustbin where it belongs.

It takes more than intelligence and commitment to speak honestly and clearly; it takes courage. It is an act of good faith between the politician and audience. Given the poor state of political discourse, improvement would be a welcome revolution.

Soundbites

A great speech is known by a phrase. Sometimes that phrase is a line from the speech; sometimes it is the occasion. Leon Trotsky said that capitalism will be consigned to 'the dustbin of history'. Abraham Lincoln spoke at Gettysburg.

The soundbite offers several advantages. It is a good phrase for the media to use to report a speech. The soundbite can also be a shorthand way of referring to a speech. And it can help people remember a speech. But the most important advantage of the soundbite is that it condenses the entire argument of the speech into a few short words, even if those words are locational, like Ronald Reagan's speech at the Berlin Wall, situational, such as Richard Nixon's resignation speech, or occasional, as in Pericles's Funeral Oration.

One book that shows the great power of a soundbite is Brian MacArthur's *Penguin Book of Twentieth-Century Speeches* (see also Chapter 8). This is an exceptional collection, my personal favourite. One reason is that each speech in the anthology is known by a phrase. In the table of contents MacArthur lists the speaker and then the soundbite, followed by the date.

This demarcation of each speech is more than a convenience. It is a profound recognition of the proper use of a soundbite. If you know the famous phrase, then you know the content of the speech. When you hear the phrase you know the entire argument. When you hear the phrase 'I have a dream', you remember large portions of the speech. When you hear the phrase 'We will bury you', you recall the speech by Nikita Khrushchev at the United Nations where he said that communism would triumph over capitalism.

Your ideal soundbite will fill as many of the tasks below as possible.

1. Condense the speech
That is what a soundbite should do: condense a speech. Tell the

story. The soundbite should be the speech in miniature, the speech frozen in verbal amber, transparent and understandable. The MacArthur book shows the twentieth century in progressive phrases: Theodore Roosevelt's 'the strenuous life', Mahatma Gandhi's 'there is no salvation for India', Roger Casement's 'in Ireland alone . . . is loyalty held to be a crime', Adolf Hitler's 'my patience is now at an end', Neville Chamberlain's 'peace in our time', Winston Churchill's 'this was their finest hour', and so on through the rest of the century, speech after speech, each with detailed and developed arguments, known through a phrase.

2. *Use few words*
Ideally, a soundbite is less than a full sentence, perhaps just a few words. In my view, a good soundbite contains five words or less, but that is a rule made to be broken. The key item is to have a phrase that says it all, like 'Mr Gorbachev, tear down this wall'. That was six words. Neil Kinnock had a great phrase that was extremely long: 'Why am I the first Kinnock in a thousand years to be able to get to university?' It breaks my five-word rule, but to masterful effect. But there is preferable brevity in Prince Charles's 'monstrous carbuncle' or Geoffrey Howe's 'conflict of loyalty'. One of the best phrases for a speech, full of hope and glory, is from Nelson Mandela's inaugural speech: 'Let freedom reign.' For me, those are the best soundbites: short and punchy, persuasive and memorable.

3. *Be organic*
There are innumerable failed soundbites. A phrase was good, its potential evident, the energy ready to be released. But the soundbite was not faithful to the speech. It must authentically condense the speech. It cannot be artificially grafted on. The soundbite must emerge from within the context of the speech. In my own writing I often find the soundbite is already there after the first draft, or at least the idea for it is there. Rarely does a phrase come from outside the writing process, thrown in after the speech is drafted. When a phrase is added because it 'sounds good', it almost invariably sticks

out with neon lights, saying 'Somebody put this in as a soundbite and it doesn't belong' or, in keeping with a condensed message, the alien phrase is 'dangerously diverting'.

4. Look with a journalist's eye

The speaker wants to persuade an audience to adopt an opinion or undertake an action. A journalist is looking to tell a story in few words. The soundbite should help do that. In fact, the soundbite should be a perfect match of message and story. So in the writing phase the soundbite should begin to emerge as the message. That is why so many soundbites are either the thesis of the speech or a locational phrase. The message is in the argument or the purpose of the event. When Jesse Jackson said 'Keep hope alive' in 1988, you know what he wanted to say and the journalist had a great phrase for telling the story. So as the speech is constructed, the soundbite should organically emerge in the text. It should be identified, possibly reworked or reworded, designed to condense the message for both the audience and the journalist.

In conclusion

A great speech must have a strong introduction and conclusion. I have written about introductions earlier. A veteran speechwriter once told me that a conclusion must have the same kind of finish as a symphony: it must take the audience to a new level of thinking and inspiration, literally lifting them out of their seats into a standing ovation. He counselled me to listen to the end of each movement, especially the final one, to learn this aspect of speechwriting. He called those finales a 'Schubert finish', thinking of his own favourite composer. I have since listened to rock music in the same way, looking for a conclusion that is as mighty and moving as a sustained power chord from Pete Townshend (think of the last explosive, soul-searing moments in 'Won't Get Fooled Again').

Yet, commonly, strangely, we are often told that a conclusion must sum up the speech at the end: sum up and then shut up. A typical strategy found in many speaking manuals is this: 'Tell the audience what you are going to say, then say it, then tell them what you said.' The conclusion is then the point of summation. After summation, say 'thank you' and just end it. That is the way many people view the conclusion.

I have another view, hopefully better, one that seeks to get more out of the conclusion. With respect, policymakers need to look at the conclusion as more than 'the summing up'. A conclusion should be the final step in the construction of a persuasive argument that aims to change the beliefs of an audience or to compel the audience to action. More specifically, the body of the speech should lead to the point of collective agreement, where the audience finds itself convinced that the status quo must be changed for the better. At that moment the speech must answer the question 'What should we do?' The speaker then explains the action steps that outline what the audience should do to make change happen. The conclusion follows and answers the further question 'When should we do all this?' The answer provided in the conclusion is 'Now!' That means the conclusion is the place where you advocate a sense of urgency, right now. The word that must be in every conclusion is 'now'. That is a clear, concise, compelling and necessary word. And you should use it. And the speaker must motivate the audience to act now, inspire them to join together and act as one. So the conclusion is not a summing up as much as the capstone of the argument of the speech. In other words, the conclusion is still working to develop the speech, not just repeating it. That is a vital distinction. In my view, the speech must still be unfolding, building and expanding until the very last line.

Here is a checklist of essential elements in a good conclusion.

1. A sense of urgency
There is a phrase from Dr Martin Luther King, Jr's famous 'I Have a Dream' speech, 'the fierce urgency of *now*' (his italics). Every

conclusion must discuss 'the fierce urgency of now', showing that inaction or delayed action is unacceptable, folly, potentially disastrous. Only action at this moment, immediate action, will resolve the problems presented in the body of the speech. In his 1988 Democratic Party convention speech, Senator Edward Kennedy employed a similar call to action, hearkening back to history:

> [President Kennedy] was my brother. But he and Dr King were also in the deepest sense brothers to us all . . . if they were here with us, two decades later, I think I know what they would say: 'Now is the time.' Some men see things as they are, and say 'Why?' We dream things that never were and say 'Why not?' Now is the time.

2. Inclusivity

If you have united the audience in the speech, then the call to action now must include everyone. In his masterful inaugural address in 1994, Nelson Mandela ended his speech with a powerful vision of unity:

> We understand that there is no easy road to freedom. We know it well that none of us acting alone can achieve success. We must therefore act together as a united people, for national reconciliation, for nation-building, for the birth of a new world. Let there be justice for all. Let there be peace for all. Let there be work, bread, water and salt for all . . . Let freedom reign. The sun shall never set on so glorious a human achievement. God bless Africa.

3. Audience empowerment

The unity of action should lead to more freedom and choice for the audience. It should empower them. In his own inaugural address, Václav Havel reached back past the years of communist dictatorship and Nazi occupation to the birth of Czechoslovakia and the democratic vision of Tomáš Masaryk. History and empowerment are found in Havel's dramatic and emotional conclusion: 'The most distinguished of my predecessors opened his first speech with a quotation from the great Czech educator Comenius. Allow me to round off my first speech with my own paraphrase of the same statement: People, your government has returned to you!' And he was right. The Czech people were now free.

4. Vision

Through inclusive action now, the audience can cross into a better future. At the start of the Obama administration, there was much discussion in the United States about Abraham Lincoln's second inaugural address in 1865. Its conclusion is among the most famous in the annuals of political commentary, even cited by Margaret Thatcher in her own conclusion before the US Congress in 1985. Lincoln ended his short speech with a vision of an attainable future after the Civil War:

> With malice toward none, with charity for all, with firmness in the right as God gives us to see the right, let us finish the work we are in, to bind up the nation's wounds, to care for him who shall have borne the battle, and for his widow and his orphans, to do all which may achieve and cherish a just and a lasting peace among ourselves and with all nations.

5. Choice

A vision also presents a choice: the vision or worse alternatives. In his 'Finest Hour' speech, Winston Churchill offered this choice:

> If we can stand up to [Hitler], all Europe may be free and the life of the world may move forward into broad, sunlit uplands. But if we fail, then the whole world, including the United States, including all that we have known and cared for, will sink into the abyss of a new Dark Age made

more sinister, and perhaps more protected, by the lights of perverted science.

The stark contrast of this choice, easy to see in the imagination and fearful to contemplate, made the end of that speech more profoundly powerful.

6. Energising and inspiring the audience to accept the vision

One person lauded John Kennedy's inaugural speech as 'the greatest since Cicero'. High praise. . . the highest. The inspiration of that speech reverberates down the years, especially the conclusion. It is a great example of igniting the optimism and commitment of an audience:

> And so, my fellow Americans: ask not what your country can do for you – ask what you can do for your country. My fellow citizens of the world: ask not what America will do for you, but what together we can do for the freedom of man. Finally, whether you are citizens of America or citizens of the world, ask of us here the same high standards of strength and sacrifice which we ask of you. With a good conscience our only sure reward, with history the final judge of our deeds, let us go forth to lead the land we love, asking His blessing and His help, but knowing that here on earth God's work must truly be our own.

Now some might object that this conclusion is so well known that it could have been omitted from this article, that I should have found something more obscure. But the fact that almost every reader knows these words by heart tells you something: this is a conclusion that did its job extremely well.

7. 'Thank you'

Please remember to thank the audience for listening. It shows respect and regard for their time and their presence. It is also the recognised verbal cue to the audience that the speech is over. This appreciation is so universally expected that its absence would end the speech catastrophically.

A template for such a great conclusion may be found at the end of Tony Blair's well-remembered, high-octane speech to the Labour Party conference in Brighton on 2 October 2001, delivered in the aftermath of the 9/11 attacks on New York and Washington. He said:

> This is the moment to seize. The kaleidoscope has been shaken. The pieces are in flux. Soon they will settle again. Before they do, let us reorder the world around us. Today, humankind has the science and technology to destroy itself or to provide prosperity to all. Yet science can't make that choice for us. Only the moral power of a world acting as a community can. By the strength of our common endeavour we achieve more together than we can alone. For those who lost their lives on 11 September and those who mourn them, now is the time for the strength to build that community. Let that be their memorial.

That conclusion has everything: inclusive language that shows all of us must be involved and 'the fierce urgency of now'. It lays out a vision and mentions alternatives of salvation or destruction, both explicitly and, even more effectively, implicitly. It is a brilliant example of vision and speechwriting.

Diana DeGette (Bloomberg/Getty Images)

4. DELIVERY

Cicero said that an orator's power depended on three things: 'delivery, delivery, delivery'. That thought has been endlessly reworked and ripped off ('education, education, education'). Cicero's view was based on a lifetime of excellence in masterful rhetorical ability. He knew that delivery could shape circumstances, create a new reality, channel thinking, touch the heart and remake the world. For him, delivery was the key element in a persuasive speech. As a student of rhetoric, he understood that the act of persuasion was a human interaction between speaker and listener, a very personal exchange of information and trust. In turn, an audience listens to good delivery with more interest and enthusiasm. Good delivery will turn a speech into a memorable event.

But delivery is not just standing up and talking or, worse yet, standing up and reading. Delivery is a sharing of the self, using both the voice and non-verbals, an understanding of the mission and message of a speech, a utilisation of the power of words, and a strategic enterprise that persuades an audience, bringing them to the point of collective agreement and uniting them with the speaker, using language to heal division and to create unity in a community. Good delivery is an act of good faith, evidence of preparation and proof that the audience matters.

Delivery is also not acting, although elements of an actor's trade are involved. A typical criticism of Ronald Reagan or Tony Blair was to attack their background in acting. But such an attack entirely missed the point. Both learned key skills from acting: understanding the meaning and use of every word, developing a pleasant and clear voice for projection of language, recognising the power of pausing and the profound impact of the sound of silence, interpreting a writer's words so they become natural and conversational, learning the ability to make a text written by someone else their own, and using delivery to reach out to an audience and become one with them. These are all skills needed by any speaker. Reagan and Blair should be praised for having them, not condemned. The 'acting' criticism somehow suggests insincerity, a masking of self through verbal ability, a practised deception. But an acting background can give a valuable appreciation of language, or, as the actor Richard Burton once said, 'a love of language'.

There is some excellent advice in *Hamlet*. Late in the play Hamlet instructs a group of actors about how to speak their lines:

> Speak the speech, I pray you, as I pronounced it to you, tripping on the tongue . . . Be not tame either, but let your own discretion be your tutor; suit the action to the words, the word to the action; with this special observance, that you o'erstep not the modesty of nature.

Indeed, a speech must be delivered with a natural confidence that is authentic and persuasive. The delivery must be smooth and clear, enabling the audience to understand and evaluate everything said. There must be a transparency of thought, allowing the audience to follow the reasoning of the speaker and the argumentative progress of the speech. As I have said elsewhere, leaders are transparent; good delivery is an indispensable part of that transparency.

So good delivery is important, and should be essential, in public life. Sadly, there is often a low bar for delivery, especially in the United States, where good delivery is viewed suspiciously as a trick or an invitation to deception. A few years ago, a British historian wrote an article about rhetoric in the 'Age of the Osbournes', suggesting that Ozzy and Sharon, Austin Powers and *South Park*'s Eric Cartman were the real rhetorical models of America. I can think of no sadder commentary (I'm sure Ozzy would put it more colourfully). I know some speakers who have said they don't want to have good delivery, because it is not 'authentic', not 'who they are'. They proudly embrace verbal mediocrity. It is the equivalent of saying 'I have an illness and I don't want to be cured'. It is also arrogant and petulant, dismissing the needs of a listening audience. Sometimes a refusal to improve is just an overwhelming fear of public speaking. And sometimes it is laziness and smugness, a statement of ego and self-centred childishness. Their frailties are obvious every time they speak, which may explain why fear or some other failing trumps the search for quality.

But a weakness can be overcome, a failing turned into a strength. As Barack Obama has most recently demonstrated with such effect, good delivery can be a powerful, profound tool in the right hands. It literally can create a new dynamic, elevating those with little experience into the ranks of the contenders, even bring victory in a campaign or advancement in business.

Voice

If one wants to be a good speaker, there are five assumptions in delivery.

First, a speech is an oral activity. So communication depends, in part, on the quality of voice, clarity, emphasis and richness of timbre.

Second, every speech is a persuasive activity. The speech is being used to try to persuade an audience to adopt an attitude, change a belief, undertake an action or make a decision. The voice is a vital element in that persuasion. There is no such thing as a purely informative speech.

Third, every voice is different. A great speaker recognises the strengths and limitations of his or her own voice, and works to balance the presentation with complementary elements, such as good writing or expressive non-verbals. Every speaker has a unique rhetorical persona. Great speakers find the right mix of variables to make a lasting, singular impression. Dr Martin Luther King, Jr had a unique, defining voice. So did Winston Churchill. When you hear the voice you know the speaker. That is the end result of the creation of a unique rhetorical persona, as I mentioned in Chapter 1.

Fourth, delivery makes a speaking event human. The voice is the thing. It creates emotion, empathy, sadness, joy, love, hate, even hope. Especially hope. The words are important for sharing meaning. But the voice makes the words work, makes the interaction human. Think about listening to an electronic voice in a communication network, not a human voice recorded, but an electronic voice simulating a human voice. It seems alien and makes us angry that we aren't talking 'to a human'.

Fifth, a speech is made up of other messages besides words. The words are not the entire speech. In fact, they may not be the speech at all. There are messages coming from non-verbals (see below). The speech also must employ pausing, spacing and silence to effect. Delivery helps transmit the verbal message and is part of the message transmission for non-verbals, too.

Put another way, the words of a speech set up the delivery. But the delivery makes the words come alive, instantly making a speech three dimensional, an event with shades of grey, depths of meaning and vastly more levels of communication. Cicero wrote that 'a leading speaker will vary and modulate his voice, raising and lowering it and deploying the full scale of tones'. The speaker must know how to do that. Without effective delivery, the speech text remains two dimensional. A wonderful Greek rhetorician named Dionysius once made that point in a very revealing way. He compared the Greek orators Isocrates and Demosthenes:

> When I read a speech of Isocrates, I become sober and serious, as if I were listening to solemn music; but when I take up a speech of Demosthenes, I am beside myself, I am led this way and that, I am moved by one passion after another: suspicion, distress, fear, contempt, hate, pity, kindliness, anger, envy – passing successively through all the passions which can obtain a mastery over the human mind . . . and I have sometimes thought to myself, what must have been the impression on those who were fortunate enough to hear him?

Indeed, while the words show the possibilities, Demosthenes's delivery would have made the speech come to life, explore the human condition, connect with the audience and therefore become vastly more effective. A great speaker knows how to create the right impression at the right moment with word choice and delivery, never sliding into farce, never seeming to act or manipulate. The speaker is letting the words do their job, unleashing them to rush out and begin the work of persuasion.

Good speaking is a necessary part of political or business training. Those who excel at it, like Tony Blair, former Conservative leader William Hague, Israeli Knesset member Natan Sharansky, Nicolas Sarkozy, Russian Duma deputy Alexander Lebedev, Colorado representative Diana DeGette or New York senator Chuck Schumer, are exciting to hear and observe, masterful in their ability. They are persuasive, educational, entertaining, relaxed and congenial. They have likeability, in large measure because of their communication skills.

So what are the elements of good delivery? Here is a partial list.

1. Find your voice
Every political speaker must know who they are and what they

represent. Each politician is symbolically representative of certain messages. In political 'self-help' language, a politician must not try to be all things to all people. But they should not try to polarise audiences either. A political leader should become the voice of the audience, giving voice to their hopes, aspirations, dreams, fears, worries and troubles. A good politician will try to unite the audience in common purpose. Personally, I don't think a speaker should pander to an audience. I also don't think a speaker should use wedge politics to polarise and divide an audience. Rather, a political speaker should let the audience see that he or she is comfortable with his or her message and position.

2. Vary rate and volume appropriately

This helps the listening audience stay interested. The changes should be strategic, giving the most impact to the words and ideas in the speech. A speaker should know the point and purpose of every word, and every pause, in a speech. That is how a speaker displays what I call 'the intelligence behind the words', which means that he understands the point and purpose of every word in a speech, and every pause or silence between the words.

3. Enunciate clearly

A missed word can change the entire message of a speech, causing the audience to hear a different speech from the one given by the speaker. The goal should be complete shared meaning. Imagine the disaster for the message if the word 'not' is not clearly heard in the following: 'We must not raise taxes.' The speaker should also project to make sure everyone can hear.

4. Know why the words are there

Delivery improves when there is a clear understanding of the reason for every word in the speech. A good speaker knows the job of the word, which helps adjudicate how to phrase that word. Knowledge of the speech should improve delivery. I think Blair excels at this. He has the intelligence behind the words.

5. Use pausing as a tool

A speech is made up of words and pauses, sounds and silence. Good delivery uses pausing to effect, allowing the words to settle into the minds of the listening audience. Few speakers know how to use silence to gain impact. But a pregnant pause may be just as important as a devastating word.

6. Emphasise key words

Delivery guides the audience, explaining how to listen and highlighting what is important. Certain words are vital for persuading the audience. These words deserve to be set apart through emphasis. So, emphasis can make the speech more powerful and profound.

7. Practise and think about the speech

Now, combine it all together. Here is an example from a speech of 1936, in the dark days when Winston Churchill was warning of Germany's danger and Britain's lack of preparation. Read it out loud. There are several 'readings' possible, each displaying the potentialities inherent in the prose. Churchill was a master at letting the words take over, so this passage has nuanced possibilities, with divisible differences of rate, volume, pausing and emphasis.

> The First Lord of the Admiralty in his speech the other night went even further. He said: 'We are always reviewing the position.' Everything, he assured us, is entirely fluid. I am sure that is true. Anyone can see what their position is. The government simply cannot make up their minds, or they cannot get the Prime Minister to make up his own mind. So they go on in strange paradox, decided only to be undecided, resolved to be irresolute, adamant for drift, solid for fluidity, all-powerful to be impotent. So we go on preparing more months and years – precious, perhaps vital to the greatness of Britain – for the locusts to eat. They will say to me: 'A minister of supply is not necessary, for all is

going well.' I deny it. 'The position is satisfactory.' It is not true. 'All is proceeding according to plan.' We know what that means.

This is a good paragraph for demonstrating the shades of grey in delivery. The words could be given at different rates and volumes. Emphasis could be placed on some words in one reading, a completely different set in another. A light touch gives a different reading from heavy treading. Yet, because of the way the paragraph is written, almost any reading will produce a shared meaning between speaker and audience. This is an instance of how the words can take over (see Chapter 3).

For example, one reading would be just that – simply reading the text. The speech has a power of its own and doesn't need much from the speaker. Merely reading the words is enough to make the speech work. Another reading would allow for a shocked and surprising reading of the line 'I am sure this is true'. Nothing else needs to be done. This would set up the rest of the speech nicely. A third would read along with little variation until reaching the response lines. Then there could be emphasis for those lines: 'I deny it', 'It is not true' and 'We know what that means'. There could be slight, extra emphasis on the words 'it', 'true' and 'means'. Or the emphasis could be on the verbs: 'deny', 'is not' and 'know'. In fact, the last line has incredible, delicious possibilities. I would love to give it with strategic pausing, emphasis on 'that' and a sly look: '. . .We know. . . what *that* means!' You could even have a Marlon Brando reading, from his early 'Streetcar' or 'Waterfront' or 'Julius Caesar' days. He would rip through it, torn and tortured, fluctuating between anger and tears, feeling frustration and torment. Or you could have a Clint Eastwood reading, from the 'Dirty Harry' days, providing a great moment with the climax (narrow eyes and steady delivery): 'We know what that means. . .' (followed by a sneer and silence).

Then there is that fantastic line 'for the locusts to eat'. That needs its own spacing and silent pausing both before and afterwards. There are countless ways of doing that one. Think what Michael

Caine could do with that line as part of *Get Carter* or Anthony Hopkins in *The Silence of the Lambs*.

And so on. There are an infinite number of ways to interpret and deliver this wonderful passage, first lightly with little verbal difference, then with more and more variation and emphasis, until reaching an extreme of heavy-handed delivery, with fireworks and anger.

Cicero was right about the importance of delivery. Good speakers are students of delivery, always thinking and watching, learning and maturing. Good speakers are constantly working on their craft. This has a tendency to create a much more developed appreciation of the human condition, a deeper insight into the lives of others and a more developed understanding of the self. Far from being a tool of propaganda or a device of deception, good delivery should lead us to a more authentic and aware rhetorical persona. This is why Aristotle and others stressed the importance of character in public speaking. Good character is essential for public trust. Audiences determine character from what they see and hear. The speaker must earn trust and faith through the human interaction of a speech.

Non-verbals

A speech is both verbal and non-verbal. There are some studies that indicate audiences are more suggestive to the non-verbal over the verbal, so appearance, clothes, backdrop and gestures matter. . . perhaps a great deal. They may be the message. The non-verbals may be the real speech for the audience.

Again, delivery includes both verbal and non-verbal messages. That is why the speech begins *when the speaker enters the room*. Already non-verbal messages have begun. Is the speaker confident? Does the speaker's appearance inspire hope and faith? Does the speaker look like a leader? Is the speaker a person of good character? The answers to these questions and more are being transmitted straightaway, creating a deep first impression with the audience. The audience is immediately determining likeability, personability, warmth, sincerity, transparency and, most important, trustiness.

Non-verbals include everything the audience sees. Cicero says a good speaker

> will avoid extravagant gestures and stand impressively erect. He will not pace about and when he does so not for any distance. He should not dart forward except in moderation with strict control. There should be no effeminate bending of the neck or twiddling of his fingers or beating out the rhythm of his cadences on his knuckles. He should control himself by the way he holds and moves his entire body.

That is sound advice to this day, highlighting the importance of gestures and body language. And all of that does matter, because the audience receives messages from every aspect of the non-verbal in a speech.

In fact, in public speaking there is a presumption in favour of non-verbals. Studies have shown that when the words conflict with the body language, or, in other words, there is a contradiction between the verbal and the non-verbal, the audience will accept the non-verbal message as more genuine and authentic. This may be because audiences are so used to the devaluation or twisting of words that they believe body language is more immediate and sincere. Words may lie; body language may be more honest. That is why the spoken words and non-verbals must be consistently harmonious. If they are not, the speaker becomes his or her own self-contradiction, resolved by the audience through belief in the non-verbal.

So, here are some things to keep in mind.

1. Dress appropriately

In other words, dress for success. The speaker will be judged by appearances, everything from tattoos to toe-nail polish, bling to belt. I suggest dressing a bit better than the audience, but don't go over the top.

2. Good posture is important

Credibility is often correlated with posture in the minds of the audience. But a speaker shouldn't be 'stiff assed' either. Comfortable good posture is best. Good posture also sets up a more intimate gesture, leaning forward to show engagement and earnestness.

3. Maintain eye contact with the audience

The audience is watching the speaker's eyes throughout the speech. Real eye contact creates a moment of connection with the audience. I suggest a speaker should try to have three to five seconds of eye contact with each member of the audience. In my view, eye contact is the most important non-verbal because of the power of such a connection. But don't stare with a glazed or threatening look. Your eye contact should be normal and engaging, not scary or alarming.

4. Use appropriate gestures

The point of a gesture is to highlight or enhance a message, not overwhelm it. Repetitive or unnecessary gestures create confusion and actually diminish the power of a speech. Gestures should be used with economy to enhance the message.

5. Employ some limited physical movement

Step away from the podium on occasion. Turn and look at different sections of the audience. Shift your torso. Even take a step closer to the audience. This variety helps with active listening for the audience and helps create a more intimate, dynamic delivery. It also helps everybody stay awake.

6. Set the tone

The speaker should adopt an appropriate demeanour at the beginning of the speech to signal how the audience should listen. The speaker should set the tone and create the atmosphere for the speech. A joyful face sends one message, a perplexed face another, a sad face yet another. The audience will take cues from the speaker's face, initiating a process of listening. The speaker must make sure the audience is listening in the right way.

7. Stay confident and in control
The audience likes measured confidence. By staying in control the speaker becomes the master of the event.

8. Become distinctive
Your unique rhetorical persona includes non-verbals. The way you dress may set you apart. In the United States columnist George Will is known for his bow tie. Politician Ken Salazar is noted for his cowboy hat (he is a rancher by profession). Winston Churchill had his cigar. The risk is that the distinction becomes a joke. But the right non-verbal can strengthen credibility, enhance believability and provide leadership credentials.

Think about non-verbals with every speech. Everything you wear, or don't wear, sends a message. Every gesture sends a message. Eye contact sends a message. Make sure you are sending clear, consistent messages. Make sure you are sending the right message. And here is a piece of advice that may make a difference: practise your non-verbals. Get them right. Leave nothing to chance. Make them meaningful, natural and persuasive. Your non-verbals just might be even more important than your delivery. You would be very foolish to ignore the powerful impact of non-verbal communication.

Overcoming speech anxiety

Early in his life, Cicero wrote:

> Personally, I am always very nervous when I begin to speak. Every time I make a speech I feel I am submitting

to judgement, not only about my ability but about my character and honour. I am afraid of seeming either to promise more than I can perform, which suggests complete irresponsibility, or to perform less than I can, which suggests bad faith and indifference.

Cicero's problem is common. Even Winston Churchill suffered from speech anxiety throughout his entire public life.

Almost everybody experiences some form of speech anxiety. It has a physical explanation. Virtually every speaker feels an adrenaline rush before speaking, and that may explain the symptoms of anxiety: dry mouth, sweating, loss of voice control, physical shaking and minimal eye contact.

But there are other reasons for anxiety. A speech is a rarity for many people, and there is a fear of the unknown. Some people focus on what could go wrong and then become obsessive about it. Some speakers become anxious because they are facing a hostile audience and are expecting the worst. Many people have anxiety because they aren't prepared to give the speech or don't really understand what they will talk about. Sometimes there are deeper problems, such as low self-esteem, a dislike of facing other people, worries about physical attractiveness, or fear of criticism by others. And some people go through anxiety as a ritual, a habit, a pattern of performance. It is a way of working themselves up for a speech. It is a 'me-centred' approach, a way of gaining attention from staff and loved ones. I have noticed this last trait in novice politicians and junior executives, who then don't grow out of it as they move up the public or corporate ladder. And staff often enable the anxiety ritual by allowing the boss to sustain the tension and pressure.

Most people overcome anxiety. But some are disabled by it for years, maybe a lifetime.

Because so many people experience anxiety, with so many different causes, there are countless theories about how to deal with it. Some of the theories are grounded in hearsay examples, such as 'I knew somebody who knew somebody who downed a shot of vodka before a speech, and it worked'. Some are based on studies of anxiety, such as academic analysis and quantitative results published in journals like *Communication Education* or the *Quarterly Journal of Speech*. Some experts have written books about the problem and its solutions, volumes often found on the self-help or public speaking shelves in bookshops. And some people even go so far as to prescribe medicines, therapies, hypnosis, exercise or lucky charms. Sometimes things get really weird, such as one person who makes a 'lucky pterodactyl noise' before speaking: 'Accckkkk!!!!' I know one woman who conquered anxiety by giving a speech stark naked in front of several hundred people. As she said: 'After that you will never be afraid again, because nothing could be worse.' That is a way of thinking about it, I suppose. But surely there should be some qualifying standards.

So, what works? What can be done? I would recommend the following actions.

1. Burn off the adrenaline

Sadly, you are usually sitting before speaking, and the adrenaline builds up, ready to rush through you. Exercise before the event, if possible. Walk around before speaking, if you can. Even if you are seated, have some physical movement. When standing at the podium, use a controlled gesture to productively address the adrenaline. Don't give in to repetitive gestures that are actually charged by your anxiety. Walk away from the podium a bit if the microphone will let you. Turn from right to left every three to five seconds to make eye contact and to get some physical movement. Changes of rate can help, too. Start slow and measured so you establish strong voice control. Then move to a slightly more rapid rate in parts of the speech for emphasis. I would especially encourage a more rapid rate in the conclusion.

2. Become familiar with the speech.

Make sure you understand every aspect of it. Make sure there are no surprises. Know the speech top to bottom.

3. Practise the speech

In my experience, this is one of the places where most speech fright can be effectively addressed for executives and politicians. For all the angst about major speeches, most people do not practise. Reading over a speech silently is fine, but it is not practice. Giving the speech to a few friends is nice, but it is not practice. Real practice takes place with a microphone, podium, substitute audience of unfamiliar people, use of gestures and voice inflections, and efforts at projection. And the whole thing should be videotaped for later review. There are some who will object that such an effort is not feasible, that there isn't time on the schedule, or access to a studio, or the chance to gather an audience, blah blah. My answer is simple: if you don't make the effort to practise in real conditions, you can't expect to be fully prepared for the event. Imagine a footballer who didn't practise on the field with teammates, or the boxer who never sparred. They wouldn't be well trained and ready for the big time. Training is essential in almost every form of public endeavour, and speaking is easily an activity that benefits from coaching, vision, direction and problem correction. Plus, the video is great. It helps you see what the audience looks at during the speech: you!

4. Have confidence

Signal confidence with a smile, relaxed manner, bold language and a commanding presence. Study the delivery of Tony Blair, David Cameron, William Hague, Nelson Mandela, Barack Obama or even Arnold Schwarzenegger (even with his inability to use articles or find proper pronunciation, he is surely the most daring and entertaining speaker of our time). I would even recommend the conversational style of Diana DeGette, former New York governor Mario Cuomo, or former Czech President Václav Havel. Think about those who are good at the college debate union or parliamentary discussion. They have a quick-witted, audience-sensitive, enviable confidence. These figures can be rhetorical role models; although you can learn from them, try not to become a clone. Develop your own unique rhetorical style. Be yourself.

5. Want to give the speech

Become passionate about the speech. Feel a sense of urgency to share your material with the audience. This is really important. If the speech is drudgery and you don't want to do it, then you will resent the event and the words. You won't want to practise. You won't feel confident. Rather, get enthusiastic about it. Make it an event where you want to share, you want to persuade and you want to educate. Visualise giving it well. Think about how the audience might be affected by a good speech. Consider the behaviour change that is possible if you connect with them. Think about how wonderful it will be to give a successful speech that is well received.

6. Make the speech a well-worded conversation

You have lots of experience with conversations. Make this speech a conversation that just involves more people. Since audiences respond well to a good conversational presentation, you have a better chance of giving a good speech. Make the speech authentically yours, a thoughtful expression of your worries, aspirations and solutions. Speak from the heart. Share a bit of yourself with the audience. In turn, they will warm to you and find your humanity refreshing. This is a good way to establish common ground.

7. Work towards improvement with each speech

'What doesn't kill you will make you stronger,' they say. So each speech should be an improvement over the last. Don't become self-satisfied; strive for greater excellence. Set new goals. Make your speeches personal benchmarks for your own communicative improvement.

If you do these things, then you will help address speech anxiety. You will make the speech more enjoyable for yourself and the listening audience. And you will be a more successful speaker, becoming one with the audience.

Of course, if none of this works, you can always consider doing the speech naked. . .

John Kennedy (Time & Life Pictures/Getty Images)

5. IMPACT

When I was learning my craft, older speechwriters talked about 'impact'. I didn't really understand. They would say vague things like 'You know, persuasion' or 'Lasting results' or 'The audience was moved'.

Finally, I began to get it. Impact is about the speech doing its job of persuasion. But more than that, impact is about the penetration of the message into the brain. A speech performs only part of its job if the audience is initially persuaded. The speech also has to keep persuading over time. That means the message has to dig in and keep working constantly, over days and weeks and months and years, still forcing the audience members to think about the issue and find themselves in agreement with the speaker, motivated to take action again and again.

So a speech has to be as powerful and persuasive as possible. It is important to get the message right and keep the speech on message.

Think about the lasting impact of Dr Martin Luther King, Jr's speech on the Washington Mall in 1963. That speech reverberates nearly fifty years later, its relevance undiminished and its profound power still working to make the world more just, fair and equitable. Consider the impact of Jesus's Sermon on the Mount, still doing its job 2,000 years on.

Every speech – every speech – has that potential. The message is important. But there are other aspects of the speech that can contribute to its impact. In this chapter we will discuss controlling the setting, the need for a good briefing book, manuscript preparation, handling hecklers and going for the jugular. These aspects deserve attention.

Control the setting

A few years ago, Mother Teresa spoke at the National Prayer Breakfast in Washington. She was introduced by President Clinton. The event was broadcast live to the nation over C-Span. There were several hundred people in the audience. This was a big speech by any definition.

But the speech failed; it flopped. The delivery was good. The message was clear. But the height of the podium was set for the tall Clinton, not for the significantly shorter main speaker. When she walked to the podium, Mother Theresa disappeared. You could hear her give the speech, but you couldn't see her, just the tip of her hat and an occasional disembodied hand that would rise in gesture to the top of the podium, wave, then evaporate.

Stories about the physical setting are legion. For example, recently a cabinet minister spoke from a podium that looked like it was designed for little children, only rising to his belt. The microphones were taped onto it and he had to bend down to give the speech. There have been other well-known occasions where the speaker was placed in the middle of an enormous stage, which itself was many feet from the first row of chairs in the audience.

The speaker looked like a miniature figure seen through the wrong end of the telescope. The physical division between the speaker and the audience was too vast to overcome.

These are mistakes that undercut the speech itself. After all the time spent preparing and practising (I wish), the speech is ruined because other people made poor decisions about the physical setting, decisions on behalf of the speaker but without regard to the actual needs of the speaker. I want to emphasise this: the speaker was passive, not involved or present beforehand, allowing others to make important decisions about the speech then just accepting the physical setting at the time of delivery.

Most speakers just show up and give the speech. This is typical. You put the speech on your schedule and then maybe show up a few minutes early to look over the room and the audience. This forces you to immediately adjust to the room, podium, microphone, cameras and other aspects of the setting of the speech. And sometimes those adjustments are wrong, because you are giving the speech and can't see your image or hear your words from the perspective of the audience. And if you have to ask 'Can you hear me?', then the magic of the speech is already gone.

Very few speakers ever preview the physical setting. I mean that. Few actually look over a room and try to understand it before giving the speech. Few speakers walk around the room looking for possible problems. Few speakers have an advance person to look over all of the elements of the physical setting of the speech and the means of transmitting the words and images that make up the speech. And, frankly, many advance people don't know what to look for when they preview the setting. The rest of us, the speakers who don't have 'people' to help us out, often don't have the time to check out the location beforehand, nor do many of us have the desire to do so.

So what can we do? In my view, we must become more paranoid, worried about Murphy's Law, because if something can go wrong it probably will. We must eliminate the passive approach and seize the setting. We must make it our own. I literally mean that: we must make the setting most advantageous for the speech through direct and strategic decisions and adjustments about every significant aspect of the physical setting. Rather than simply accept decisions made by others, *speakers must become more aggressive in altering the setting to suit the needs of the speech.*

Here are some things to think about.

1. Change the backdrop

Find out about the backdrop. Get a photograph if possible. This will allow you to know the message displayed behind you. Make sure that message is consistent with your own. There have been many occasions where the backdrop actually contradicted the message of the speech. You should consider changing any backdrop to better emphasise your own message. That backdrop can be creative. It doesn't have to be a waving flag or a dot.com address. It can be a photograph, an emblem, a slogan. It can be anything. It can also be nothing. . . a neutral, solid black or blue. The point is to make sure it is what you want, not what someone else thinks you want. And dress to stand out from the backdrop, to make you look good. One famous comedienne for whom I wrote came to a ballroom to be filmed. Her dress was exactly the same pattern and colour as the backdrop. When she stood in front of it her body was gone, with only a head and hands remaining. She looked out at me and said: 'Always tell someone about the backdrop.' Good advice, that.

2. Get the podium you need

The podium anoints you as the speaker. It is a functional tool to hold a manuscript and a symbol of your task to be the speaker, to be the expert or advocate for a position or party. The podium may also display a logo or emblem of office or a message on the front. So you have to think about the podium, just as a church minister has a pulpit or a teacher the desk. This is where we will work from, the place that makes us different from the audience. There are podiums of every shape and size. Some are wooden poles and planks from another era. Some are so technologically advanced you need an instruction manual. There are thousands of possibilities in between. My advice is to get a podium that will adjust to your height, will look good in a photograph, allows you enough room for your work and gives you control of the technology, such as the microphone or the Powerpoint remote.

3. Use a microphone that makes you sound good

Microphones are not all equal. There is vast variation. Some make your voice sound deep and rich, like James Earl Jones. Some raise your voice and make you sound like a heavy metal rocker hitting those falsetto notes. Some microphones make the sound muddy, others clear. You need to know which make and style of microphone works best for you. That comes with trial and error. With each one you have to discover how to use it, whether to speak across it or right into it, or whatever. You should extend this well beyond fixed microphones for the podiums. Look into clip-ons and headset models, too. When you find that one that works for you, insist on it for your speeches. Obviously, the sound system in each room will vary. So you want to have the right microphone that provides the best overall sound quality, with 'quality' defined as the best presentation, in your view, of your voice. If you have any doubts about any of this, consult your local rock star or special events coordinator. They have a lot of knowledge about microphones. I would imagine Rod Stewart knows as much about microphones as he does about hair gel or spandex outfits. You might want to get that kind of background (on microphones).

4. Fix the lighting

Recently, one of my clients was scheduled to speak before a large audience. The day before I went to the room and tried out the podium. When the lights came on I couldn't see anything. I couldn't see more than two feet in front of the podium. The lights were blinding and created a wall of glare. I spoke to the events people who replied: 'Well, we have to illuminate the speaker so everyone can see him.' Yes, they do have that task. But the solution to their problem is not to create a visibility problem for the speaker. So the lights had to be configured a new way. I know many speakers who complain about lighting that blurs the manuscript. That needs to be fixed beforehand. Some lighting is too hard, making us look too old or weary or wrinkled. I know that some celebrities bring their own lighting people to interviews and speeches, replacing the usual bulbs to produce softer lighting that makes their skin glow and look younger. That is good control of the physical setting.

5. Mind the gap

There is space between you and the listening audience. Make sure it is the right amount of space, close enough for connection without violating any territorial imperative. Think of the back row as well as the front row. How close is too close? At this moment, the trendy answer is to place the speaker among the audience, the 360-degree look, creating an image of intimacy and contact. When the audience is all the way around you it also gives you a backdrop of people. That may be the backdrop you want.

6. Understand the room

Where should you stand so the audience can see you best? Move the podium there. If you don't have a microphone, find the acoustic 'sweet spots' where your voice sounds best and speak from there. Where will the cameras be placed? Do they have a good visual angle to get their pictures? Alter the setting to give the photographers what they want. Where will the media be seated? Look often in that direction during the speech. Show you care about them. And, of course, know how to get in and out of the room. Nothing is more pathetic than a speaker who cannot find the way out of the room.

This list is abbreviated. There are many more worries about the physical setting. You need to see it beforehand. You need to study the setting. You need to make decisions that empower you as a speaker. Don't let others make key decisions without consulting you. Change the setting to best suit the needs of the speech. Control the setting; don't let it control you.

The briefing behind the speech

For important speaking events there are two products: the speech and a background briefing book. Behind every successful politician or corporate CEO is a hard-working, often unacknowledged staff. One or more staff members help to prepare important public speeches, especially speeches given at annual conferences, civic clubs, union gatherings or other events. And the speech is the finished product that the public hears or reads. But behind the speech, especially if it is professionally presented and well constructed, is a prodigious research effort. The speech reflects that research. It is a product of numerous decisions on topics, arguments, references and word choices based on that research. The background briefing book helps prepare the speaker for the event. It explains the direction, construction and content of the speech. It provides essential information about the event itself and the audience. It will also help the speaker prepare informal conversation and chit-chat, as well as provide possible answers to questions that might arise during the event.

It helps to gather as much audience information as possible. You need event information, too. Here is a checklist:

1. When is the speech (date/time)?
2. Who invited the speaker?
3. What is the purpose of the speech?
4. What is the specific point/theme of the speech?
5. Who will introduce the speaker?
6. How many people are in the audience?
7. What are the general characteristics of the audience?
8. What do they want to hear?
9. What is the audience's attitude to the speaker?
10. How much time is allotted for the speech?
11. Will there be Q&As?
12. Who should the speaker recognize?

The briefing will need to contain the answers to those questions.

So what should a good briefing book look like? Well, the briefing book is a collaboration between the scheduler, the advance staff, the speechwriter and available experts and advisors. Each responsible party has vital information that should be contained in the briefing book. The material must be gathered together in a quickly accessible, understandable, concise manner. Many offices already have a designated format for preparing the book. Below is a suggested format based on the best briefing books I've seen in the White House, in the cabinet agencies, in Congress and in the corporate world.

Imagine the principal speaker is someone named Bertie Wooster.

Cover letter and tables of contents

The briefing book should start with a cover letter attached on the outside or preferably enclosed as page 1. It should be dated on letterhead. The next line should be addressed to the principal, as in 'To: Bertram Wilberforce Wooster'. The line after that should identify the sender, as in 'From: Reginald Jeeves'. The following line would be about the purpose of the briefing book, such as 'Re: Speech before the Drones Club Fine Arts Committee'. Then we get to the body of the letter, which is a brief sketch of the event, background and circumstances. All of this should be summarised in one or two paragraphs. The time and date of the event, address and room must be included. The cover letter should then indicate who will introduce the principal ('Mr. Richard P. "Bingo" Little, a member of the club, will provide introductory remarks of about five minutes.') It is also advisable to then add in the expectations of the audience: 'You have been asked to speak for about twenty minutes. The event organisers hope you will address the upcoming purchase of wine and spirits for the annual golf tournament, the repair costs to the library after the Boat Night festivities, as well as the particulars of the annual darts tournament. Questions will follow your speech.'

The cover letter should also have an outline of the subsequent tab divisions.

Tab A: Letter of invitation/agenda

The letter of invitation should follow the cover letter. It makes sense because the speaker may want to consult it to answer any lingering issues from the cover letter. Also include after the invitation letter the agenda of the event. The need for the agenda is obvious, allowing the speaker to see how the speech fits into the overall layout and progression of presentations. Often the agenda is composed at the last minute. This may have the advantage of allowing your office and staff to make suggestions about when and where on the agenda the principal should speak.

Tab B: Speech

The speech is next. There should be two versions. One should be in a 12-point font for easy reading prior to the speech. The second should be the reading copy in 22–26-point font (I recommend Times New Roman bold) for easy use during the speech. The reading copy should be double spaced, scaled to fit the upper two-thirds of the page, with unbroken sentences on each page, and page numbers at the top right (and at bottom right or centre if you need them there too). Last-minute changes should be made on this version.

Tab C: Background on organisation

Then there is information about the organisation and the audience. The summary should be extensive without too much length. So it is a good idea to condense the information. You need the relevant data and background, just not too much of it. For example, a short version could look like this: 'The Drones Club, of which you are a member, is a gentlemen's club in Mayfair on Dover Street, off Piccadilly. The club records show that you have been a member since at least 1923. The Fine Arts Committee meets over snooker or cards to provide planning for forthcoming events. The members of the committee and invited guests will be in attendance, numbering about twenty people. For your additional information, a list of the forty-four members of the Drones Club, compiled by Daniel Garrison ("Who's Who in Wodehouse"), is attached.'

Tab D: Biographies of key leadership

Biographies of those involved in the event should follow. These are usually available from their organisations or from biographical dictionaries such as *Who's Who*. The Internet is also a common tool (although beware relying on Wikipedia. . . even they recommend you double-check all information). The biographies should be limited to one page each. You could have a brief initial explanation of the choice of biographies that looks like this:

> Enclosed are biographies of members of the Fine Arts Committee: Mr. Richard P. 'Bingo' Little, G. D'Arcy 'Stilton' Cheesewright, Baron Chuffnell (Marmaduke 'Chuffy' Chuffnell), Hildebrand 'Tuppy' Glossop and Alexander C. 'Oofy' Prosser. The benediction will be offered by Reverend Harold P. 'Stinker' Pinker, who is not a member. Also, in attendance will be Sir P. G. 'Plum' Wodehouse, whom you may encounter at the dinner. Remember, he fancies himself responsible for your prominence. Humour him, if possible. Stephen Fry has called his work 'the sacred text', so you might want to quote a few lines. Please also remember that at the last meeting Augustus 'Gussie' Fink-Nottle put a newt in your restorative snifter, which you discovered as it descended past your tonsils on a downward trajectory, providing some stark amusement for those in attendance. A covert revenge newt has been procured by Rogers, a member of the club staff, who will silently serve it to Mr Fink-Nottle as part of the concluding toast by Cyril 'Barmy' Fotheringay-Phipps. Perhaps you might prepare strong denials.

Tab E: Summaries of reports and other publications

A speaker must demonstrate expertise on the subject and familiarity with the organisation in the words chosen in a speech, the references made and the solidarity with the views of the audience. So it is important to provide executive summaries of key reports or short explanations of the organisation's legislative agenda.

Tab F: Background record of support

The speaker also needs to know about votes or actions of interest to the audience. So here is an example: 'Your encounters with the Drones Club and its members may be found among the material in *The Penguin Wodehouse Companion* by Richard Usborne. A short summary of those encounters is attached at this tab.' The summary would then follow. An outline in talking points or bulleted format probably would be the most useful way to provide this information.

Tab G: Questions and answers

Most speeches are followed by a Q&A session. Even if not, questions do arise in informal conversation or during press availability after the speech. So a summary list of numbered questions should begin this section. Then the questions, with short answers, would follow. The questions should be briefly worded, as well as the answers, which may be structured as brief talking points. The questions might be as simple as: 1. May women enter the darts tournament? 2. May we place wagers to show a proper sporting spirit? 3. What is the budget for the event? and so on. The questions may be formulated after extensive research on the interest of the organisation and through conversation by the principal's staff with people familiar with the audience.

Other tabs may be added for press releases, specific background materials for the speech, conference materials, airline schedules or anything else important for the speech.

Remember, there is an art to constructing a good briefing book: the shorter the better without leaving out key material. Too much material can deter the speaker from even making an effort to read and absorb it (I've watched speakers literally walk away from a big briefing package). If read at all, it can overwhelm the speaker. In preparing for the first presidential debate with Walter Mondale in 1984, President Reagan was given a stack of briefing books (some place the figure as high as ten). He read them all and experienced information overload, performing poorly in the debate. For the next

debate, the volume was substantially reduced to one book, which
he read. The result was a sharper, more effective performance. In
preparing a briefing book, sometimes less is more. It is important to
have the broad policy objectives and overall vision clear. The details
don't matter as much. Statistics, names and references often get
in the way. So limit the information to what is essential and what
can be absorbed in the allotted time for principal preparation. For
instance, many principals schedule time to read the briefing book.
That is a really good idea; it forces the principal to actually read the
briefing with the compilers/experts still at hand. Be suspicious of
those who say 'I'll read it at home tonight' or 'I'll look at it in the
hotel room'. The former almost never happens and the latter might
be too late for necessary additions or clarifications.

So here is a rule of thumb: if the briefing book requires more
than one binder, then it is too long. If it would take more than
thirty minutes to read, then it may be too long. But sometimes
this rule should be violated. Never sacrifice quality or necessity
for shorter length. If it has to be longer to satisfy the needs of
the principal, then err on the side of caution and include the
questionable information. But use discretion and good judgement.
Good briefers develop a strong sense about length and material.

Briefing books should be labelled, indexed and retained when
the event is over. There should be a library of briefing books for
reference about the event and for consultation for similar upcoming
speaking opportunities.

If the briefing book is small enough it can actually be carried
to the podium, functioning as a binder for holding the speech.
This gives the speaker the chance to have materials available for
questions and answers after the speech. But a well-prepared
speaker shouldn't 'need' the briefing book at the podium, and given
the choice I would urge good preparation before the speech versus
undue reliance on the background material during the speech or in
discussion afterwards, especially for the Q&As.

A good briefing helps the speaker focus on the audience, the
message and the expectations for a presentation. It helps smooth

the way for an effective, mistake-free presentation. It is an effort to rationally manage and condense information. A sloppy briefing effort invites risky, sometimes uninformed remarks that could alienate an audience, ignite a damaging press story or even end a career. The absence of a briefing book for an important speech is simply stupid, unforgivable staff laziness.

The background briefing material must reflect a deep understanding of the audience and the event. It must be a Jeeves-like effort, outstanding staff work. In other words, the information needed is always there. But, if outside help is required, the noted nerve specialist Sir Roderick Glossop is on call. He is familiar with the Wooster file.

Preparing the manuscript

A great speech requires more than composition, audience analysis and memorable prose. Often successful public speaking is a matter of the way you prepare your delivery manuscript. Murphy's Law is at play here too: if something can go wrong, it will. So in an effort to improve delivery and to avoid mistakes, here are some ideas for the delivery of the manuscript and the actual text before you as you speak.

1. Increase the font size
Typically a draft speech in preparation is constructed and circulated in 10–12-point size. Yet, for delivery, the font size in the manuscript should be much larger, between 22 and 36 points. This allows for easy viewing of the manuscript, which in turn allows for more eye contact and fewer verbal gaffes. If you are squinting to see the manuscript or have to break away from eye contact to read the text more closely, then you need to increase the font size in your delivery manuscript. Personally, I like the size of the text to be around 22 points. It allows you to see the text very well, even if you walk a couple of steps away from the podium.

Here is an example of the larger font size from a speech Cicero gave against Catiline in the Roman Senate in 63 BC:

When, O Catiline, do you mean to cease abusing our patience?

That is 22 point size. Since the main text of this book is 10 point, you can easily compare the difference.

Now, think of what this means as you are standing at a podium, the speech 2–3 feet away, and you are speaking to a room full of people you want to persuade to adopt an action of belief. You are fine-tuning the language to the atmosphere of the room, gesturing meaningfully, sometimes walking away from the podium, leaning forward, moving back, searching every face, sensitive to the feedback from each person in the audience, interpreting that feedback and making adjustments in your eye contact and emphasis. You don't need to be reading small print or losing your place. You need the words to pop out at you in a user-friendly fashion. When a speaker cannot see the words then I judge that to be a self-inflicted problem, rhetorical stupidity, easily avoidable, often fatally dooming the speech.

Yes, larger print size does mean more paper. But the trade-off is worth it because the speech is delivered more fluently, which should mean more effectively. If you think that 22 point is too large for you (or too small) then experiment until you find the right text size. And that means the right size for you at the podium, not while formatting the speech in the office or using a portable printer on the road. You need to find the text size that works best for you in the action of delivery itself, not what looks good to you before the action starts. You may hesitate to use more pages, but you will become a believer after your next failed speech that died because you couldn't really read it easily enough to deliver it well.

2. Increase the spacing between lines

You may want to create space between lines of larger text to see it better. Some speakers like double spacing, which is what I recommend, although I know some speakers who triple space. Again, the reason for this is to create more ease of viewing the text during the speech.

Obviously, if you increase the size of text and space more, you would be well advised to use shorter words and shorter sentences. One of the great advances in public speaking during the twentieth century was the use of more concise sentences. If you doubt this happened, compare speeches from the eighteenth and nineteenth centuries with those given today. Look at speeches by William Pitt the Younger or William Gladstone, both great speakers, and both speakers who typically liked to use punctuation to string together epic sentences that never seemed to end, although often it looked like they might, but such expectations were merely an illusion, a mystery of missed opportunities, savaged by the need to speak more profusely and stretch out the allotted time (just like this sentence). Even our verbally generous speakers today would be hard pressed to maintain the long sentences of the past, although there are some modern speakers who need to learn the value of concise language. Shorter is better. It is certainly better for the text of the delivery manuscript.

3. Use only two-thirds of the page

Every part of every page is not equal. The top is better than the bottom. With each line that gets closer to the foot of the page the speaker lowers the face to read it and sacrifices eye contact. In order to maintain eye contact you don't want your head to bob up and down. Also you don't want to cut off your air intake as you speak.

So, many speakers only use the top two-thirds of a page. Good idea. This allows them to keep their head level and to better coordinate the reading of the manuscript with eye contact.

4. End each page with a complete sentence

If the idea in preparing the manuscript is to increase the effectiveness of the speech, then the sentences must flow. If the sentence is interrupted by the. . . turn. . . of. . . a. . . page, and the continuity of thought is lost, then the speech starts to lose its effectiveness. Avoidance of such an interruption can be easily addressed, pre-empted, by making sure that each page ends with a complete sentence, not merely a fragment or a clause.

5. Place page numbers on the top right-hand corner

That way you will always know what page you are on and what page comes next. Amazingly, with page numbers at the bottom of the page, many speakers don't pay attention and then miss a page as they move on. Equally amazingly, the audience rarely realises this because the speeches are usually so muddled that clarity has been lost long before such a mistake. But if one really cares about the message and wants the audience to listen, then page numbers should be in a place of prominence (top better than bottom) and usefulness.

6. Underline or highlight the key words in each sentence

The underlining helps you remember to emphasise certain words. It can assist you to make the sentence livelier. A sentence without emphasis is sterile. Delivering a sentence with no emphasis on key words is reading, not speaking. One of the great gifts of Reverend Jesse Jackson in his prime was his tremendous ability to emphasise words, sometimes even adding syllables or stretching out the endings. Tony Blair has the ability to change rate, volume and emphasis from word to word, while most great speakers only do this sentence to sentence, and bad speakers use little or no emphasis at all. Underlining can help. It can work wonders for some speakers.

Here is an example with one possible interpretation from the 'Iron Curtain' speech delivered by Winston Churchill in 1946:

> The <u>Dark Ages</u> may <u>return</u>, the <u>Stone Age</u> may return on the gleaming wings of science, and what <u>might</u> now shower, shower <u>immeasurable</u> material blessings upon mankind, <u>may</u> even <u>bring about</u> its <u>total destruction</u>. <u>Beware</u> I say; <u>time</u> is plenty <u>short</u>. Do not let us take the course of allowing events to drift along before it is <u>too late</u>.

That is just a sample of what one might do. The emphasis could be different for each speaker, idiosyncratic and personal. It could be placed on proper names, verbs or direct objects. The choice is yours. But each choice dictates the way the audience hears the speech. Consistency might be helpful in forming patterns that construct listening habits for the audience. Underlining might also be helpful for difficult words or facts. Some speakers like to underline or highlight proper names or statistical facts. It helps them to get the words right during delivery.

7. Structure pauses in speech for better control of rate
In his inaugural address John Kennedy confronted a very tricky passage near the end. Successful delivery required great understanding of the text. Here are the words:

> Now the trumpet summons us again – not as a call to bear arms, though arms we need – not as a call to battle, though embattled we are – but a call to bear the burden of a long twilight struggle, year in and year out, 'rejoicing in hope, patient in tribulation' – a struggle against the common enemies of man: tyranny, poverty, disease and war itself.

That passage requires some directions about how to pause in order to maintain the coherence of the idea. Remember, the audience does not have the text. So people in the audience need verbal cues to help guide their listening. Some speakers like to engineer the pausing in the speech, using a method called the 'slash' or 'diagonal' (it looks like this: /). They put the slash in between words to help remind the speaker to pause. Typically the slash is used in place of hyphens or at the end of sentences and paragraphs. But it can be used for more than pausing in those circumstances. The slash can be used to indicate pausing anywhere it would be effective for the listening audience: commas, prepositional phrases, using the conjunction 'and' or the disjunction 'or', giving a list of reasons or names, or for emphasis to allow an audience a few seconds to think about what has been said. Using the slash method, the passage might look like this on the delivery manuscript:

> Now the trumpet summons us again// not as a call to bear arms/ though arms we need// not as a call to battle/ though embattled we are// but a call to bear the burden of a long twilight struggle/ year in and year out/ 'rejoicing in hope, patient in tribulation'// a struggle against the common enemies of man// tyranny/ poverty/ disease/ and war itself///

You can do exactly the same thing with dots doing the same work as the slashes. It would work like this: two dots for a brief pause, three a longer one, and a quartet for a full stop. The use of dots method might work better for some people as a device to guide your pausing and pacing. The number of dots governs the amount of time for pausing.

So, the Kennedy passage might look like this:

> Now the trumpet summons us again. . . not as a call to bear arms. . though arms we need. . . not as a call to battle. . though embattled we are. . . but a call to bear the burden of a long twilight struggle. . year in and year out. . 'rejoicing in hope, patient in tribulation'. . . a struggle against the common enemies of man. . . tyranny. . poverty. . disease. . and war itself. . . .

Try giving that passage out loud without pausing, guided by the hyphens and the punctuation. It would be incoherent. But it can be understood with guidance from the slashing or the dots. The important thing is to know when to pause and for how long. Each slash is one unit of pausing, for example one second for some speakers; the double dots function in the same way, offer the same unit of time. Once a speaker becomes used to engineering the pausing, the speech itself becomes composed of words and pauses, or, in my mind, words and silence. The pausing is built into the speech.

By the way, this method is better than actual stage directions, which often confuse the speaker or sometimes are even uttered inadvertently, such as the speaker saying 'In conclusion, pause two seconds, I would like to remind the good people of Laramie that. . .' Disaster!

8. Anticipate problems and prevent them

The extra effort to prepare the manuscript is worth it. One bad speech is more than momentary failure; it can cost a job, end a career, or stop a policy from being adopted.

Years ago, an American cabinet member was giving a speech at Mount Vernon, the home of George Washington. The speech was outdoors and it started to rain. Drop by drop, the water started to wash away the ink on his manuscript. Soon, rivulets of black flowed down the paper; the speech washed away, the soggy pages blank. Murphy's Law: if it can go wrong, it will.

Over time, speakers confront the unexpected in a speech. But prepared speakers prevent problems.

Hostile audiences and handling hecklers

A speech is always, always, always about the audience. Your job as a speaker is to persuade the audience to do something, like adopt a belief, support a position, vote for something or someone, or take up an action. Sometimes that audience is friendly and very willing to be persuaded by you. Sometimes the audience is persuadable, which means they generally haven't made up their minds but are willing to give you a fair hearing (this is increasingly rare). Sometimes the audience is simply hostile, which means they come to the speech already in disagreement with you, and don't want to give you a fair hearing at all.

In this last case you hope to change minds or behaviour. This is extremely difficult, but not always impossible. There are some strategies that can be persuasive. But this kind of change of attitude requires much sustained effort. In this situation every word, every symbol on the stage or in the backdrop, everything you wear and every gesture you use must be calculated for its usefulness in the enterprise.

I am not counselling that you reinvent or redefine. You still must be yourself. You want people to respect you for who you are and what you represent. Do not change the core message or pander to the audience. People see right through that. Do not grovel or beg. That is just sickening.

The most important thing is to start your speech by identifying common ground with the hostile audience. Show that you have shared beliefs, interests, positions and values. Indicate the times you have worked together. You will use this common ground to pivot away later, indicating how those shared beliefs led you to your position. Show them how they can follow you. I remember a great phrase from one of Margaret Thatcher's speeches: 'Come with us then.' You will use the common ground to lead them to your view.

An effective way to start this change of attitude is with an example. An example humanises the abstract and tells a story. I once heard an effective example before a hostile audience that went something like this. The audience was in favour of the 'exclusionary rule' in courts of law in the United States, excluding evidence that is gathered illegally, thereby protecting the rights of a defendant. The speaker was in favour of eliminating the rule and the audience didn't agree. So he started with this example:

> Here is how the exclusionary rule works. A woman [whom he named] was kidnapped, beaten, raped, chained to a tree and shot six times with a shotgun. She lived. She identified her assailant. The bullets pulled out of her body and the tree matched the shotgun found in the back seat of his car, registered to him with only his fingerprints on it. But he is walking the streets today because the evidence was gained illegally. That is how the exclusionary rule works.

I was sitting in the audience and people were simply stunned by the injustice of that. They were ready to think about changing the rule. And that is how an audience begins to move towards the position of the speaker. The right example can work wonders.

Some people come to the speech to personally express their hostility to you: hecklers. I don't just have in mind somebody in the audience who just raises a good point spontaneously. I am also thinking of what I call the 'professional' heckler, someone who is skilled in the chess match of argumentation and its development, and knows how to manoeuvre a speaker into a fatal checkmate in the mind of those listening. The heckler has many goals: disrupt the speech, steal time and attention away from the speaker, persuade the audience that the speaker is wrong, force the speaker into a serious gaffe, create news, or generally be a backdrop of opposition for photo images or verbal reporting by the media. In fact, many hecklers are trained by political or advocacy groups, so they are quite skilled, mindful of timing, message focus, media concerns and audience manipulation. Often the heckler has put considerable time and thought into the strategy of disrupting a speech, with multiple traps laid and early warning to reporters that something is going to happen, and when.

You should take hecklers very seriously. Calculate where the heckler might strike and how. In other words, think about where the heckler will try to interrupt the message and what might be said. Preparation should include constructing 'impromptu' remarks to counter the heckler's message, turning the interruption to advantage. This often means making a list of responses and memorising it (or simply laying that list next to the speech with the best responses prioritised, giving the speaker an array to choose from when the time comes). Identify possible strategies beforehand, prepare responses, test the quality of each response, and then judge the media's potential coverage of that response. It is imperative that the response to the heckler, taken out of context, does not create a negative story in the media. There was a catastrophic instance of this in 2006, in the US Senate re-election campaign of George Allen of Virginia, who through a careless, stupid comment about an opposition cameraman who was filming his speech narrowly lost his seat and thereby the Republicans' control of the Senate. And that was just a comment about someone's presence! Since what you say is the story, be sure what you say to the heckler doesn't achieve the aims of your opponent.

The standard approach to hecklers is to initially ignore them, at least for the first interruption. You don't want to give the heckler the audience's attention. Often the audience will take care of the heckler for you, expressing strong disapproval of the interruption. But if the heckler interrupts again, you need to respond.

There are two kinds of response. The first is the quick and deadly one-liner (like President Gerald Ford's amazingly vitriolic 'Young man, get a job' or the commonplace 'If you don't like our country, go home' or the witty 'I'd expect you to say that' or the pleading 'People came to hear me, not you'). This is where you would use the list of responses you generated prior to the speech. I would suggest ten possible responses, each of a different type that you can apply as the situation warrants.

A second response is to fully engage the heckler, to take them on and use the interruption to further develop your message. A good example of this was provided by President Bill Clinton in the mid-1990s during a speech on HIV/AIDS research. Someone shouted at him: 'You're not doing enough.' He flashed back: 'That's not true.' He then took the heckler to task for not knowing about a number of programmes and initiatives, all of which he explained in some detail. In other words, he gave the speech he would have given anyway and used the heckler as a convenient foil. The heckler became the embodiment of what the speaker was against, giving the opposing message a physical manifestation for the audience to see and hear.

Of course, this is a dangerous strategy. Remember, I said that these hecklers are often well trained. If you turn the focus to them, the audience may be lost to you. You give the audience a chance to hear someone else, not you. These hecklers may be better able to control the situation and persuade the audience. In short, you may be falling into a carefully laid-out trap with immediate repercussions for the audience and longer-term problems in the media later. You have to be very good and very lucky if you undertake this second kind of response.

Of course, the bottom line in all of this is audience analysis. A speech is about the audience. Hecklers challenge your preparation of the message and its appeal to the audience. Remaining on message when they strike, and retaining control of the situation, demands discipline, focus and skill.

They are out there, thinking. . . waiting. . . plotting.

Are you ready?

Going for the jugular

Searching for the jugular looks like this. In 2004, Prime Minister Tony Blair was defending his government in the aftermath of the Hutton report and the controversy over raising university fees. When Michael Howard, then leader of the opposition, asked pointed questions in Parliament, he wasn't just after the Secretary of State for Defence or lesser figures. The *Independent* reported (10 January 2004) one minister as saying: 'Dracula is going for Blair's jugular.'

Finding and cutting the jugular looks like this. In the 1980 campaign for president of the United States, there was only one televised debate between the two major candidates. Jimmy Carter spoke repeatedly about governmental solutions to the nation's problems. At one point, he began an eloquent appeal about health care: Medicare for the elderly, cost containment measures and catastrophic-care insurance for those facing unexpected and expensive treatments – all leading to government-financed national health insurance. He said Reagan was initially against Medicare and concluded: 'Governor Reagan, again, typically, is against such a proposal.' Reagan, smiling throughout Carter's remarks, responded, delighted, almost laughing: 'There you go again!'

That comment said it all. It was more than a dismissive line. Carter advocated more governmental programmes, more federal spending, more taxes and more erosion of individual freedom – almost as a knee-jerk reaction. Reagan, of course, stood for less government, lower rates of public spending, lower taxes and less intrusion on individual liberty. The contrast was clear; the comment said it all. And with that one comment Reagan did more than note a difference. He went for the jugular! And he found it later, when he asked these memorable questions:

> Are you better off today than you were four years ago? Is it easier for you to go and buy things in the store than it was four years ago? Is there more or less unemployment in the country than there was four years ago? Is America as respected through the world as it was? Do you feel that our security is as safe, that we're as strong as we were four years ago? And if you answer all of those questions 'yes', why then, I think your choice is very obvious as to whom you will vote for.

Reagan advisor Lynn Nofzinger remembered: 'We didn't have to wait for the debate to end . . . Everybody in the room knew we had won.' Discussing the debate nine years after, Reagan said it showed 'my approach was based on the promise of a better

America'. Journalist Bret Schulte, reviewing the debate in 2008, said Reagan's lines 'pierced Carter's presidency' and the conclusion was a 'knockout punch'.

When someone says they are 'going for the jugular', it doesn't mean vampirism and blood-sucking so much as rhetorical blood loss. Typically it means that the politician is going to slice the jugular vein in an argument to weaken it, grabbing the open vein, ripping it out and swinging it in every direction until eventually so much blood is spilt that the argument loses life-sustaining credibility and dies. By winning this argument the opponent loses more than a single point. The argument must be so important, so vital, that losing it means total defeat. Going for the jugular is ultimately about victory, a defining conquest. It is a phrase that actually defines a rhetorical strategy and spells out a plan of action.

How to do this? There is a strategy for political haematologists. It usually has five stages of development.

1. Look for a devastating weakness
Of course, every political opponent should analyse the strength or weakness of the arguments under discussion. But not all arguments are equal. A sense of proportion is needed. Most arguments in the public arena are about the give and take of policy, tradeoffs, a mixed bag of winners and losers among the electorate. But a few arguments attack fundamental and foundational beliefs. Going for the jugular is an attempt to expose a weakness that is lethal. When you have found it, allow no diversion, no resuscitation, no transfusion, no staunching and no tourniquet! The whole idea is to let it bleed!

How to find it? Well, sometimes you have to look behind the headlines or outside the flow of events. Often, political rhetoric is designed to deflect attention away from weakness, like a magician's trick. So don't follow your opponent so much as look for what you need. And the weakness in your opponent's argument may come from a spontaneous mistake. One such mistake occurred in the United States in 2004 when the Secretary of Education, Rod Paige, responded to a question in a closed press event for state governors at the White House. When asked about the National Education Association, the teachers' union, and its opposition to a law requiring schools to guarantee that all students meet reading and mathematics requirements before graduating, Paige compared the union's lobbying tactics to 'a terrorist organisation'. One governor (from another party) slipped the remark to a reporter waiting outside the room and a raging nuclear firestorm began, with teachers, students, parents, reporters and politicians levelling Paige for the comment. He received hundreds of thousands of letters from teachers, many of whom also wrote to newspapers saying 'I didn't know as a teacher that I was a terrorist'. It was a devastating mistake for both the policy and the politician.

Stay alert. One mistake can change the rhetorical dynamic. In 2005, in a debate on the Iraq War at Baruch College in Manhattan, opponent George Galloway MP was clearly winning against supporter Christopher Hitchens. The debate was winding down to its conclusion, Galloway doing well with an audience that mostly agreed with his position. But then, inexplicably, he seemed to claim that the United States deserved the attacks on 9/11 (there is some debate about what he actually meant – I'm sure he didn't think that is what he said). Hitchens immediately interrupted and noted that this was a bad argument to make to people in New York. He was right. You could feel a shift in the audience towards Hitchens, who was then able to get back into the debate. There was no declared winner or loser, but the debate was much closer after the Galloway gaffe. Mistakes often happen when your opponent is doing well – often they over-reach and then stumble.

So look for a weakness. Be patient. If it isn't obvious in your preparation, it will probably come out during the course of a discussion.

2. Seize the moment

And when the mistake is made, pounce on it. Reach for the jugular. Pull it out and perform the operation. Don't let a rare, defining opportunity go by. Timing is everything. The opportunity may not come again.

Here's an example. In 1990, the American cabinet member for health and human services was Louis W. Sullivan. Dr Sullivan was, and is, an eminent haematologist (a real one of much distinction) and former president of the Morehouse School of Medicine, one of the historically black medical schools in the United States. He is also a noted civil rights advocate and, as a Morehouse undergraduate, a student of Dr Benjamin Elijah Mays, the mentor of Dr Martin Luther King, Jr.

Sullivan was attacked in early August of that year by Pete Stark, a representative in Congress from northern California. Stark, who is white, called Sullivan, an African American, a 'disgrace to his race' because he 'doesn't have the courage' to oppose Bush administration policies that hurt poor and minority citizens. Sullivan responded immediately, within minutes, demanding an apology and saying, with explosive effect: 'I don't work on Pete Stark's plantation!' That angry comment changed the debate and sliced the jugular. Sullivan added: 'I wish he had the guts to make his comments to my face.' The White House called Stark's comments 'bigoted' and a media feeding frenzy followed. Stark, disavowed even by his own party members, later said: 'I blew it.' Yup!

3. Blow it up
It isn't enough just to identify the mistake and go for the jugular. The rhetorical focus must be stationary. Don't go to other arguments. Stay on the mistake and blow it up. Collapse on the argument. This is the place to vastly expand your response – make it bigger, much bigger! This is where you use your time, only leaving the argument behind when you have done as much damage as possible. This is the location for massive impact. So don't just mention your reasons for opposing – destroy the opponent's argument. By winning here you may win everything. And the lingering impact may stay in the voters' minds for weeks, even years, becoming part of the cultural matrix.

Here's a classic case of jugular slicing, pumping and dumping, a case that lingers in the mind to this day. In 1988, in the televised vice presidential debate, Republican senator Dan Quayle noted that he had just as much experience in Congress as John Kennedy when the latter ran for president. Quayle's opponent was Democratic senator Lloyd Bentsen, a seasoned veteran of political argumentation. He could have responded to this claim about experience in a number of ways, such as saying that Kennedy had a better record or that Bentsen himself had more experience by far. But sensing a critical weakness, Bentsen went right for the jugular and produced an iconic moment. Slowly, with measured cadence, and a big smile on his face, he said: 'Senator, I served with Jack Kennedy. I knew Jack Kennedy. Jack Kennedy was a friend of mine. Senator, you're no Jack Kennedy!' Now, this is how iconic the remarks became: a year later I went to a Billy Bragg concert a few blocks away from the White House. The concert opened with a recording of that moment, echoing over and over and over again 'You're no Jack Kennedy!'

Jack Kennedy himself knew how to give a jugular argument maximum impact. In late June of 1960, former President Harry Truman, a member of Kennedy's own party, gave a speech arguing that candidate Kennedy was too young and inexperienced to be President. Rough stuff from a respected figure. Kennedy countered in a televised press conference. He argued that there should not be a 'maturity test' for politicians in their forties (Kennedy was forty-three). Then he went for it. To do so, he said, would have denied people the contributions of Theodore Roosevelt, William Pitt the Younger and others. But he didn't stop there. He piled on:

> To exclude from positions of trust and command all those below the age of forty-four would have kept Jefferson from writing the Declaration of Independence, Washington from commanding the Continental Army, Madison from fathering the Constitution, Hamilton from serving as Secretary of the Treasury, Clay from being elected Speaker

of the House and even Christopher Columbus from discovering America.

He then added that, up to that moment, America had had six presidents in their forties. So if these people wouldn't be qualified to serve, then who would be? And if only the old could serve, then the vigour and stamina of youth would be lost. Certainly, Kennedy won that argument with a 'who's who' of American leaders. He had severed the vein. Truman had to give in and his credibility in the election was lost.

Kennedy had another powerful jugular moment in his acceptance speech at the Democratic convention in July 1960. Positioning his opponent, Richard Nixon, as committed to maintaining the status quo, Kennedy said Nixon was a Richard I trying to follow 'bold' Henry II, or Richard Cromwell 'not fit to wear the mantle' of his father, Oliver. He then followed with this passage:

> Perhaps he could carry on the party policies . . . But this nation cannot afford such a luxury. Perhaps we could afford a Coolidge following Harding. And perhaps we could afford a Pierce following Fillmore. But after Buchanan this nation needed a Lincoln – after Taft we needed a Wilson – after Hoover we needed Franklin Roosevelt . . . And after eight years of drugged and fitful sleep, this nation needs strong, creative Democratic leadership in the White House.

By mentioning the instances when America elected successive Republican administrations, with mixed results, he suggested that such a succession in 1960 would be risky even in the best of times. But in a time demanding change, the country needed to follow history, with Democrat following Republican, as happened with Lincoln, Wilson and Roosevelt. This is a powerful use of history that blows up the argument.

Blood attracts attention. You don't have to do all the work. At some point let the media take over. That is part of the art of politics.

The media can smell blood. Let them pound and pound away. Let them show the video again and again. Let the think tanks get involved (I remember a great, devastating session on 'plantation politics' at a think tank in Washington after the Stark–Sullivan exchange). And, of course, the blogosphere will be at it, relentlessly, 24/7. More and more we see the media following the blogosphere, not the other way around (witness the unfolding of events with the recent Damian McBride scandal).

4. Tell them what to do next

Don't just leave the argument gushing blood. Tell anyone listening what must happen next. Take the rhetorical ground. Take it! Define the debate. Make it clear that the next response must be on your own terms, according to your own demands. If you do this effectively, you will own the issue. And your opponent will have no place to go, no way to squirm out. I had a debate coach, Jed Richardson, who once called this moment the time to 'justify or deny'. Make your opponent either justify the bad argument or deny having said it (or deny holding the view). In a jugular moment, when you are right and you have blown it up, neither alternative will be possible. There will be no acceptable explanation or no possible way to deny holding the view. This is a powerful moment in an argument. The other side is trapped by their own words and actions. You can see that you've won, feel it. So can everyone else, except those who somehow believe their own spin.

5. Follow with hope and vision

If all you do is exploit weakness you have done only half the job. Politicians cannot be effective if they are only attack dogs. Style is important. A jugular moment may be more effective without anger. Some of the most devastating examples have been delivered with a smile. The best debater I've ever heard, a skilled speaker named Mike Anderson, used to say 'Kill them with kindness'. And he would do that. He didn't have a slick smile or a Cheshire cat one. He sincerely displayed enormous kindness and civility as he filled the room with blood. And his opponents and the audience actually liked Anderson, even admired him and loved him, as he performed the operation. You don't have to be mean spirited, out of control, angry or upset to be effective. Civility in discourse is essential to governing after election and for getting along with opponents in other situations. Subtle, surgical, tender and magnanimous slicing may be in order.

You must think about the aftermath of argumentation. Winning an argument is not necessarily proof that you should be an opinion maker or leader. It is not necessarily the qualification for government. Effective jugular arguments are followed by positions and policies that are full of life and promise, glowing in good health by contrast. Kennedy understood this in his party convention speech in 1960. After going for Nixon's jugular, he said:

> But I think the American people expect more from us than
> cries of indignation and attack. The times are too grave, the
> challenge too urgent and the stakes too high to permit the
> customary passions of political debate. We are not here to
> curse the darkness, but to light the candle that can guide us
> through the darkness to a safe and sane future. As Winston
> Churchill said on taking office [as Prime Minister]: 'If we
> open a quarrel between the present and the past, we shall
> be in danger of losing the future.'

*

So next time the 'Dracula' moment comes, be ready. Discover your inner Bela Lugosi. Go for the jugular! But blood-letting isn't wisdom. Also be ready to offer new direction, better programmes, optimism about the years to come, hope for moving forward and an inclusive vision, a vision that even generously includes someone whom you've just drained dry.

Tony Blair (PA)

6. TYPES OF SPEECH

During the course of a business or a political career the average speaker gives several kinds of speech. Verbal success often leads to more speeches. . . and more work. So a mastery of various speaking formats is essential.

Campaign speech

The late comedian Peter Sellers had a routine in the 1950s called 'Party Political Speech'. It was a brilliant series of trite, vacuous remarks, given with serious, sincere purpose, such as:

> My friends, in the light of present-day developments, let me say right away that I do not regard existing conditions lightly . . . I am more than sensible of the definitions of the

precise issues that concern us all. We must build, but we
must build surely . . . Let us assume a bold front, and go
forward together.

Actually, it sounds similar to most modern campaign speeches,
which offer platitudes and generalities in the hope of attracting
the widest possible support. The vacuous campaign speech reflects
a kind of strategy, to be sure: stand up, be vague, don't commit
to anything, push the right emotional buttons (family, prosperity,
patriotism and hope) and try to become all things to all people.
And, with this strategy, the campaign speech is an exercise in
obscurantism, illusion, delusion and sleight-of-hand prose and
promises. Even if it produces victory, there is no mandate. Even
if successful, there is no ability to lead or to govern. The common
complaints about this type of campaign speech reflect electoral
disappointment: the words are insincere, the candidate will say
anything to get elected, the promises won't be kept and the speech
is more about ego than service. And, frankly, many, if not most,
campaign speeches deserve such suspicion and dismissal. Most
are infinitely forgettable, failing to arouse trust, faith, loyalty or
inspiration. They fail on multiple levels: vague policies, lack of
vision, nothing interesting and absence of commitment. No wonder
people don't remember most of these speeches! There is nothing to
remember! It is all about showing up, being a personality, shaking
hands and striking a balance by avoiding the risk of actual content.

There is another approach to campaign speeches, one that is
more concrete and precisely focused. The campaign speech can
be an evolving, powerful weapon. The message must expand and
grow over time. This development must be strategic, following a
careful and well-conceived plan to simultaneously increase voter
awareness of the candidate and increase voter support. A campaign
should know weeks and months in advance where it wants to be
in terms of reaching out to voters and gathering electoral support.
A good campaign will develop its ideas on taxes or immigration
one week, then is ready to move ahead before the opponent has

a chance to develop a coherent response. Ideally, the campaign is always one issue ahead of the opponent, forcing the media to also play catch-up. This allows the campaign to control the message and use it most effectively. The strategy should be structured with the voters in mind – how best to maximise the impact of each issue to gather electoral support. So the strategy may be developed with national holidays in mind, or important historical anniversaries, or even with local events like school graduations or gatherings of like-minded people at trade conventions or technology conferences. A campaign that doesn't have a strategy is simply brain dead from the start, hoping that intuition and luck will somehow work in its favour. But a successful campaign is a matter of engineering and planning, followed by disciplined development of the message and competent performance.

Of course, it is easy to say 'Develop a strategy'. But it is difficult to stay on track with the strategy as your opponent attacks you, the media pursues its own agenda and unexpected circumstances intrude. These combine to make a campaign reactive, responding to the demands of others and not remaining focused on its own needs for victory. Many elections are lost through a lack of discipline, or because the campaign is overwhelmed by an opponent's attacks or by poor handling of the unexpected. It is vital to have a disciplined approach which not only handles the daily twists and turns of political fortune, but also remains on point and on message.

With this strategy the campaign speech becomes an integral part of a well-conceived and mission-driven road to victory. Here is an outline of how to construct such a speech.

1. Know what the speech must do
A great campaign speech is targeted. The speech is an effort to reach out to certain defined groups of potential voters. A careful analysis of the voting population, including the use of focus groups and private surveys of voters, determines the strategy of the campaign. There must be an accurate, detailed answer to this question: 'What must we do to win?' And there must be a roadmap

that follows. In other words, does the demographic analysis reveal that the road to victory lies in energising our supporters, because they outnumber the opposition? Must the campaign do more than that, such as draw converts from the centrist fringe of other parties? Must the campaign get more supporters to the polls than the other parties? Or does the campaign have to change the entire political landscape and reframe the issues, in the belief that a new battlefield is advantageous? The campaign staff must construct a long-term strategy to victory. If they do, the campaign stump speech becomes the right tool for reaching supporters or new converts, or motivating voters to cast ballots, or reconfiguring the issues, or some or all of these. This means the speech has a definite point and purpose, using words and arguments to help engineer victory according to a pre-determined strategy. And the speech may change with new information, needs and issues. The speech can also work in harmony with efforts on Twitter, YouTube and other websites and media.

In addition, a campaign should have a progressive movement forward, with some new topics and new information week to week. This helps it to remain proactive and in control of issues and events, rather than reactive and defensive. The speech then is a tool for moving the campaign forward.

2. Develop the message for the target audience(s)

The campaign stump speech should develop a coherent message that will persuade the target audiences. Explain the failures of the opposition, although don't let that be the major focus of the speech. The speech should be more about the future than the failures of the past. Becoming the anti-Bush, the anti-Brown, or the anti-anything is not enough to win with a mandate. The voters must have a reason to vote *for* a candidate, not just against someone else. So a great campaign speech outlines policies. It explains what will happen after the election. And it gives hope. The speech must be clear and straightforward. Details enhance clarity and show good faith. The voters know what they are getting.

Whatever the message is, the candidate must stay on it, constantly pounding the message home to each and every audience. This is one key to victory: stay on message! Every political consultant I know would counsel this: stay on message. . . don't go off message and debate other issues on the opponent's ground, or get drawn into irrelevancies. And the speech should be short: five to fifteen minutes, depending on the setting.

Of course, the press always wants something new. So the stump speech should be continually tweaked and modified in a few paragraphs, or some modular paragraphs added on. New language could be specific for the audience or the location, or for new issues. Variation in language and content, if it is slight, say about 10–20 per cent of the speech, keeps the candidate alert and focused on the stump, yet allowing for the majority of the speech to remain on message, with the new bits for the press to report. New language helps control the frenzied needs of a 24/7 news cycle. I want to stress that word: 'control'.

3. Brand yourself

Capture and use key words. Tony Blair did this very effectively in his 'Modern Constitution' speech in 1994. The speech started: 'A belief in society. Working together. Solidarity. Cooperation. Partnership. These are our words.' Barack Obama won the 2008 presidential election by owning the word 'change', the most important word in an election. But choose the right words, because they may have immortality. As Winston Churchill said: 'Words are the only thing which lasts forever.'

This is the way political strategists talk now, using the language of marketing. A candidate has to establish a recognised 'brand'. That means the voters have to equate a face, name and presence with known policies and positions. As an example, if the candidate is a tax reformer, voters must see that person as the 'anti-tax man' or the 'fix-the-taxes woman'. These policies and positions must set the candidate apart, giving that person a unique political persona. Too many politicians see their relationship with the voters through ego gratification or the politics of personality. This is a mistake, an old-fashioned way to go glad-handing and back-slapping through an election. Modern elections are not primarily about a politician standing there and accepting adoration. Now, voters want to know more about the candidate, what they stand for and what they will do. There is a more detailed examination of positions and policies than in the past. So electoral politics must start with a core set of ideas and work from there.

In recent campaigns there has been some interesting brand identification. Some politicians want to be viewed as progressive, so they build their brand on aggressive environmental protection, development of Silicon Valley-type businesses in their districts, creation of free enterprise zones (with lower taxes and other incentives), eco-tourism and other policies. For example, in the United States, the late congressman Jack Kemp was long associated with the notion of free enterprise zones. Some politicians talk about quality of life, focusing on education, development of mixed-income communities, more housing for the poor, health care reform and other domestic issues. Blair once said that there were three priorities for him: 'education, education, education'. That line has now become iconic, successfully giving brand identification; everybody knows that line and that he used it. Or the brand can be with international issues, such as immigration policy, trade, human trafficking and national defence. The Greek actress and politician Melina Mercouri did this effectively as an advocate for human rights. Civil society and reconciliation can be another way to establish brand identification, as Nelson Mandela did so effectively in South Africa. The question is this: who are you? The answer is: your brand. And that answer is not a biography, although that can be part of it. Rather, the answer is about what the candidate represents, what ideas or policies the voters will associate with that person.

Once your core set of ideas is articulated, then brand identification comes through repetition of your ideas. Message development means focusing on word choices and condensing the message into simple, understandable, provocative sentences. These sentences may become slogans, like 'Effective change now!' or 'From the Past into the Future: Britain Steps Forward' or 'A Green, Sustainable Britain'. Repetition doesn't mean dullness or lack of imagination. Rather, the right kind of slogan can be the thread that holds together numerous ideas, policies and positions. The condensed message is the bond that gives cohesion to the proposals you offer on taxes, job creation, building infrastructure, access to health care, the war on terror and any other proposals you want the electorate to consider.

Often the message itself is nothing more than 'Change'. This is the most powerful word for a new politician, as proven yet again by Barack Obama in the 2008 presidential election in the United States. Change is the comparison of a known present with a possible future. The skilled politician can make change seem like a step forward, a move towards a better world, even an inevitable stride toward an historical ending point. Voters always want something better. . . always. So they are prepared to accept change if convinced that it will give them more freedom, increased income, better protection, more effective delivery of health services, or any other components of a better life. The Obama campaign used this word, 'change', with greater and greater effectiveness with the downturn of the US economy. 'Change' became a simple word with a powerful impact on the minds of the voters.

4. Use inclusive language
Unite the audience. Become the voice of collective assent. The pronouns to use are 'we' and 'us'. Show leadership through language. Don't divide to conquer; unite to win.

5. Develop a vision
A vision is not a series of platitudes, such as 'We must get Britain working again' or 'Britain must be fixed'. A vision is a picture of what could happen if voters support a candidate. Ronald Reagan talked about his 'shining city on a hill', a bastion of freedom that led

by inspiration and example because of its goodness and greatness. After his election in 1997, Blair spoke of a vision of Britain:

> Today I want to set an ambitious course for this country: to be nothing less than the model 21st-century nation, a beacon to the world. It means drawing deep into the richness of the British character. Creative. Compassionate. Outward-looking. Old British values, but a new British confidence.

He also spoke of a vision for the European Union. He said: 'We want a people's Europe: free trade, industrial strength, high levels of employment and social justice, a democratic Europe.' The vision must be lofty, inspirational, recognisable, principled and attainable. The absence of a vision is damaging for a campaign speech; its absence is disastrous for government after victory.

Vision ties policies together and gives them rational coherence. Vision shows policymakers the direction of government. It gives civil servants guidance in how to handle their own work in the continuity of government. A great campaign speech simply has to have a vision. One cabinet member in the United States told me that vision 'helps us know how to make decisions and the course those decisions should follow'. Without it, 'energy is scattered and policies fly off in different directions'.

6. Address issues head on

There will be moments when new, unexpected issues flare up. Some can be easily handled, others perhaps ignored. But some are significant and dangerous, and demand immediate attention because of their corrosive effect. John Kennedy faced such an issue in 1960 when his Catholicism became divisive. Would he make decisions based on his faith or the direction of the Vatican? In addressing the Greater Houston Baptist Association, he confronted the issue directly and said: 'I believe in an America where the separation of church and state is absolute . . . I believe in a President whose religious views are his own private matter.' The issue went away for most Americans.

7. Make the speech memorable

One of the greatest-ever campaign speeches was given by George H. W. Bush upon accepting the Republican Party nomination in 1988. He was not noted for his eloquence, but in this speech the words came to the forefront. The speech argued for a compassionate conservatism, racial harmony, 'peace through strength', more literacy programmes, environmental protection, 'zero tolerance' for drug use and a number of other positions. But all of that was overshadowed by three memorable statements. Bush called for a reliance on community and non-governmental action, 'a brilliant diversity spread like the stars, like a thousand points of light in a broad and peaceful sky'. He said there would be no tax increases under his administration: 'My opponent won't rule out raising taxes. But I will. The Congress will push me to raise taxes, and I'll say no, and they'll push, and I'll say no, and they'll push again, and I'll say to them: "Read my lips: no new taxes."' And through America's renewed prosperity, and the growing action of compassionate communities, Bush called for 'a kinder, gentler nation'. All three of those ideas – and the words that expressed them – are now part of shared memory, quotations that are part of the common culture of America and Europe. A campaign speech should do that, should give the audience ideas and phrases they will never forget, that will be with them for decades, ideas that bring out the best in a nation and its people.

8. Connect with the audience

A good, well-written speech can fall flat if the delivery is less than exceptional. Maximum effort should be made to enhance delivery, even if that takes time away from other campaign necessities. The candidate should invest time in a studio and practise repeatedly. Feedback is vital. Improvement is a constant goal. Poor verbal skills can doom a campaign from the beginning. The public wants to know if the candidate has a mastery of detail and can explain the direction and advantage of their policy proposals. In other words, can they articulate who they are and what they want? Good delivery is demanded in such situations; poor delivery guarantees failure.

Peter Sellers could get a good laugh from a speech that just filled the air with words. But a finely tuned speech can help engineer victory. Political language can become action that changes the world. The campaign speech can do that, especially if it is strategically and surgically targeted to the demographics of specific audiences. That is how the campaign speech becomes a profoundly powerful tool for victory. Then who's laughing?

9. Coordinate with other forms of communication

As I said earlier, a speech is part of a campaign strategy. It should integrate well with other forms of communication. For example, a candidate must develop interpersonal skills. The candidate will shake countless hands and attend hundreds of events. The candidate must do more than 'grip and grin'. In addition, the interpersonal skills must connect with the voters. The candidate must stand for something. He or she must symbolise a set of issues and solutions. The candidate must persuade voters that change is needed. The candidate must be associated with answers for positive change. There must also be party identification. But the candidate must become unique in the eyes of the voters. The candidate must establish a level of comfort with the voters, making them feel that he or she can handle the job and represent their best interests. There is a bonding between a successful candidate and the voters, with the candidate uniting with constituents, becoming their voice, reflecting their views. The candidate must learn how to work the media and contain some sort of control over the stories and reporting.

The Internet age has made that task even more demanding. New technology provides valuable, perhaps unparalleled opportunities to connect with voters. So the candidate must learn the low-tech techniques for connecting with voters on a human, interpersonal level, and must connect through the filtered medium of the media and the Internet. It has now become axiomatic that a politician must use the Internet to advantage. So a website is required. Obama effectively used text messaging and Facebook to decisive advantage. But most political websites are still poorly developed and confusing. People turn to websites for information. They must be able to find it. An article in the British political magazine *Total Politics* graded the websites of the three political parties. The highest grade was a C+. That is a stunning result, given the importance of this information vehicle. In my view, politicians and consultants understand the need for a good website. But they don't have high standards for the creation and function of these sites. There needs to be much more attention paid to the creation of a compelling and informative web presence. Perhaps a good model right now would be the website for the White House. It has just been substantially renovated by the Obama people and offers a good example of how to structure a site with substantial information.

Everyone will want to know the candidate's positions on a number of issues. The campaign can control that information as part of the campaign's strategy, revealing views through speeches and interviews. There can be longer responses through position papers and even book-length manuscripts (most American politicians on the national level put out a book at the start of the campaign). This must be an ongoing process that is part of each event. When I worked for the Reagan administration we had a press release to announce an event, and then followed up the event with talking points, a position paper, editorials by leading experts supporting our views, and a list of experts who were willing to be interviewed by the press. It is interesting how this information works its way into a story. Lazy reporters just use it to construct the story, which means you are effectively writing the story for them. More industrious reporters use the information as a baseline to start, which still means that you are helping to channel their thinking. In any event, the information you provide can help keep the message on point and the strategy moving forward. It is a lot of work to do this for each event. But it pays off.

10. Get a good pollster

Get someone who is really good at this. Polling is no substitute for brand identification or message development. But it tells you what works and what doesn't. Initial focus groups are extremely helpful on the front end of your message development, telling you the reaction and acceptance of potential voters. But there is a limited use for focus groups, although some politicians never understand that and become simply captured by their groups. Rather, once the message identification and branding takes place, polling can tell you how your strategy is doing. It can identify areas that need modification, even suppression. It can highlight elements of the message that need to come to the forefront of speeches and events.

It is important to have a private pollster that is reliable and accurate. The campaign's own polling will compete with the polls run by opponents, by public polling agencies and by commissioned polls for the media. The campaign's polling must tell the truth with a high degree of reliability and validity. The media will run stories about their own polls or polls conducted by others. These polls may have a built-in bias or reflect support for opponents. In other words, there may be competing agendas here, and the public polls may be wrong. The campaign must know the real story. Based on your own polling, the campaign must make decisions about strategy and the future of the campaign. So there must be complete trust in the pollster.

Again, it is tough to stay disciplined if the polls become the story. As polls rise and fall, the media will make them a story. The campaign's electoral strategy must take this into account. But it cannot become a hostage to stories about polling. The campaign must use polling, not be used by it. The polling must help direct the evolution of the speech, but not capture the speech or divert the core messages. There must be politics with a purpose.

11. Control the non-verbals

In the Reagan White House there was a genius named Mike Deaver. He was brilliant at the planning and the staging of an event. He often said 'News is entertainment', so he would make sure the event itself was compelling for both the media and the public. There would be much discussion about the backdrop behind the speaker, the other people on the stage and the visuals of the crowd. There was always an attempt at complete harmony of message, verbally and non-verbally. It is important to recognise the power of the non-verbal: some communication studies say that people give the non-verbal more credibility than the verbal and take away more information from the non-verbals. Richard Nixon is a good case in point. His non-verbals – the sweating, the shifty eyes, the lack of comfort, the crooked body posture – still to this day define him in the eyes of the American public. So there must be careful thought given to the non-verbals. The Obama campaign put a great amount of thought into them, scoring a hit in Berlin with the speech there, but missing the mark with a party acceptance speech in a football stadium with fake Doric columns behind the candidate.

12. Reach out to youth

There is a base of support that could be decisive. The speech must reach the young – voters between eighteen and thirty. The Obama campaign literally won the election with the youth vote. Because young voters are idealistic, demand change and possess superior understanding of technology and new uses of that technology, they are amenable to new political voices and to those who want a new order. Make common cause with young voters. Their energy will invigorate your campaign.

How to get young people involved in politics? That has been a question that challenges every political campaign. Young voters are a key to victory. It has long been a maxim in American politics that young voters could be decisive in many local and national elections, if they would just vote. This is also true in most other countries, even in elections for the European Parliament. But the young could often be discounted because of their own apathy, which led to low turnout and indifferent participation in politics. Of course, there have been exceptions: great student leaders like the young William Hague in Britain, who eventually became the head of the Conservative Party, or Bill Clinton, who was a strident young politician in college. But the rule is that students and young professionals are usually politically apathetic.

But that apathy can turn to activism under the right circumstances. Barack Obama won the 2008 US presidential election with 8 million more votes than John McCain. Notably, he had 8.4 million votes more than his rival among the 18–29-year-old voting population. Young voters were the margin of difference. They elected the President.

How did Obama do it? Well, one key reason was the use of technology, which led to the mobilisation of young voters. Facebook, Twitter, texting, the Internet and other new means of communication have now become part of political campaigning in the United States, perhaps worldwide. Rapid advances in software and portable devices are now assumed as part of the political equation. The party that has a technological advantage will be in a superior position to mobilise voters, raise money, rapidly respond to the other parties and disseminate messages at the touch of a keypad. In other words, harnessing technology is an important way to win. Technology can empower young voters and make them feel involved in the campaign.

Obama also reached out to young voters through tightly organised grassroots efforts, on campuses and in urban areas, to generate intense interest and participation in his campaign. He established youth organisations, employed young Americans in his campaign in unprecedented numbers, set up ongoing voter registration efforts, visited campuses and community centres and made young voters believe he represented their interests better than the other party. The resulting 'Obamamania' is just one measure of his comprehensive efforts to involve the young – he is the leader of their generation, a political rock star (and I don't mean this in a negative way. . . he is the voice of those under thirty in America, which may mean that he has changed the political landscape because those voters will be active for several generations to come).

With the Obama campaign we witnessed a clinic in how to involve the young. Technology and outreach are important, perhaps decisive!

13. *Rousing finish*
The speech should end with energy and power, bringing people to their feet in applause and support. And this should happen twice: once at the end of the speech and once at the end of the Q&As. The conclusion must involve positive emotive words that express ideas of unity and greatness. It must empower the audience and make the speaker one with the audience in an historic endeavour to transform a troubled present into a more prosperous and safer future. The conclusion should tell the audience that 'now' is the time for action, that change will only happen if the audience acts now, demands results now. And remind the audience that change only happens through voting; they need to vote on polling day!

Conference speech

I know one famous politician who thinks that a conference speech is just about 'showing up: 90 per cent is just going to the conference'. Respectfully, I think that's wrong. You have been invited to speak because of what you have to say, unless you are a celebrity. Here's my rule of thumb: if you are Bono, Madonna, Angelina Jolie, Václav Havel or Nelson Mandela, you can say whatever you want. Everybody else had better bring a great speech.

This attitude that 'presence is performance' does explain the dross in most conference speeches: for many politicians and executives, they just say the right loaded words, push the right emotional buttons, get the audience cheering over the required slogans and end the speech before anyone notices the lack of substance or style. For some people, a conference speech isn't about quality, it is about checking an item off a list: 'OK, went there, spoke, did that. They should be grateful I came. Check!'

Here we will explore unknown territory for many speakers, famous and infamous: the making of a good conference speech. They are tricky. They demand a lot of work. It is easy to fail. Most conference speeches are really bad, just filling the air with meaningless sounds and taking up rhetorical space before the lunch break. Think about how many of these you sat through and then forgot. Think about how many you avoided because you anticipated they might be a torture to endure. Ugh!

But there is always hope, because when they work, good conference speeches set the tone, become memorable landmarks, change lives and redefine the political or business climate. The landscape itself is different. And the speech becomes a benchmark in the evolution of the topic, the latest definition of the cutting edge.

So, here are some ideas about how to construct a good conference speech.

1. Have a compelling topic

Most conference speeches have boring, unimaginative topics. Here's an example: 'The Future of the Housing Market'. The words tell us little. There is no imagination. There is nothing to draw us to the speech. The topic needs to attract people, give them a reason to come. A better alternative is 'Equity, Wealth Creation and Ensuring Your Financial Security'. That might be important for you. Here's another bad example: 'The Challenges of the Twenty-first Century'. A better alternative: 'Ending Poverty Now!'

2. Don't tell the audience what they already know

Every conference veteran I spoke with passionately mentioned this one. For most, it was number one to avoid. Most speeches offer a laundry list of programmes or accomplishments. This is precisely the approach most likely to turn off an audience. It is old news. The audience only needs a passing reference to what they know. It is much more important to push into new territory. That means offering new ideas, new words, new programmes, a new vision.

The watchword is 'new'. It should be the guiding word for every sentence, every paragraph. When President George W. Bush gave his speech to Congress after 9/11, virtually every line was about something new. I remember people gasping when he spoke of the doctrine of pre-emption or the view that 'you are either with us or with the terrorists'. Tony Blair's Labour Party conference speech in 2005 is another example. Look at the second half of that speech. There he described the way a proactive government must operate in our time. The language was amazing, bold and fresh. It offered a new vision of the social contract. I know many politicians on the western side of the Atlantic who mined that speech for ideas and phrases. Remember: new, new, new!

3. Use powerful, positive emotive words

In each arena of business or public life there are good words and bad words. Make a list of them. Use the powerful good words to strike an emotional response in the audience. Use the bad words to paint the picture of your opponent. Here is an easy contrast: 'I'm for choice, for freedom, for progress, for the future. My opponent wants to take us back in time, enslave us to bureaucracy, steal the gains for women and minority communities, robbing us of a promising future like a thief in the night.' In the current election cycle in the United States there has been much written about the word 'change'. It is one of the most powerfully emotive words in politics, as we have already seen. That's why almost every politician tries to grab it, to use that word to define themselves. I remember when President Ronald Reagan stopped Walter Mondale cold in the 1984 re-election campaign by saying that the Democrats keep asking for change, but 'we Republicans are the change'. This from a sitting President! He then proceeded to remind his audiences of what life was like before the Reagan administration. He knew the power of that word and wouldn't let his opponents have it as a rhetorical tool.

4. Go easy on the audience

A conference speech is given to a tough audience. Yes, you are usually speaking to a large number of people who generally agree with you. But they have travelled great distances, stayed up much too late, often drinking way too much, eating strange food, surrounded by the distractions of the city and the conference. Many have trouble listening, paying attention, staying awake and hanging in there. Some are on sensory overload, thinking more about shock coffee or the nearest toilet than about your speech. And this goes on for speech after speech. If you survive the first speech, repeat and repeat again! By the seventh or eighth speech their brains are fried and their enthusiasm lost; they become zombies, the listening dead. This is the worst part: sitting through speech after speech after speech after endless bloody speech, the vast majority instantly forgettable, repeating the same facts and figures about the same programmes that you hear about each day and at each conference.

5. Give them a reason to listen

One conference veteran asked: 'What's in it for me? I want to know that in every speech.' Most members of the audience want the answer to that question. This is how a speaker justifies the time spent listening. In my view, every speech is about the audience, persuading them to adopt an opinion or to perform an action. So unless the audience sees the benefit of the speech material to them, they won't listen, or won't even come to the speech.

6. Finally, be bold, be brief, be seated

Give the audience a vision. Use bold language. Give them a sense of urgency. Take them into the future. Do it within ten minutes, fifteen at most. Less is more. The shorter the speech, the better. The audience will not remember most of the speech, even in the best of situations. But they always remember the length of the speech, both on the clock and how long it felt to those sitting there.

Showing up isn't enough. You have to set the audience on fire. You have to change their world. Leave them wanting more, not wanting you to leave.

Debate remarks

No one will forget the vice presidential debate in 2008. Republican nominee Sarah Palin asked Democrat Joseph Biden: 'Can I call you Joe?' That question was part of a strategy which reflected an endgame that didn't happen.

Given their importance, mastering debating skills is a necessary part of political training. Those who excel at it, like Neil Kinnock or William Hague, race ahead of their opponents and marshal arguments that support their viewpoints. Whether in a parliamentary setting or as part of political campaigns, debates can be persuasive, educational, entertaining. . . even decisive. They are also memorable. Many years ago, sitting in the public gallery of the Commons, I watched Harold Wilson and Margaret Thatcher go at each other in one of the most exciting exchanges in my experience. It was intense, breathtaking and electric. I thought you could see the sparks. Thanks to the availability online of Prime Minister's Questions, millions of people around the world witnessed the outstanding exchanges between Tony Blair and David Cameron. Debates can cut to the core of an issue and expose difference, leading to clarity and understanding. That is why debate is an essential check against tyranny and injustice. It is a powerful weapon for free thought and democratic choice, which is why it is feared in so many countries.

Strangely, few politicians are actually good at debate. For most, it is unnatural, difficult to understand, a source of anxiety and dread. They lack the persuasive ability to carry an audience. Most politicians do not have a good turn of phrase or the ability to condense difficult issues into a comprehensible sentence. Many of them treat debates as nothing more than events for prepared mini-speeches, totally missing the cut and thrust of a direct clash of ideas. Sadly, some are clueless about how to prepare for a debate; others over-prepare and find themselves lost in the details. And some arrogantly, and wrongly, believe that all they have to do is show up, that preparation is unnecessary because their personality and presence will carry them to victory. Because of these problems, and others, many politicians find themselves ill suited to the format and cautious to engage in debate.

But these worries can be overcome with a sound strategy of preparation and skilful participation. The following list may be helpful.

1. Know the format

Start by finding out everything you can about the event. Be comprehensive. Details are vital. What is the format? What do you know about the room and the podium? What kind of microphone will be used? What do you know about the lighting and the acoustics? Who are the other debaters? What do you know about them? What are their positions on current issues? Who will moderate? What do you know about the moderator? Does the moderator favour one party over another? What media will be present? Where will the television cameras be? Who will be in the audience? Where will your supporters sit? Can the audience participate? Will they be able to ask questions too? These are not trivial or idle questions. The answers are powerful determinants of your success.

2. Prepare properly

You want to be prepared. And good preparation is comprehensive. But there is a right way and a wrong way to prepare. The wrong way is to get too caught up in the small details and lose sight of the big vision. Too much detail is worse than none at all.

A good debate answer starts with a general statement of your policy proposal, such as 'I am committed to lowering taxes for the middle class'. You start that way because you want the audience to think about an issue along certain pre-determined lines of thought. This first statement of position narrows their thinking right away, enabling you to channel thought towards your desired conclusion.

You follow the general statement with a small collection of facts that support your view, maybe two or three factoids. Then you offer up your proposal and show why it will work. Give an example of a real person who will benefit from your plan. Then compare your plan to your opponent's, showing how that same person would not benefit, and that this person is typical of those who will be affected by your opponent's plan.

Since most debate answers are limited by time, you should look at your answer as a 2–3-minute speech that must condense some difficult problems and proposals into understandable, concise and memorable statements. That is part of the trick to debate: finding a way to make complex discussions into comments that are clear and persuasive.

Now, how to prepare? Begin by writing out every possible question that could come up in the debate, from policymaking to personal preferences. I know some debaters who will put each question on a single page of paper and then index them and file them in a binder for easy reference. Then, as you craft every answer, start with a clear, concise statement of your view.

After the question, write out the answer following the format suggested already. Edit, rework, condense and memorise your answers. But most importantly, memorise the initial statement of your position. That is the most important sentence of your answer.

If you have to ask a question, there is a three-step format: identify the issue, state your opponent's position and then ask the question. Here is an example: 'On climate change, you advocate a higher carbon tax for Edinburgh. Would this have an impact on profitability for local businesses?' And whether you are asking or answering, watch out for loaded or leading questions, such as 'Why would you advocate such a dangerous and provocative response to Islamic fundamentalism?' That question is actually a statement. You need to reword such questions to remove or address such embedded statements.

3. Debate strategically
Don't become obsessed by your opponent or what that person says. Stay on your point. Develop your argument. Keep talking about

the debate from your perspective. Don't be led away to debate on your opponent's ground. That is an old trick, baiting someone into talking about an issue from another perspective, one that is stronger for an opponent than for yourself. There is a saying in debate: 'If you shift to your opponent's ground, you will lose the debate. If you stay on your own point, you will win.' I believe that is true – when you shift away from your own rhetorical ground you will lose.

Think about this from a strategic standpoint. You should choose the strongest rhetorical ground for your position; 'strongest' is defined as that ground which places your opponent on weak ground if they make the direct opposite argument. Here is an example. You say: 'Air pollution is dangerous to public health.' The direct opposite argument is to deny it, which would be unbelievable to an audience, or to claim that air pollution is good, which is also hard to believe. So, the opponent would probably shift the argument, to claim that you don't know what you are talking about or that you are the worst polluter of them all or that the pollution really comes from France or Ireland or blustery politicians ('ha, ha, ha. . .'). Don't be led off your point. Rather, come back to it again and again, and show how your opponent is non-responsive, that you are the serious one who will cut pollution and help the citizens of London breathe better air.

Also, a point once made by Aristotle should be kept in mind: don't debate common ground. In other words, don't debate everything that is said. You and your opponent probably share considerable common ground. So only debate the points in contention and agree on anything that you share in common. This helps keep the focus on the points of contention and helps the audience see your position more clearly with less confusion. Here is an example: 'Yes, we both agree that the situation in Iran is serious. Where we disagree is whether or not to pursue diplomacy through the European Union or the United Nations.'

4. Control your non-verbals
Establish eye contact with the audience. If there is a television camera, periodically look directly at it to create the impression

of eye contact with those watching at home or in the office. The audience will be looking at your eyes and mouth, so use the full range of facial gestures (as appropriate): smiles, frowns, surprise or perplexity. Stand upright, relaxed, with good posture to convey confidence and credibility. Use your hands for an occasional gesture to highlight a point, but don't over-gesture, because that will become a distraction. Don't grip the podium. I would also recommend that you put considerable thought into the way you look: competent, understated, elegant, successful and tidy.

The audience will look at you to watch your reactions to the other speakers. Remember to keep control of your non-verbal responses. Don't do anything that can be used against you. Don't make any gesture or facial expression that undercuts your credibility or likeability. I am convinced that former Democratic presidential candidate Al Gore lost to George W. Bush in 2000 because of his arrogant, self-defeating non-verbals in their presidential debates. The Vice President rolled his eyes, loudly sighed during Bush's answers, showed impatience and was extremely condescending with his head shakes and facial grimaces. It was obvious that Gore couldn't believe Bush was a viable candidate or that his answers were plausible. The cameras caught it all. That means the American people saw it. Gore's attitude was widely debated in the press. And enough Americans were offended by it that those non-verbals surely cost him the election. So don't do anything rude or foolish. Stay focused. Stay on guard. Keep a serious, respectful demeanour when the other debaters are speaking. Your success may depend on it.

By the way, the lights are usually too bright. You will end up blinking a lot, which will become a distraction, unless you become accustomed to the brightness. You might want to practise with the most accurate reproduction possible of the debate setting. Try to get unintentional non-verbals under control.

5. *Never lose your cool*
Debates are a test of temperament. There is a lot of pressure on the debaters. Aristotle also said that people come to see a speech

to assess the character of the speaker. If you are hot headed, easily offended or pushed to anger, unable to remain calm and rational, people will probably think that you lack the temperament for high office. As well, if you say or do anything offensive, the audience will be put off, determined to vote against you. Be polite. . . always. Remain cool and collected. Let your opponent feel the pressure and lose control. My watchwords for debates are ease and elegance. Never let them see you sweat or get angry. Show the audience that nothing will get under your skin. You cannot be flustered. And that is why they should vote for you. You can handle the pressure.

6. Don't do anything stupid

Don't over-reach! Don't get arrogant, over-confident or giddy! Many debates are lost because of stupidity. By this I mean that the debater tries to become funny or cute or condescending or flirtatious. When you do this, you take unnecessary, dangerous risks. Sometimes less is more. Avoid unnecessary risks.

7. Capitalise on mistakes

When an opponent makes a mistake, seize the moment. Go directly to the mistake and blow it up. Direct the audience's attention to it. Hold your opponent to what he said. Make the mistake an issue. Go for the jugular vein. Clamp on it. And don't let go.

8. Spin the debate

Stay confident throughout the debate. Smile often. No matter how disappointed or defeated you feel, never show it. You may think that you only performed at about 30 per cent of your capability. But to the audience you may be doing extremely well. Don't signal to the audience that you are failing in the debate or that you could have done better. If you send a negative signal, the audience may start doubting because your non-verbals signalled to them to do so. Stay confident.

After the debate is over, the media will be looking for commentary and assessment. Your supporters will spin the debate your way by pointing out your virtues and the promise of your proposals. It is vital that you stay confident long after the debate is over, because the spin after the debate may actually determine how it is reported the next day. I have a saying: 'There are two debates – the one before the audience and the one after with the journalists. No matter how you performed in the first debate, you can win it by winning the second.'

9. Lead, don't follow

A debate is an exciting format. Everything happens quickly. It is easy to become distracted and sidetracked. Mastery of debate requires sound strategy, solid and clear thinking, comprehensive preparation, disciplined presentation and a good understanding of the arguments as they unfold. You must know where you want the debate to progress, and then lead the audience to that pre-determined end. Don't be led elsewhere. One of the best compliments I've heard from one debater to another is this: 'You were always five seconds ahead of me.' In other words, one debater led the debate and the other followed. Lead the debate to the place you want it to go, persuading the audience that you have the vision, ability and leadership skills to get the job done.

A good debate performance may not win an election by itself, although that has happened. But it can get you closer to a successful election. A bad debate performance has often, more often than not, doomed a candidate. So don't under-estimate the format or the results.

Polling day speech

In his book *Rendezvous with Destiny*, Craig Shirley describes Ronald Reagan as 'a study in adrenaline and cool' during the last days of his 1980 presidential campaign. Those are good words, words that show a campaign is going well, demonstrating leadership in action, reflecting Reagan's inner strength and self-understanding. The words suggest vigour and control. A campaign ramps up to a frantic pace in those last few days, the final push after long weeks and months, even years, of travel, meetings, handshakes, interviews and speeches. The adrenaline takes over, but a candidate in control is still cool, with grace under pressure, elegant while focused, confident, not arrogant. There is no panic visible.

Polling day ends the campaign with finality: victory or defeat. But there is one task left: the polling day speech. These remarks, often given late at night, sometimes very late at night or in the early morning, offer a declaration of victory or a disappointed concession.

1. Prepare a speech

Strive for a great speech. Don't, don't, don't and don't put off preparations. Work on the speech in the days before the election, not the night before. Amazingly, given its importance, many candidates don't even prepare a polling day speech. Many who do often just piece together platitudes and worn-out phrases, sound barks without the bite, providing a ho-hum, 'who cares', instantly forgettable set of remarks when there is the possibility for inspiration and vision. This is a chance for greatness. Give a speech worthy of the moment. History is calling.

2. Be humble

On polling day, genuine humility is refreshing, especially when combined with a commitment to service. Ronald Reagan started his election night remarks in 1980 with this in mind. He said: 'There has never been a more humbling moment in my life. I consider the trust you have placed in me sacred, and I give you my sacred oath that I will do my utmost to justify your faith.' He understood that this is a time for graciousness and character. Time to be a good winner or loser. Time to show you understand the responsibility and the duties of the office. Don't gloat. Don't pile on. Don't twist the knife or sling mud. Don't say something like 'This election is a complete repudiation of everything the other parties stand for.'

Don't be a mean-spirited bastard (like Alan B'Stard). Move beyond the pain and trauma of the election. This speech is about the voters asking you to represent them, to work for them, on the great task of building and governing a country. After his second electoral victory in 2001, Tony Blair said: 'I want to say what an enormous privilege and honour it is to be entrusted with the government of this country.' Good words. That's the right approach.

3. Dress for leadership

Time for the look of leadership. Don't look tired. This isn't the place for pity or sweat. Balance the adrenaline and cool. Be confident in an understated manner. Display strength of will and good character. The victor must be up for the job, not ready for a stay at Fawlty Towers. Rest during the day. Let me repeat that: rest, rest, rest. The cameras will be on that night. The entire nation will be watching, even for local elections. Even if defeated, go out a winner. By the way, remember that this is one of the candidate's most visible photo opportunities. Treat the visuals with respect. Give consideration to the backdrop, the setting and the lighting. Leave nothing to chance. . . don't screw up.

4. Start by thanking the opponent

This should be the start of the speech. By talking about respect and regard for the opponent, the process of reconciliation begins, win or lose. In 2001, Blair began his remarks with a few words about William Hague, praising his 'stoicism and resilience'. Be generous with goodwill. And there is an order to the speeches. The concession speech should come first, with words to the effect that 'I've just called my opponent to congratulate her on her victory. I wish her my very best as she represents us.' Then, after the concession speech is finished, the victory speech should be given, starting with words such as 'I have just received a call from my opponent congratulating all of us on the election results.' Obviously, if there are three or more parties, it is ideal if all of the concession speeches have been given before the victor makes her remarks.

5. Thank the family

Yes, the family is important. The candidate couldn't have done all this without Uncle Shane and Aunt Brittany. But don't overdo it. Thank the spouse or partner ('Matt has given me unselfish support'). But with each additional name the speech loses momentum and the crowd gets bored. Introducing the entire extended family is just plain self-indulgence and kills the speech. I would counsel not introducing anyone beyond your significant other.

6. Thank the supporters

That's what the people in the audience want to hear, that their work is appreciated. Thank them for their hard work, faith, commitment and participation in the electoral process. Many will be true believers in a philosophy or party. Many gave of themselves because they sincerely want a better country. Many found the meaning of democracy in their work. That means that they discovered the value of handing out leaflets, working blogs and chat rooms, text messaging and twittering, attending meetings, walking door to door, speaking at clubs and colleges and union meetings and displaying campaign badges and stickers and lawn signs and banners. Put the spotlight on the supporters. They've earned it.

7. Thank the voters and look for a mandate

The tone of a campaign often affects the ability to govern. A large victory margin based on acceptance or rejection of a personality is not a mandate for government. It is giving someone their P45. But an election victory after a debate about principle or vision results in a mandate. The larger the election margin, the greater the mandate. Every victory speech should be searching for the words or actions that claim a mandate. John Kennedy realised the importance of this. He remarked at a press conference a few days after his victory that 'the margin is narrow, but the responsibility is clear . . . a margin of only one vote would still be a mandate.' Claim the mandate immediately, if you can, starting with the polling day speech. . . especially with the polling day speech.

8. Place the election in historical context

Here is where you can grasp at greatness. Nelson Mandela understood this. He started his election victory speech in 1994 by saying:

> This is one of the most important moments in the life of our country. I stand here before you filled with deep pride and joy – pride in the ordinary, humble people of this country. You have shown such a calm, patient determination to reclaim this country as your own. What joy that we can loudly proclaim from the rooftops – free at last!

The historical significance can be a reaffirmation of principle. Barack Obama did this the night of the 2008 presidential election. He started his speech with these words: 'If there is anyone out there who still doubts that America is a place where all things are possible, who still wonders if the dream of our founders is alive in our time, who still questions the power of our democracy, tonight is your answer.'

9. Restate the vision

Reagan did this very well in 1980. He outlined his vision, coupled with hope for a nation fighting malaise, at home and abroad. He said: 'I aim to try and tap that great American spirit that opened up this completely undeveloped continent from coast to coast and made it a great nation, survived several wars, survived a great depression, and we'll survive the problems we face now.' Often a polling day speech is used to briefly state the policy objectives of a new government, explaining how they fit into an overarching vision. These policies can help generate renewed hope in the future.

10. Look to the future

A polling day speech is about the future. Nelson Mandela in his great election night speech showed the adrenaline would start pumping with the dawn of the new day. He said: 'Tomorrow, the entire ANC leadership and I will be back at our desks. We are rolling up our sleeves to begin tackling the problems our country faces. We ask all of you to join us – go back to your jobs in the morning. Let's get South Africa working.' Memorably, standing outside 10 Downing Street on 4 May 1979, Margaret Thatcher closed her brief remarks by quoting St Francis of Assisi: 'Where there is discord, may we bring harmony. Where there is error, may we bring truth. Where there is doubt, may we bring faith. And where there is despair, may we bring hope.' She added the words of Airey Neave: 'There is now work to be done.' A polling day speech should end with that thought.

The day after polling day is the start of a new chapter. The campaign was about politics and party. Now, with the election results known, the need is for reconciliation, healing and national unity. The victorious party must govern. They must show leadership and wisdom, placing citizens and country first. The parties in defeat must form a 'loyal' opposition, which means a constructive opposition. All parties must now work for the good of the country. Mandela said as much at the end of his speech: 'Let our celebrations be in keeping with the mood set in the elections, peaceful, respectful and disciplined, showing we are a people ready to assume the responsibilities of government.'

Every polling day speech should remind us that politics can be noble and enriching, respectful and decent, the means to a better world. This is a speech that requires humility and vision, acceptance and commitment, thankfulness and wisdom, with some adrenaline and cool. The candidate owes it to supporters, party, constituents and the nation to give a memorable speech. That doesn't mean a long speech – shorter is usually better. But this is one of the best opportunities for an historic speech that can set direction and tone for the victor, and highlight purpose and meaning in defeat. The polling day speech can be one of the most important speeches of a campaign, even though the campaign is over.

Government policy speech

In 1979, five months after electoral victory, Margaret Thatcher warned the Conservative Party at Blackpool that 'winning an election is a splendid thing, but it is only the prologue to the vital business of governing'. After the votes are tallied, government begins. Unfortunately, most politicians with power just sound like politicians with power, huffing and puffing for the media, in search of soundbites and demanding attention, stuck in campaign mode, rewinding slogans and reliving old moments, rather than leading the nation into the future. The prose is already tired and worn. The speeches do nothing but absorb time and space, becoming instantly forgettable, cast aside by history because they are unworthy of remembrance. The prose is dead on arrival: leaden words that fail to inspire, bureaucratic acronyms that dull the mind, commonplace and disposable terms, often laced with weasel words that kill through over-qualification, and clever manipulations of language that just hide the truth. And those problems with language are compounded day after day, news cycle after news cycle, until the next election.

However, there are some politicians who use the opportunity of power to lead through words, marshalling a language of leadership. It is a use of language that is authentic, organic and contemporary, yet shared by Winston Churchill, Franklin Roosevelt, Ronald Reagan, Margaret Thatcher, Nelson Mandela, Václav Havel and Tony Blair, to name a few. Even before the modern media age, leaders needed to master language. Now, it is a central, indispensable part of any governmental responsibility. The absence of an ability to communicate dooms even the most competent exercise of power. You don't want to hear someone like the prison warden in the movie *Cool Hand Luke*: 'What we have here is a failure to communicate.'

So, what do great leaders do with language?

1. Leaders talk differently
They have gravitas. They know who they are and what they stand for. Great leaders do more than welcome the challenge of government;

they rise to it. Great leaders slow down, speak with a humbling authority at a rate that is clear, transparent and conversational. They are confident without becoming arrogant. Great leaders know that language is action, that words create our world. They choose words that draw on the strength, symbols and history of a nation. And they do this in a way that is credible and accepted, not phony or contrived. That is why great leaders must speak at times of tragedy or change. Their words help us understand and frame events. We need them to speak, and speak well.

2. Leaders put the needs of the country first
Party politics drive a campaign. Election demands new priorities. Yes, the success of the party remains important, crucial over time. But there are now additional needs, overriding needs, national needs that must become central, to thought and language. At Blackpool in 1979, Thatcher explained: 'Now, more than ever, my responsibility is not only to the party but to the nation.' That's right, and any office holder who places party above nation is reckless, arrogant and irresponsible. For, as Neil Kinnock so famously warned, 'you can't play politics' with people's lives or jobs.

3. Leaders become bigger than the moment
Look to history. This is one of the great traits of Winston Churchill, who was always aware of the historical antecedents of an issue and always mindful of the opportunity for an historical legacy. Great leaders rise above immediate circumstances and the 24/7 news cycle. They explain the value of a policy over time and show its historical implications. In Brighton, after the 1997 victory, Tony Blair argued for the historical importance of the election:

> The result is a quiet revolution now taking place. Led by the real moderniser: not me, the British people . . . The British don't fear change. We are one of the great innovative peoples. From the Magna Carta to the first parliament to the Industrial Revolution to an empire that covered the world.

> Most of the great inventions of modern times [come] with
> Britain stamped on them: the telephone, the television, the
> computer, penicillin, the hovercraft, radar. Change is in the
> blood and bones of the British.

Place decisions in an historical context. Use the symbols and
achievements of a nation to show historical importance and, if
desired, historical continuity.

4. Leaders explain the agenda

Great leaders lay out the legislative agenda. They tell the nation
what will be accomplished in the years to come. This helps focus
expectations. The agenda gives structure and scope to policy
decisions throughout government. It provides a criterion for
measuring success and failure. Here is a simple example. When
Churchill became Prime Minister of a nation at war in 1940, he
communicated with clarity of purpose. His explanation is still
known, seventy years later, by millions of people around the
world:

> We have before us many, many long months of struggle and
> of suffering. You ask: What is our policy? I will say: It is to
> wage war, by sea, land and air, with all our might and with
> all the strength God can give us . . . That is our policy. You
> ask: What is our aim? I can answer in one word: Victory
> – victory at all costs, victory in spite of all terror, victory,
> however long and hard the road may be.

5. Leaders heal division

Great leaders heal division. Because language shapes and moulds
our world, it must be mobilised to stitch a society back together.
In his inaugural speech in 1994, Nelson Mandela seized every
opportunity to unite through language, employing inclusive
pronouns, adjectives and nouns again and again: 'We understand
. . . that there is no easy road to freedom. We know it well that

none of us acting alone can achieve success. We must therefore act together as a united people, for national reconciliation, for nation-building, for the birth of a new world.' Through such language he avoided civil war and undoubtedly saved millions of lives. Great leaders do not divide and rule; they legitimate their power through unification.

6. Leaders seize the mandate
Closing the divide between voters is important to governance. The election provides choice. Moving forward from that choice requires a mandate. So great leaders explain how the results provide that mandate. In the 1979 Blackpool speech, Thatcher said that she had been accused of 'waiving a phony mandate'. She strongly objected to that:

> When a voter takes his decision and slips his paper into the ballot box he does know, broadly speaking, what the party of his choice stands for . . . in voting for us they were voting for all those policies. That was and is our mandate, and we have every right to carry it out, and we shall.

The mandate is the set of policies that address the nation's needs. It must be central to the legislative agenda. When the mandate falls by the wayside, government becomes directionless, reflecting reactive drift and a stagnant agenda.

7. Leaders speak of the vision
Churchill, Reagan, Thatcher, Blair and other recognised leaders all had a vision of the future. They explained that vision to the voters. And, importantly, they wrapped the vision in constitutional principles. The vision must be consistent with the constitution, even help expand, strengthen and defend it. This makes it easier to fulfil the agenda and apply the mandate. So when Reagan spoke of the 'shining city on the hill', it became a powerful aspiration for the United States to lead through freedom and democracy, which

was a direct reference to the constitution and the unique history of the country.

8. Leaders remain bold

One commonality between great leaders is that they continually use bold language. They don't hedge or qualify. They lead through language. They decisively and proudly use bold language at every opportunity. So when Churchill talks about having nothing to offer but 'blood, toil, tears and sweat', or explains that the British defence of freedom was 'their finest hour', or calls to the United States to 'give us the tools, and we will finish the job', there is no misunderstanding of his intention. Boldness is not something that has a shelf life of 100 or 500 days. It must be a linguistic preservative for the length of government. It also helps drive the media coverage because it gives soundbites that condense the policy.

9. Leaders involve constituents

Franklin Roosevelt established a close relationship with the American people through 'fireside chats' on the radio. Churchill built his bond through honestly explaining the dire wartime circumstances daily in his speeches. Reagan enjoyed a communion with the American people through a shared thought process of the meaning of the American experience. Great leaders become the 'voice of collective assent', which means that they give expression to the hopes and dreams of constituents, literally becoming the voice for those who have none, or who have no opportunity to raise it. This makes the relationship between political leaders and constituents much more immediate and lasting, bypassing the media if necessary, and surely using the media to accomplish the task. This allows the people to govern through leaders. In Prague in 1990, Václav Havel explained that the restoration of freedom did more than remove a 'contaminated moral environment'. It enabled people to become more prosperous, honest, decent and human. That is why the end of that speech spoke volumes about the changes taking place: 'People, your government has returned to you!'

10. Leaders empower people

The late novelist and MP John Buchan once wrote that 'true leadership is not to put greatness into humanity, but to elicit it, since the greatness is already there'. In other words, great leaders make others great by helping them find their humanity. He continued: 'That truth is the basis of all religion, it is the only justification for democracy, it is the chart and compass of our mortal life.' That is one other trait that separates Churchill, Reagan, Thatcher, Mandela, Havel, Blair and other great leaders apart from others who merely hold power. Great leaders transform the world by empowering those around them. Constituents don't lose their freedom. By displaying their humanity they find it. Great leaders help all of us become better, nobler and more human, which also means becoming more tolerant, inclusive, understanding, fair, just and compassionate. Great leaders educate, inform, share, motivate, inspire and heal. They move us forward into a safer and saner world. A great leader helps a nation become and remain great.

Fundraising speech

Probably the hardest speech to give is the fundraiser. Fundraising speeches are often a lifeline for an organisation, especially non-profits. So speakers are under considerable pressure to be successful. They must stimulate philanthropy.

There are some speakers who are great, 'Class A' fundraisers: Bill Clinton, Newt Gingrich, Elton John, Bono and Bob Geldof, among others. And there are common elements to their excellent fundraising speeches.

1. Start with an example

Every good speech is a morality tale, with heroes and obstacles and a quest for a better world. Audiences love stories and easily relate to them. So start with a story. Engage the audience right away. A fundraising speech is the perfect type for this approach. Explain the nature of the problem you confront with a story about someone who has made a difference. A good instance is Margaret Thatcher's Clair Booth Luce Lecture in 1991. She started with comments about Ambassador Luce and others to show the link between public service and philanthropy: 'Among the legitimate aims of philanthropy is the nourishing of the values of freedom and the free economy that underpin the prosperity of this country and of the West as a whole.' Such a beginning shows the importance of the event and the potential contributions of each member of the audience. This will allow for immediate audience interest and a strong emotional response.

Another beginning is to give an example of someone in need. Give that person a name and tell their story. You may recall that television fundraisers, especially for organisations that work in developing countries, regularly use this approach. It provides a human interaction rather than a faceless statistic. Of course, there are some uses of examples that are plastic or contrived. Here less is more. Just tell the story without a breaking voice or rhetorical tricks. The power is in the story itself, if it is a good one.

2. *Explain the scope of the problem*
Explain the complexity and depth of the problems the organisation is trying to confront. You may be talking about poverty, hunger, landmines, homelessness, global warming, species extinction, domestic violence or hundreds of other issues. Whatever it is, explain its importance and the necessity to address it. Tell the audience the problem reaches out to harm thousands, maybe millions of people. Tell them we live in a global village, where the problems of one or the many are the problems of all. In a speech at the official opening of the Cape Town SOS Children's Village in 1996, Nelson Mandela said: 'The children of South Africa have assumed a responsibility beyond their years, both in the freeing of our country and in building its future.' That is a good way to broaden the scope. Now, show what that means! Mandela continued: 'Our children have borne the brunt of apartheid's ravaging deprivation.

Most were robbed of their right to a decent education, adequate health care, stable family lives – and sometimes of their entire childhood. And this applies to the majority of children.' This is where you lay out the issue in some detail, indicating the causes and implications of the problems.

3. Explain the importance of the work
But there are organisations trying to address this problem. Yours is one of them. Tell them about the accomplishments registered and the hard work underway. Explain the plans for the future, how with support more could be done, and more quickly.

And tell them about the people involved. Name names. Humanise the presentation. Show how the organisation is boldly fighting for a better future. Speaking to the American Cancer Society in 1977, the journalist William F. Buckley, Jr spoke of Alfred Sloan, who was a biomedical scientist, inventor and businessman, eponym of the Sloan-Kettering Institute for Cancer Research and president and chairman of General Motors. Buckley noted: 'Even since the death of Alfred Sloan, some ten years ago, the odds [of cancer survival] have begun, slowly, grudgingly, but exhilaratingly, to change. Because of his work, his determination, his philanthropy, because of the efforts of those fired by the same resolution, progress is made every day.' At the Heritage Foundation in 1999, Buckley told the audience of the organisation's value in American history: 'The masses of material generated by Heritage flow out into the major arteries of American thought.' That is the kind of language needed to explain how the person or the organisation is of vital importance to our world.

4. Show linkages to other organisations
A speaker greatly increases the possibility of a donation by showing partnership and cooperation with other accepted groups. For example, if you show that your organisation will work in harmony with other well-known groups, you can appropriate some of their credibility and prestige. You shine brighter in their borrowed light. I remember one passage from George Herbert Walker Bush's party

acceptance speech in 1988 (the 'no new taxes' speech). He said 'This is America: the Knights of Columbus, the Grange, Hadassah, the Disabled American Veterans, the Order of Ahepa, the Business and Professional Women of America, the union hall, the Bible study group, LULAC [League of United Latin American Citizens], 'Holy Name' – a brilliant diversity spread like stars, like a thousand points of light in a broad and peaceful sky.' He is borrowing a lot of light in that passage.

5. Involve the audience

Now, show how each one of them can become part of this great work. Do not under-estimate the necessity of this part of the speech. Remember, every member of the audience wants to feel important, that their efforts are needed, that they can make a difference. Crudely put, each person is asking 'What's in it for me?' Tell them. Explain how each person's involvement will make the organisation better, more effective and more successful. In a speech at Eisenhower College in 1969, then-Governor Ronald Reagan explained that the involvement of the audience would make a profound difference. He said: 'You – ladies and gentlemen of the world of commerce and the professions – you can make no greater investment in freedom than your contributions to independent schools and colleges in this country.' He used a key fundraising word, 'investment'. An audience must believe that their money is not destined to be wasted or to help someone in the organisation to live the high life. Rather, they want to know – they want guarantees – that the money will go directly to help address the problems cited in the speech. That is why so many organisations mention the percentage of donations that are used for administration, such as 'only 5 per cent of your donations are used to run the programme; the rest go to help end poverty and fight disease in sub-Saharan Africa'. The lower the percentage for operation costs, the better the persuasive possibilities for donations. You have to show that the organisation will be careful, prudent and responsible with donated money. This is a fiduciary duty.

6. Ask for money

This is the major point of the speech. It is called 'the ask'. Ask for it openly and directly. Don't hint. Don't be evasive. If your organisation is worthy of support, then there is no shame in asking for support. It helps the audience become involved in something bigger and more lasting than one person or one moment. Financial support is a way for people to join together to make a difference. Yet it is hard to ask. In one recent fundraising speech I heard, the audience was told that donations were not expected during these troubled economic times. I almost fell out of my chair. The audience was there to support the organisation, precisely because funding was tight. Ask for the money without any qualifiers, without any weasel words that diminish the strength of your message.

And show your own commitment. Tell the audience that you do more than work for your organisation. . . you are a donor too!

Also, research your target audience. Find out where the donations have gone in the past. Use that information as part of the ask. Show you understand the immense demands for a corporation's or individual's donations. Demonstrate how your work has a priority. If that work is successful it may help alleviate other problems and curtail the necessity of donation in other areas. For example, if homelessness is addressed, then it might improve the health status for those without a permanent place to live and reduce violence against them. You are competing for a piece of the philanthropic pie – show that giving your organisation or campaign some of that pie makes sense in terms of the overall goals for a donor.

You can take two approaches to the ask. One is to include it in the speech and try to collect funds on the spot. That is easy for small sums, for pocket money. You see this approach in religious services that set aside time to pass around the plate after the sermon or homily. Frankly, a cynical view of many religious speeches would conclude that they are fundraisers more than moralising commandments. For larger sums, the ask is performed at a follow-up meeting, often one to one between the fundraiser and the corporate or philanthropic person designated to handle donation requests. In this case, the expectation is that, if the follow-up meeting is scheduled, then the ask is the main item of discussion and some level of commitment will be made. Of course, the two could be combined. I recently heard a fundraising speech that attempted to raise $40,000 for a project. There were approximately forty people in the audience, each of them reasonably wealthy and intensely engaged in the topic. If the speaker had said then 'Well, if each of you could give a thousand dollars, we could do this', I'm sure they would all have pulled out a cheque book. But the speaker instead scheduled follow-ups and asked each of the forty for the full amount. The result: nada. So don't overlook the possibility that the speech itself could generate instant donations. Build that possibility into the speech and the process. And spread the pain. Generally it is not a good idea to try to get everything from one person. Make your support diversified and collective. Remember, if one person bankrolls the project, the organisation becomes enslaved to that donor.

7. Ask for other forms of support
You can also ask for volunteers, resources like buildings or equipment, in-kind services such as printing or transportation, or anything else that you would use funds to buy. This might be easier for many organisations. In the recent presidential election in the United States, union assistance and college volunteers were major factors for the election of President Obama.

8. Explain any tax advantages
Always, always, always do this.

9. Thank the audience
Even if they don't donate now, each member of the audience may donate in the future. So thank them for their interest and involvement. In a speech in London for the Nelson Mandela Children's Fund in 1996, President Mandela included these comments:

Broad partnerships which harness our nation's resources are the key to achieving our goals, because they give each and every person the opportunity to be part of bringing about change . . . Assembled here are distinguished members of British society and South Africans, joined in their commitment to alleviate the plight of South Africa's youth . . . I wish to thank you all assembled here for replying to my call.

10. End with a sense of urgency
The donations are needed right away for the work to continue. In fact, it would be catastrophic if funding dried up. So the watchword is 'now'.

One more thing. . . choose the right person to give the speech. That may not be the CEO or president. It could be that the best fundraiser is lower in the organisational food chain. So find the best person for the job. Most people are naturally, sincerely eager to help others. But parting with hard-earned money is difficult, even in the best of times, much less during times of economic struggle. However, in many sectors philanthropic donations are rising. So it can be done. Make sure you get your proper share of the philanthropic pie.

Graduation speech

The graduation speech is a sober affair, in theory. At least, parents and administrators view it as a moment of recognition of accomplishment. The graduates may have a different idea.

Each educational institution has its own culture and history. It is a massive mistake to assume that all graduations are the same. Investigate the event thoroughly. Look at past graduation speeches. Talk to past graduates, faculty and administrators. Look at media accounts. Try to get a sense of the event. You don't want to be too stiff or too loose. It is vital to make a good impression on all concerned.

The speaker is generally a famous or accomplished person with a message for the graduates. That is a key fact. The speaker must have a message, usually about the importance of service and making a difference. That is the general theme of almost every graduation, at least the good ones.

1. Set the right tone

Based on research and interviews, the speech should be constructed to set the appropriate tone immediately. Here are two disparate examples of variation in tone. The first is from Dr Arthur Burns, former chair of the Federal Reserve Board in the United States. In 1970 he spoke at Hebrew University in Israel. He started the speech by recalling earlier visits and warnings of danger: 'This is my third visit to Israel. I remember, just before my first visit here, in 1958, being admonished not to come by several United States ambassadors.' Contrast that with a graduation speech to law graduates at Catholic University in Washington, DC by humorist Art Buchwald, who spoke in 1977. He asked: 'What does a speaker say to a fresh-faced, well-scrubbed graduating class of neophyte lawyers? Your studies are over, and now you leave these hallowed halls, this ivy-covered campus, to go out and practise the second-oldest profession in the world.'

The speaker sets the tone right away.

2. Congratulate the graduates

The event is really about the graduates. If they listen to any part of the speech, this is the bit they must hear. It might be helpful to mention a few items about their academic experience: the number of courses taken, the amount of time in lectures, the number of really bad meals consumed, the hesitation on the first day of the first year, the confidence of the last day, study abroad, community service and milestones in inter-school sports. It might be helpful to mention the names of lecture theatres, halls of residence, the sports arena or local pubs. Remember that there are parents in the audience, so keep the focus on scholarship. The words might be something like 'I want to congratulate the class of 2010 on graduation. This is a hard-earned testament to your commitment, your learning and your achievement.'

3. Thank the leaders of the educational institution

They run the place. They were the ones who invited you. They may actually be the only members of the audience who want to listen to you.

4. Thank the faculty

There are probably several faculty members in the audience. They may all be seated together. You can tell. They are the older members in academic robes. Thank them for their scholarship, their sacrifices to educate the graduates and their commitment to the third-oldest profession, teaching. One philosopher called teachers 'the soldiers of democracy'. They deserve thanks for being idealistic enough to work for low wages and little appreciation. But they make a profound difference every day through education and example. They surely should be recognised.

5. Thank the parents

The parents, family and friends of the graduates have made extraordinary sacrifices for them. These sacrifices involve more than money. There have been moments of choice where the family did without. The students' absence has changed the dynamics of home life, often leaving parents with an empty-nest feeling and an extra room they would rather have filled. There have been sacrifices of emotion, time, convenience and ease, all because parents want something better for their children. Actually, the parents may have a greater appreciation of the meaning of graduation than the graduates. It is a step towards maturity. It is a recognition of growing wisdom and independence. This moment would not have happened without the parents. Perhaps it is also important to explain to the graduates that parents want that independence, as comedian Bill Cosby once noted. He said at one graduation: 'Parents want you to know, graduation does not mean "move back home"!' Former New York state governor Mario Cuomo gave the graduation speech at Iona College in 1984 directly to the parents, with only a brief mention of the graduates. It is said that he 'spoke over the heads' of the graduates.

6. Discuss a life of service
This is the core of most graduation speeches. It is a sound, time-honoured message. It may also be the last time graduates hear about the need to help others. This is the time to mention Emmeline Pankhurst, Mahatma Gandhi, Dr Martin Luther King, Jr, Mother Teresa, Oprah Winfrey, Nelson Mandela and others who have made a difference with their lives. Name names. Cite the famous and the infamous and the everyman/woman. Examples help to explain a life of service. Cuomo told the parents to tell their children

> that the philosophers were right. That St Francis, Buddha, Muhammad, Maimonides all spoke the truth when they said the way to serve yourself is to serve others; and that Aristotle was right, before them, when he said that the only way to assure yourself happiness is to learn to give happiness.

Challenge the students to seize every opportunity to remake the world. Tell them that a better world is in their hands, a world of mutual respect, kindness, compassion, tolerance, wisdom and love. Convince them that achieving those traits is the way to measure success.

7. Add some philosophy
Not too much. . . just enough to give the speech focus and elevation. This is the time to mention Plato, Aristotle, Bertrand Russell or John Rawls. Maybe add in a few figures in literature or the arts. The American labour leader Lane Kirkland, speaking at

the University of South Carolina in 1985, offered a chestnut from George Santayana, that 'those who cannot remember the past are condemned to repeat it'. But he also cited the philosopher Sidney Hook, who said: 'The difference between a truth and a deep truth [is that] a deep truth is a truth the converse of which is equally true.' That kind of reflection will get everyone thinking, even if they don't understand it.

8. Make news
Some speakers use the occasion to make a specific point or to make news. In 1994, Colin Powell spoke at Howard University, one of the historically black colleges and universities in the United States. The president of the school had just resigned over an anti-Semitic rally involving a few students who attacked Jews and spoke of the sins of white Americans. Powell used his graduation speech to call for tolerance, compassion and an end to hate speech. At one point in the speech he argued:

> African Americans have come too far and we have too far yet to go to take a detour into the swamp of hatred. We, as a people who have suffered so much from the hatred of others, must not show tolerance for any movement or philosophy that has at its core the hatred of Jews or anyone else. Our future lies in the philosophy of love and understanding and caring and building. Not of hatred and tearing down.

The audience sat in silence and listened. Powell made news and the situation became less heated.

9. Be brief
In his graduation speech at Iona, Mario Cuomo started by saying:

> It was an Irishman who gave me the best advice . . . about the art of delivering a commencement speech. Father Flynn was the president of my alma mater, St John's, and the first

time I was asked to speak at a graduation, I asked him how I
should approach it. 'Commencement speakers', said Father
Flynn, 'should think of themselves as the body at an old-
fashioned wake. They need you in order to have the party,
but nobody expects you to say very much.' That's the advice
I intend to remember today.

It is good advice. A graduation speech is long at ten minutes. A
well-received speech should last between five and eight minutes,
the shorter the better.

A graduation speech is a great honour. Such a speech is usually
printed and made available to the public, placed in the institution's
archives and made available on the Internet. So it must read well
orally and verbally. Such a speech becomes part of the record. It
must be an inspiring effort with a lasting impact.

Memorial speech

The most famous memorial speech is by Pericles. Other great
recognised memorial speeches include Marcus Antonius's words
at Caesar's funeral, Edmund Burke's lament on the death of Marie
Antoinette, Abraham Lincoln's address at Gettysburg, Jawaharlal
Nehru's speech about Gandhi, Ted Kennedy's eulogy for his
brother Robert, Ronald Reagan's Challenger speech and Boris
Yeltsin's remarks on the burial of Tsar Nicholas II and his family.
These addresses would be on anyone's list of greatest speeches ever
delivered. Why? Because the memorial speech allows for sombre
reflection, deep appeals to the human heart, discussion of loss and
sadness, and hope arising out of adversity. The memorial speech
looks at the meaning of life and our ability to make a difference.
A memorial speech often reveals the soul of a community and a
nation. Speaking of the poet Robert Frost, John Kennedy said: 'A
nation reveals itself not only by the men it produces but by the men

it honours, the men it remembers.' The life remembered is a life of importance to others. As Kennedy said of Frost: 'Because he knew the midnight as well as the high noon, because he understood the ordeal as well as the triumph of the human spirit, he gave his age strength with which to overcome despair.' Given in times of sorrow and grief, a memorial speech is an opportunity to unite the audience in its appreciation of those who have passed away. This unification can then be used to ask the audience to initiate change and continue the good work of the deceased.

This type of speech requires nerve to maintain composure and a sensitive touch to adequately gauge the feelings of those in the audience. In a time of grief, less might be more. That means a lighter touch might be best, avoiding any risk of upsetting or alienating an emotional audience, especially family members and close friends. Here are some things to do.

1. *Explain your presence*
Tell the audience why you have been asked to give a memorial speech. It helps the audience understand your remarks, giving credibility and reflecting intimacy with the deceased. One of the most powerful memorials ever given was by Dr Benjamin Elijah Mays, the president of Morehouse College in Atlanta. He gave the eulogy at Dr Martin Luther King, Jr's funeral at Morehouse. Mays had been a close friend and mentor when King was an undergraduate at Morehouse. Perhaps a better way to put that is that Mays was a profound influence on King, directing his reading, forming his philosophy and counselling his later civil rights activism. So Mays started by explaining that he had been requested to give the eulogy by the family, and that it was like being asked to 'eulogise a dead son – so close and so precious he was to me'. He also mentioned that King himself had asked for the eulogy if he preceded Mays. That is a powerful way to begin.

2. *Reach out to the audience*
Explain that your presence is symbolic. You speak for the audience,

giving voice to each person in attendance. You express the grief and loss felt by each person, not so much by words as by your willingness to stand up and speak.

3. Find a theme

Some lives can be explained with a phrase, a thought or a quotation. Look for a theme that can be used as a thread to hold the speech together. A haunting theme may be found in a speech given by General Douglas MacArthur at his alma mater, West Point, in 1962. He spoke of the code of the corps: 'Duty, Honour, Country'. Those were the themes of his life, the words he lived by. He said at the end of that speech that 'the shadows are lengthening for me. The twilight is here . . . In the evening of my memory, always I come back to West Point. Always there echoes and re-echoes in my ears – Duty, Honour, Country.' He understood that great lives are motivated and channelled by great themes and great messages. When Martin Luther King died, Robert Kennedy gave impromptu remarks wherein he revealed his own thematic justification. He said: 'My favourite poet was Aeschylus. He wrote: "In our sleep, pain which cannot forget falls drop by drop upon the heart until, in our own despair, against our will, comes wisdom through the awful grace of God."' The theme can give coherence to the speech.

4. Talk about the life and accomplishments

Mays spoke at great length of King's accomplishments. He spoke of his civil rights ministry, ethics, philosophy of non-violence, patriotism, courage, righteousness and love. Mays also spoke of King's place in history:

> No! He was not ahead of his time. No man is ahead of his time. Every man is within his star, each in his own time. Each man must respond to the call of God in his lifetime and not somebody else's time . . . the time was always ripe to do that which was right and that which needed to be done.

Pericles spoke of the deaths of Athenian soldiers to preserve democracy; Lincoln talked of the deaths at Gettysburg to preserve the Union. This is the time to list accomplishments, both professionally and personally. Name names and dates. Give facts and figures. But above all, speak of humanity, decency and love.

5. Tell the audience what to do next

Tell them to carry on the important work. Time stops for no one; the need for our best efforts continues. Use the deceased as a role model for the living. Robert Kennedy told his audience that the best way to respond to King's death was to 'dedicate ourselves to what the Greeks wrote so many years ago: to tame the savageness of man and to make gentle the life of this world'. Mays, also speaking of King, said:

> If we love Martin Luther King, Jr and respect him, as this crowd surely testifies, let us see to it that he did not die in vain; let us see to it that we do not dishonour his name by trying to solve our problems through rioting in the streets . . . let us see to it also that the conditions that cause riots are promptly removed . . . Let black and white alike search their hearts, and if there be prejudice in our hearts against any racial or ethnic group, let us exterminate it and let us pray . . . 'Father, forgive them for they know not what they do.' If we do this, Martin Luther King, Jr will have died a redemptive death from which all mankind will benefit.

Those are good words, a paradigm of speaking at a time of reflection and grief. Death helps us to change life.

Barack Obama (Adrian Sanchez-Gonzalez/Landov/PA)

7. CIVILITY MATTERS

In every recent election there have been cries for more civility, dignity and mutual respect. And those cries have been generally ignored. Lip service is offered, with hand-wringing in the media and shrugging of shoulders. But, in the hearts of some politicians and their campaign managers, as well as many bloggers and party activists, the call for civility is viewed as a diversion: weak, pathetic, preachy, unworkable and unrealistic in modern elections. They would not agree with Edmund Burke, who once said that 'manners are of more importance than the laws'.

Instead, campaign managers order up more 'red meat', which often means more character assassination, ad hominems, or rudeness. Usually, 'going negative' means forgoing civility. This has been a popular strategy, especially in the last weeks of a campaign when the loss of civility emerges into a covert part of the overall campaign message. That strategy often works. There is considerable evidence that negative campaigning is successful, often because it clarifies differences, highlights problems or intensifies voter participation.

There are good reasons to take civility seriously. Political discourse is not just a collection of ideas expressed in words and gestures; it is action, creating and shaping our world. Words are tools that can become weapons. The right words can change the lives of all who hear them; they can change history too. The words we choose to use can make a powerful, profound and positive contribution to our lives, culture and politics. The wrong words can damage, divide and destroy our polity, leaving behind hatred and polarisation.

So I urge, in the strongest possible terms, civility in politics.

1. Have good manners

Civility is a case for good manners, which are developed social and cultural norms of behaviour. Good manners are not only for blue-bloods, elite wannabes, or private club members. Good manners are how people show respect and regard for each other. An Australian speechwriter, Lucinda Holdforth, in a recent book, argues that good manners are a display of important attributes: 'Patience. Self-control. Awareness of others. Deferral of self-gratification. A readiness to make those small Emersonian sacrifices. A preparedness to comply with rules that are less than ideal or may, in truth, seem rather silly.' Yet, even if silly, these attributes are vital for a good leader, the very traits we should want in our decision makers. In addition, manners are a code of human interaction. Holdforth thinks manners matter 'because they represent an optimal means to preserve our own dignity and the dignity of others'. In a time of political correctness and extreme sensitivity to language, manners should be emphasised, becoming a required expectation and a demand of a civil, democratic and egalitarian society.

2. Employ good use of language

In the time of the ancient Greeks, good use of language was demanded by audiences. Oratorical skills were held in high regard. Good oratory was a requirement of public life. Professor Kenneth Cmiel has put it well: 'Eloquence implied far more than the ability to handle words deftly; it involved larger concerns about audience, personality and social order. Eloquence was civic.' The orator is supposed to be virtuous, leading by finding the best in each individual, helping each person to become nobler, better and greater. Political speech shaped the polity and elevated the citizens. Cmiel writes that 'to be an orator, then, was to be a certain kind of person. It implied an ethos, a character that pervaded one's whole self.'

That notion has survived into our time. For example, one hundred years ago, on 12 April 1910, Theodore Roosevelt spoke at the Sorbonne in Paris. His speech, now known as 'The Man in the Arena', was about the need for civility as a part of citizenship. Civility also required good public speaking skills, as well as a commitment to honesty, clarity and transparency in language. We must say what we mean in the clearest possible terms, not hiding behind the fear of disclosure or the vagueness of obscurantism.

Of course, good oratory could mask malice or dishonesty. There is still a suspicion that a good speaker is merely 'a smooth talker' or someone who talks well but really just wants to mislead the audience with good words. At one point in that speech, Roosevelt said:

> It is highly desirable that a leader of opinion in democracy should be able to state his views clearly and convincingly. But all that the oratory can do of value to the community is enable the man thus to explain himself; if it enables the orator to put false values on things, it merely makes him power for mischief . . . Indeed, it is a sign of marked political weakness in any commonwealth if the people tend to be carried away by mere oratory, if they tend to value words in and for themselves, as divorced from the deeds for which they are supposed to stand. The phrase maker, the phrasemonger, the ready talker, however great his power,

whose speech does not make for courage, sobriety and right understanding, is simply a noxious element in the body politic, and it speaks ill for the public if he has influence over them. To admire the gift of oratory without regard to the moral quality behind the gift is to do wrong to the republic.

Good words must have content and substance, and be followed by the promised appropriate actions.

3. *Leave significant others and families alone*
In the 2008 American presidential election, there was considerable attention paid to the family of Sarah Palin. I thought much of that attention harmful to the public interest, a case of voyeurism and crudity masquerading as the public's right to know. Many years ago, First Lady Hillary Clinton asked for a 'zone of privacy' for her family, especially her daughter. President and Mrs Obama have asked for a similar respect of their privacy. These requests are understandable and reasonable, only to be breached if the significant other or the children choose public life. The candidate's family should not be part of the political discussion, even if the candidates themselves invite press and public interest. Fundamentally decent people should leave families alone, unless those family members ask to be in the public eye and their comments part of the public record. This is part of civility too.

4. *Avoid snark*
Humour that makes a point has a place in politics, sometimes leading to the best in political discourse and action. But we should avoid 'snark'. This requires more than going hunting with Lewis Carroll. Snark is an attempt at humour that is mean spirited, personal, pointless and without any contribution to the public interest. In Snarkland, comedy is more important than truth, public welfare or good policy. And the comedy isn't very funny, as David Denby argues in his book about snark: 'It's the bad kind of

invective – low, teasing, snide, condescending, knowing.' Sadly, the political landscape is dotted with snarkers. Blogland harvests snark. Many politicians thrive and survive on it. *Mock the Week* is half an hour of pure snark.

It is corrosive. Snark's point is to attack, attack and attack. Its target: individuals through character assassination, not policies or programmes. Its aim: to be funny while trying to seem intelligent, to try to sound like the smartest person in the room without any actual mental effort. The result is sad, vacuous, mean-spirited, juvenile mush. It is the lazy person's way of talking: sound smart while saying nothing, avoid thinking or standing for something while acidly destroying efforts to construct common ground or generate coalitions. Denby argues that 'snark doesn't create a new image, a new idea. It's parasitic, referential, insinuating.'

Snark is ultimately self-defeating. Denby offers this insight:

> Scratch a writer of snark, and you find a media-age conformist and an aesthetic non-entity. Recognising no standard but celebrity, indifferent to originality or to quality, snark may be out of date or fading almost as soon as it's filed (or posted). The media are always moving, like time itself, and snark becomes time's fool – it has to scramble to keep up. Perhaps that's one reason why writers of snark seem so bitter: they know they are cutting the path of their own extinction.

5. *Be of good character*

For the Greeks, character was the end result of the desire to be ethical, a process of deliberation that calculated the virtuous action in each situation, and follow-through to actually perform the ethical act. This process of deliberation and action eventually became habitual, forming an ethical second nature of good character. So, rather than our first nature of animal desire or baseness, good character was a sign of prudent judgement that reflected the speaker's commitment to ethical dealings and a moral political system.

How important is character? Aristotle said that people come to a public speech to assess the 'character' of a speaker. The audience wants to determine if the speaker is worthy of its faith, trust and commitment. Questions swirl in the minds of the listeners. Does the speaker have good or bad character? Is the speaker the 'leader' that the audience should follow? Should the audience believe the speaker? Is the speaker honest? Does the speaker want to help and serve, or is the speaker after power for its own sake, or seeking to satisfy the needs of a select few? Will the speaker work for the audience or against it? The audience wants to know. Each person in the audience is thinking 'What will happen to me and to the country if I support the speaker?' Good character is essential for trust, faith, believability and credibility.

6. Respect your opponent

In his speech in Paris, Roosevelt made an impassioned plea for respect for those who enter public service. He said:

> It is not the critic who counts; not the man who points out how the strong man stumbles, or where the doer of deeds could have done them better. The credit belongs to the man who is actually in the arena, whose face is marred by dust and sweat and blood; who strives valiantly; who errs, who comes short again and again, because there is no effort without error and shortcoming, but who does actually strive to do the deeds; who knows great enthusiasms, the great devotions; who spends himself in a worthy cause; who at the best knows in the end the triumph of high achievement, and who at the worst, if he fails, at least fails while daring greatly, so that his place shall never be with those cold and timid souls who neither know victory nor defeat.

In other words, we should respect those who try to make a difference, even if we disagree with them. Current efforts to demonise the opposition miss this crucial point: it takes courage and commitment to live a life in public service. We should respect those traits, with a strong dose of fair play. Of course, some people may be unworthy of that respect, and so lose it. But respect should be the first instinct, the place to start. Demonising all politicians, or castigating all who disagree with a viewpoint, shows a loss of perspective and lack of imagination that could be remedied with a more prudential assessment and a more tolerant attitude.

There is a more powerful point. The loss of civility undermines the power to govern. When civility is lost the country suffers. Politics cannot perform its function to unite. So it matters how a campaign is won; the wrong kind of electoral victory may make governing impossible. I strongly support civility in politics. And I think it should be an expectation for informal public comments, formal speeches, debates, press releases, interviews, off-the-record briefings and other aspects of political communication. To put it more strongly, civility should be a part of every public political utterance to supporters, donors, press and constituents by every member of an office holder's staff. It should be a demand by voters in every campaign; incivility should be a voting issue.

Margaret Thatcher (Getty Images)

8. TOOLS OF THE TRADE

Constructing a speech requires certain tools. Some seem indispensable for those who seriously want to learn the craft of speechwriting.

When I first started out as a speechwriter, I worked with a team of veteran writers. They were a wild, unruly lot, worthy of a sitcom, something like a cross between *The Office* and *Yes, Minster*: irreverent, diabolical, deeply opinionated and unpredictable egomaniacs (you had to have a very strong ego to survive so long). But the collective wisdom was sound.

These writers looked over the new fellow, the fresh meat, very quickly. I noticed that the first action was to check out my bookcase, followed by comments and questions: 'Where did you get this? Why don't you have that? You can't be serious!' Finally, I asked about the scrutiny. 'We want to know what you use to construct your speeches,' they replied. In fact, that scrutiny is part of the tradition – speechwriters always want to know about the books and other sources of information used by colleagues or competitors. Upon entering an office, speechwriters go right for the bookcase, a gravitational pull. True, the resources don't tell the whole story by any means. Good writers free themselves from dependence on certain kinds of resources early on. But the books begin to tell you something about the learning process and the background a writer brings to a project.

So, for those just starting out, or for those who feel that gravitational pull, let me suggest some tools of the trade. More information is available in the bibliography at the back of the book.

1. Style manuals

Good speechwriters are first and foremost writers. Style manuals are required tools. Several should be in your library. They should be read cover to cover, encyclopedically. The best one is also one of the shortest, *The Elements of Style* by William Strunk and E. B. White. In less than eighty pages, this book gets right to it, instantly improving your style. No one should be without it. I have found some of the older style books useful, especially Sir Ernest Gowers's *The Complete Plain Words* or Henry Fowler's *Modern English Usage*. The big manual from the University of Chicago should also be at hand.

2. Dictionaries

Words have jobs. They are the tools in the toolbox. Expanding word choice in constructing a speech means there are more tools available. You may still rely on the same words over and over again, the same hammer and saw, but it helps to have tools that fit every job. A standard dictionary is a start, probably one of the many versions of the *Oxford English Dictionary*. But over time you may want to add specialised dictionaries.

3. Books of quotations

Every American speechwriter I know has *Bartlett's Familiar*

Quotations sitting on the shelf. It is a sentinel, guarding the office. This vast compendium of quotations is simply a 'must-have'. But because it is so well known, any of the quotations are well known and well used, so its value is limited because of familiarity. I've watched speechwriters in the back of the room look at each other when a 'Bartlett's' is used, almost with sympathy because the speaker was so obvious. So you will need to supplement that volume with others like *The Concise Oxford Dictionary of Quotations* or George Seldes's *The Great Thoughts*, which give you more variety and less overlap with other such books. You can even expand your library to include some oddities, such as *The Dictionary of Biographical Quotation*, edited by Richard Kenin and Justin Wintle. This is a book of quotations about famous people. Here's an example about James I by historian Hugh Trevor-Roper: 'An omniscient umpire, whom no one consulted.' There are also great anecdotes, such as this about Adam Smith (written by R. C. Fay): 'Be seated, gentlemen,' said Smith on one occasion. 'No,' replied William Pitt the Younger, 'we will stand till you are first seated; for we are all your scholars.' There is also a book of anecdotes by James Humes, speechwriter for several US Presidents: the *Speaker's Treasury of Anecdotes about the Famous*. This is a classic (my copy fell apart years ago), designed to provide introductions and conclusions.

Speechwriters are relying less and less on this type of book over time. But the hope of a chestnut makes every writer buy and read quotation books, almost as if the volumes represent an insurance policy against writer's block or lack of inspiration.

4. Collected speeches

Reading speeches helps develop a certain style of writing for what one of those veterans called 'the mind's ear'. Good speeches are oral masterpieces, not necessarily acceptable on paper for visual inspection (remember that when editing a speech). You have to hear the words, not look at them. A collection of effective speeches can be a helpful guide to this type of writing. There are many, many great collections out there. One old warhorse is a collection titled *Select British Eloquence* by Chauncey Goodrich, a revered scholar of rhetoric who taught for many years at Yale. The collection, which dates from 1852, starts with Sir John Eliot and has an extensive number of complete speeches from a wide range of British politicians, such as Lord Chatham, Edmund Burke, Charles James Fox, William Pitt and George Canning. There is another ancient collection, a real antique. It is called *Modern Eloquence*, edited by Thomas B. Reed. Published in 1903, it is an outstanding anthology of hundreds of speeches, lectures, after-dinner remarks and anecdotes. This collection is recognisable by its distinctive red cover. Often you can find a volume. The entire set of fifteen is extremely difficult to obtain. If you ever find it, buy it whatever the cost.

There are modern collections that are very good. Here is a partial list, selected because the speeches are excellent oral demonstrations of the craft: the *Chambers Book of Speeches*, Simon Heffer's *Great British Speeches*, Brian MacArthur's *The Penguin Book of Historic Speeches* and William Safire's *Lend Me Your Ears*. For me, the best one of all is MacArthur's *The Penguin Book of Twentieth-Century Speeches*. I carry this book with me everywhere, on every assignment, from Middle America to central Africa. There are also some useful collections of speeches by particular speakers, such as Winston Churchill's *Blood, Toil, Tears and Sweat*, edited by David Cannadine (a similar collection titled *Never Give In!* is now available from Churchill's grandson); Mario Cuomo's *More Than Words*; William F. Buckley, Jr's *Let Us Talk of Many Things*; John Kennedy's *Let Every Nation Know*, edited by Robert Dallek and Terry Golway; Ronald Reagan's *Speaking My Mind*; and Margaret Thatcher's *The Collected Speeches*, edited by Robin Harris.

The rapid advent of Barack Obama has already produced a number of books with his speeches. I recommend two of them: Henry Russell's *The Politics of Hope* and Penguin's *Barack Obama: The Inaugural Address*.

There is also a collection of pre-Prime Minister speeches by Gordon Brown, *Moving Britain Forward*.

For Australian readers, I recommend a collection edited by Rod Kemp and Marion Stanton, *Speaking for Australia*.

5. Good literature

One of those veteran speechwriters took me aside and said: 'If you want to be a good writer, read good writers. Inhale them. Study them. Try to figure out what they do.' So I started carefully reading some very good wordsmiths: W. Somerset Maugham, Henry James, Lawrence Durrell, F. Scott Fitzgerald and, especially, Ernest Hemingway (look at the sentence structure, which reads well out loud). Maybe the best is P. G. Wodehouse (just read some of *Right Ho, Jeeves* out loud).

6. History of ideas

I don't know a good speechwriter who isn't a student of history and philosophy. History gives background, context and examples. Philosophy provides a life of the mind, the ideas that shaped our culture and time. You can also find some outstanding writers in these fields, such as David Hume, Bertrand Russell, Gilbert Ryle, A. J. Ayer, Antony Flew, Peter Strawson and J. L. Austin.

7. Rhetorical handbooks

The ancient Greek and Roman rhetoricians have much to teach us. In their time, public speeches were like sporting events, attracting thousands of listeners and garnering much analysis and discussion. The rhetorical handbooks compiled a number of techniques for public speaking. The speeches by Isocrates, Demosthenes or Cicero demonstrate how to use them. If you want to find out more, you could turn to any of the books by the legendary George A. Kennedy, such as *The Art of Persuasion in Greece* or *A New History of Classical Rhetoric*. A more recent book that might be extremely helpful is Joy Connolly's *The State of Speech*, which discusses rhetoric and political thought in ancient Rome.

Frankly, one could learn everything necessary about public speaking from the Greek and Roman orators. You don't have to be a classical scholar or intimidated by the age of these speakers. They are contemporaries for those interested in good public address. Give old Demosthenes a try sometime. And don't forget Aristotle's masterpiece, *The Rhetoric*. Closer to our own time period, I have found Kenneth Cmiel's *Democratic Eloquence* to be instructive on the relationship between public speaking and character, as well as the change in speaking patterns in America. I also recommend anything by Kathleen Hall Jamieson, the scholar's scholar of political communication. Try her *Eloquence in an Electronic Age* or *Deeds Done in Words* (this last one with Karlyn Kohrs Campbell). These are masterful, enviable works that will stand alone for decades to come.

8. The Archers

I know, this is the last bit of advice you'd expect to find in a book like this. But there is something important in that advice. An old speechwriter who worked in radio once told me that writing for listening was the key to that medium. The words had to work with the imagination to paint pictures in the mind, to help people 'see through words'. He told me to buy some old radio programmes and listen to how the words work. So I did. I bought some by Jack Benny. What a revelation! These were not books on tape, with famous readers reading prose for the eye. These were programmes constructed for the ear, presented for the mind's ear. I noticed my speechwriting improved dramatically with this type of resource. For example, pick up a copy of the BBC's recent publication *From Our Own Correspondent*, edited by Tony Grant. Then, in private, read these scripts out loud. You begin to see the difference. Or listen to radio programmes like *The Archers*.

9. Public speaking books

Some books offer good discussion of delivery and putting everything together. Peggy Noonan's *On Speaking Well* is my choice as the best. However, James Humes's *Speak like Churchill, Stand like Lincoln* is also very good and widely available. I am extremely impressed with a straightforward approach by Jeanette and Roy Henderson, *There's No Such Thing as Public Speaking*, which argues for a conversational style. For simple motivational style, there is Nick Morgan's *Give Your Speech, Change the World*. This is a good book for a business audience.

I was fortunate to start my career with those experienced speechwriters. They were full of wisdom (which is one way to put it). They often spoke of the dynamics of speechwriting with reverence, because they understood that a successful speech involved more than just standing up and reading words. An effective speech could change attitudes and motivate action. A speech was almost sacred. It could reach into the soul and change each person in the audience, providing a memorable moment that did alter the course of events. Because a great speech could be so powerful, the process itself deserved respect and consideration. They demanded that I learn my craft and practise it with professionalism. Acquiring and understanding the tools of the trade was part of the learning process, an apprenticeship that was conducted under the scrutiny of the White House, the national and international press and Washington insiders. But no audience was tougher than my teachers, those boisterous and brutal speechwriters, real craftsmen of an illustrious and indispensable trade, usually conducted in the background with anxious humility. Every day, with every speech, I try to remember their advice.

Nelson Mandela (AFP/Getty Images)

9. SUCCESSFUL SPEECHES

This chapter offers case studies in effective speaking and speechwriting. In my mind, it was about how to put everything together. I know that I've learned so much from the masters of speaking and speechwriting. One way I've done this is to study techniques. I've also read some speeches over and over again. In fact, one speech by Mario Cuomo, 'A Tale of Two Cities', given at the 1984 Democratic national convention, I've read over a thousand times. I read for the 'mind's ear', trying to hear the words orally, looking at words as spoken prose, with the full dimension of ideas, words, voice, inflections, gestures, feedback and adjustments. So I have looked to see and hear what worked for others, with special attention given to those I've admired.

I should add that you can learn a lot from other mediums, especially songwriting and singing. Great songwriters use many of the same techniques as a speechwriter in crafting a song, including simplicity, spacing, silence, emphasis and subtle rhythmic structure. Singers of other people's songs must learn about the ideas, intention and contours of the lyrics and music. They must find a way to make the song their own. Singers often have to study the work of someone else, and then find a way to interpret the words to make them sound authentically their own. There has to be an understanding of a song, then a melding of the song into one's own style and voice. Just as with speechwriting, singers have to discover the meaning of words, the place for pauses, the emphasis for phrases, the cadence of the language and the overall message of the song. So I have found that you can learn much from gifted, intelligent songwriters. For me personally, Pete Townshend, Björn Ulvaeus and Benny Andersson, and Justin Hayward stand out. Yes, they write for themselves, but they offer a lot to learn about word choice, imagery, cadence, pausing and emphasis. These musicians write great songs, which is why they have an enormous body of work covered by other singers. There are other songwriters, like Burt Bacharach and Hal David, Tim Rice and Mike Batt, who write for interpretive singers. Their work is very much like speechwriting because someone else will always be singing their songs. They won't perform themselves. So, the poetry, simplicity and soulfulness of the way they write can be an education for writers in other mediums.

So when I listen to their work, I look for an edge or a new use of language for speechwriting. The same is true of singers who cover songs, like Linda Ronstadt, Bing Crosby, Tony Bennett, Ella Fitzgerald and the great maestro of interpretation, Frank Sinatra. Sinatra worked very hard to make each song uniquely his own. If only speakers worked that hard with that much intelligence, they would get the same kind of lasting results as 'Ol' Blue Eyes'. Think about what he did with 'Summer Wind'. The lyrics are simple: 'The summer wind came blowing in, from across the sea.' He finds the idea and the rhythm. He sings the song with understated emotion, with no emotion, almost, letting the song tell the story, which he makes into his story. There is clarity, thoughtfulness, understanding, longing and love. Brilliant. Effective. Timeless.

Yes, much to learn. Listening to certain music can help uncover the skills necessary for good speechwriting, good delivery and a memorable end product.

But there is plenty to learn from speeches themselves. Here are some masters of the craft and some masterpieces.

First we will start with three great speakers: Ronald Reagan, Nelson Mandela and Tony Blair.

Ronald Reagan

The Reagan administration ended in 1989. And in the last two decades his reputation has been enhanced, especially through his books and collected writings, such as his hand-written radio scripts, speeches and diary, which document his thinking, both before and during his presidency. More and more, the new impression among historians is that Ronald Reagan was a thoughtful, formidable and well-read leader who spoke to Middle America, and in a sense re-created it. We now have a much clearer idea of how he earned the respect and admiration of Margaret Thatcher, Mikhail Gorbachev and other world leaders.

But this Reagan, as a man of ideas and skills, is a revisionist view for many people, although accurate in my opinion and experience. Then, in the 1980s, and now, Reagan was called 'The Great Communicator'. But at the time, for many, this translated into the simple thought that 'Reagan was eloquent', a smooth-talking Hollywood guy with a suit and a shine, reading his lines like an actor, but away from the podium a bumbler without the mindful watch of his handlers. For some, he was just a caricature of hair and wrinkles, a nice old guy, the 'Teflon' president. In the words of one Washington insider, Clark Clifford, Reagan was 'an amiable dunce'.

But with that comment, Clifford violated the cardinal rule of politics: never under-estimate anyone. It was a ridiculous mistake to make with Reagan, and Clifford vastly under-estimated him, a former two-term governor of California, a politician who possessed formidable skills, singular gifts and an articulate vision. Reagan's presidential record disproved Clifford's faulty assessment. Under his guidance, the United States experienced a restoration of faith, values and confidence after the failed presidency of Jimmy Carter. Domestically, Reagan saved the economy from its 'malaise' and engineered staggering economic growth. Reagan's influence on world events was rapid and stunning, culminating with the fall of communism immediately after he left office. For most Americans, and millions worldwide, he was a trusted and familiar leader who communicated directly to them, someone who was larger than life, yet at the same time the guy you talked to across the fence. And, yes, he was a great communicator. Reagan respected the possibilities, power and potential persuasiveness of political speech. He was great for sound, solid reasons. He has much to teach anyone who wants to improve as a political leader.

1. Vision
One of the best books on Reagan was written by his chief political strategist, Dick Wirthlin (*The Greatest Communicator*). A vision is an 'ability to see'. Reagan had an ability to see a possible future and explain it to an audience. His vision of America was as 'the shining city on the hill', a beacon of freedom and opportunity, ready to lead the world towards peace and prosperity. This vision was adaptable to historical and modern problems, and helped highlight the heavy hand of governmental regulation, the burden of high taxation and the threat of communist dictatorship. Here's an example. At the end of the Berlin speech in 1987 he said: 'This wall will fall. For it cannot withstand faith; it cannot withstand truth. The wall cannot withstand freedom.' He was right, but in a self-fulfilling way because his vision was corrosive to anyone or anything that restricted political freedom.

Wirthlin shows that Reagan held his vision for decades before becoming president. It was a core part of the man and the leader. George H. W. Bush famously derided the 'vision thing'. But it is central, vital to both political success and successful governance, functioning as a reason for running for office and a blueprint for how to use power once office is obtained. In his last speech as President, Reagan recalled the vision. He said:

> In my mind it was a tall proud city built on rocks stronger than oceans, windswept, God blessed and teeming with people of all kinds living in harmony and peace, a city with free ports that hummed with commerce and creativity, and if there had to be city walls, the walls had doors and the doors were open to anyone with the will and the heart to get here. That's how I saw it, and see it still.

Then, when Reagan left the White House, he gave his staff a picture of himself and Nancy with the language about the 'city on the hill' printed underneath. It summed up his presidency.

2. Stories

Audiences love stories and Reagan was a classic storyteller. He understood that stories function as a way to humanise the abstract. They are also a form of proof. As Wirthlin notes, Reagan would present a rational case for a policy, and then use emotional stories to inspire and motivate. So he used stories to allow the audience to link the emotional with the rational. In other words, stories drew the human heart towards the rational, showing how a policy or a proposal would work, or, in other words, to repel the mind from bad ideas. They also allowed enough vagueness so that each audience member could read their own meaning into them. In his Christmas speech in 1982, he talked about a letter from a sailor on the aircraft carrier *Midway*. A group of Vietnamese were rescued from a floundering boat. For five days they had been in that boat, attempting to escape the repression of their own country. When they sighted the aircraft carrier, they waved and shouted: 'Hello, America sailor! Hello, freedom man!' Reagan used that story to explain why people risk their lives for freedom. And how a sailor is 'America' and a 'freedom man'. It really was a Christmas story.

3. Substance

There are some who think the Reagan speeches were lightweight. They were anything but. In fact, there is more substance and content in Reagan's speeches than those by any American President afterwards, even Bill Clinton or Barack Obama. Look and compare. Reagan talked about economic theory with commanding detail and understanding. He spoke of the threat of communism by quoting Marx and Lenin, and then explaining their views in some depth. He talked about government spending with statistics and facts that were positively wonkish. Witness his 1981 'Address to the Nation on the Economy'. It reads like an economic treatise. However, the insight extended to the human as well as the scholarly. Even in that speech, he also spoke of people with sympathy and warmth. As a student of history, he had an ability to place contemporary problems in context and perspective. A reading of his speeches today reveals a much more elevated and detailed presentation than the current style displays, which seems thin and wispy in comparison. Here is an example from that speech:

> We're victims of language. The very word 'inflation' leads us to think of it as just high prices . . . Inflation is not just high prices; it's a reduction in the value of our money. When the money supply is increased but the goods and services available for buying are not, we have too much money chasing too few goods . . . Now, one way out would be to raise taxes so that government need not borrow or print money. But all these years of government growth, we've reached, indeed surpassed, the limit of our people's tolerance or ability to bear an increase in the tax burden.

In virtually every speech you see a reliance on facts and explanation, a discussion of history and patterns of behaviour, and detail and depth in analysis. The substantial character of Reagan's speeches was strangely unnoticed by the press two decades ago and remains a surprise for many readers today.

4. Soundbites

Every speechwriter and speaker should read Peggy Noonan's book *What I Saw at the Revolution*. There is a lot of insight about Reagan and about the construction of political messages. For example, she argues that Reagan's speeches had memorable phrases because they were an organic part of the speech, authentic expressions of the messages. They actually condense the message of the particular speech. Good soundbites are not grafted on. Noonan wrote: 'They are part of the tapestry, they aren't a little flower somebody screwed on.' And she adds that there has to be substance behind the soundbite, real 'beef'. The Reagan speeches had that: clear and condensed messages with substantial policy discussions. So the Reagan soundbite becomes a way to understand and remember the message. Think about the lasting power of phrases like 'government is not the solution to our problem; government is the problem', 'a new movement is stirring', or 'Mr Gorbachev, tear down this wall'. A few years ago, I heard President Gorbachev speak in Washington. When asked what action by Reagan did the most damage to the former Soviet Union, he immediately mentioned the devastating and concussive impact of one phrase, the 'evil empire'. The condensed message helped destroy the legitimacy of the Soviet government itself.

5. Direction

Reagan was personally involved in his speeches. Every one of his former speechwriters has commented on this involvement. The general direction of his message could be understood from his time as governor, the thousands of speeches he gave before his presidency, and the hundreds of radio programmes he wrote and delivered in the 1970s. A speechwriter could start with those resources, which was a huge advantage unavailable to most speechwriters for other politicians. But Reagan was very careful with the direction he gave in crafting a message. He was also a very good editor. As Noonan and Peter Robinson have written (*How Ronald Reagan Changed My Life*), Reagan as editor made the language more lively, condensed the message and smoothed out the sentences for greater understanding.

6. *Oratory*

Reagan was a great speaker. He understood the power of words. He also knew how to say those words for maximum effect. I call it having 'the intelligence behind the words', knowing why a particular word was chosen and knowing what to do with it. The late French President François Mitterrand once said that Reagan was someone 'in communion with the American people'. That communion was established through a speaking style that was conversational, clear, bold and intelligent. It was the result of hard work made to look easy as Reagan shifted into different rates of delivery, with emphasis on key words, an uncanny ability to make prose sound alive and vital, and knowing the power of the pause. . . how a pregnant pause can have a lasting impact in highlighting words and ideas. Reagan once said to Wirthlin that for every polling number 'I saw a face'. And in every audience he saw individual faces and had a conversation with those people. In my view, that led him to emphasise inclusive language, American mythology and symbolism, simple words, short sentences and commonsense reasoning. He had the ability to inspire because he saw the good in people, understood their aspirations and dreams, and wanted to empower them to succeed. He offered encouragement, opportunity and hope. He stressed individual freedom and responsibility.

He himself downplayed his rhetorical gifts. I think that is what made him so good. He kept working at his speaking style, always trying to improve. In my view, he was never satisfied. And that is how you become better, through practice, analysis, consultation, experimentation and thoughtfulness about word choice. He was good because he wanted to be good, and knew from his days in acting that there are countless ways to say something. He wanted to find the most effective ways to communicate. That was always imperative. An effective, successful leader has to think like that.

7. *Sense of self*

Reagan's advisor and close friend, Michael Deaver, wrote in his book, *A Different Drummer*: 'The guy knows who he is.' Reagan knew what he stood for. He was comfortable with his vision. Reagan was not driven by polls or politics, unless they could get him to the goal: freedom. He was on a mission that was good for America and the world. Robinson had a good insight when he wrote about Reagan's words: they changed those who heard them but they also influenced Reagan himself. He was the product of his vision as well as the architect. You can see this in a speech to members of Parliament at the Palace of Westminster in 1982. Reagan recalled another great leader, Winston Churchill, when he said: 'Let us ask ourselves: "What kind of people do we think we are?" And let us answer: "Free people, worthy of freedom and determined not only to remain so but to help others gain their freedom as well."' Reagan not only saw the 'shining city on the hill'. He wanted it to be part of a 'second American revolution'. He wanted all of us to live there, to be citizens who made a dream our reality.

Nelson Mandela

Nelson Mandela has great moral weight. He is one of a handful of people who has given greater moral clarity to his time. He embodied the fight for freedom in South Africa. But he also became freedom's champion worldwide. His speeches reflect a great spirit of forgiveness, cooperation and humanity. And he unites people to join him on his 'long walk to freedom'.

He has also given two of the most important speeches of the last twenty-five years. One is the speech he gave on his release from prison on 11 February 1990. The other is his inauguration remarks on 10 May 1994. Both are models for inclusive language and peaceful change. There is a lot to discover in his speeches. After all, his words helped prevent civil war and the deaths of millions of people. In his hands, language is a tool of harmony, tolerance and peace. He is a revolutionary for peace, inclusion and fulfilment of constitutional promises. One can hear echoes of Martin Luther King, Jr, Mahatma Gandhi, Steve Biko and Desmond Tutu. His sounds may also carry harmonies of John Lennon, Bono and Peter Gabriel.

1. *Pride in country*

Mandela consistently urges the citizens of South Africa to see themselves as one with the country. He himself aligns his own accomplishments with the history and symbolism of South Africa. In a Freedom Day speech in 1995 he said: 'Wherever South Africans are across the globe, our hearts beat as one as we renew our common loyalty to our country and our commitment to its future.' This is a positive nationalism that transmits hope and optimism, empowering people and rejecting a weighty victimology that often accompanied post-colonial rhetoric.

2. *Inclusion*

In his great inaugural speech Mandela uses the pronoun 'I' just once, and not in an important sentence. However, the pronoun 'we' is used repeatedly. He unites with the listening audience, becoming one with them. Here are some examples: 'We are moved by a sense of joy and exhilaration when the grass turns green and the flowers bloom', 'We have, at last, achieved our political emancipation' and 'We must therefore act as a united people, for national reconciliation, for nation-building, for the birth of a new world'.

3. *Tolerance and forgiveness*

'The time for the healing of the wounds has come,' Mandela said in that inauguration speech. It is a common, and vital, theme. He does not dwell on the past, although he does not forget it either. He does not point fingers or blame individuals, although he does blame apartheid as a system. He uses his speeches and his stature to heal division and to move the country forward. You see this in speeches about education, housing, health care, social services and economic progress. Unity is the key for positive change. His message does not include partisan politics or racial gamesmanship.

4. *Eye on history*
Mandela knows that history will judge every person and every country. In a speech before the parliament in 1999, he told the members:

> I hope that decades from now, when history is written, the role of that generation [of those who struggled for peace] will be appreciated, and that I will not be found wanting against the measure of their fortitude and vision . . . To the extent that I have been able to achieve anything, I know that this is because I am the product of the people of South Africa.

5. *Vision: democracy*
As Like Reagan's 'shining city on the hill', Mandela sees his South Africa as offering a regional example of the greatness of democracy in action. South Africa stands as a beacon of freedom for countries like Zimbabwe, the Democratic Republic of the Congo and others which find themselves enslaved by dominant parties, tribal divisions, corruption, poverty or power-grabbing political personalities. In his speech to the parliament, he said: 'As for me personally, I belong to the generation of leaders for whom the achievement of democracy was the defining challenge.' Not only has he embodied democracy, even when he was in prison (especially when he was in prison), but his vision of South Africa as a regional leader in the fight for democracy is notable and defining in his speeches.

6. *Looking to the future*
This is also a consistent vision. It is manifest in his hundreds of speeches about children. He is involved in several efforts for children in South Africa and around the world. He has a special calling for children. Mandela sees his work as an opportunity to

make Africa safe for children, who have suffered in every possible way on the continent. If freedom and democracy work, then Africa must use the equity, responsibility and empowerment of democracy to safeguard children. In his Nobel Peace Prize speech in 1993 he said: 'The children must, at last, play in the open veld, no longer tortured by the pangs of hunger or ravaged by disease or threatened with the scourge of ignorance, molestation and abuse and no longer required to engage in deeds whose gravity exceeds the demands of their tender years.'

Mandela has a vision of moving to the future. He calls it the 'long walk to freedom'. He invites each of us to join him on that walk.

Tony Blair

I admire Tony Blair's approach to oratory. He has what I call 'the intelligence behind the words'. That means that he knows why every word is in the speech, or at least he knows what he wants to do with each word. Even if he doesn't, he gives that impression. He must work hard on his speeches. If he undertakes the level of preparation I think he does, then he may be one of the hardest-working and most effective speakers in the world. Love him or loathe him, he has a great talent for oratory.

He certainly is one of the best speakers in the world. This makes him very effective on most occasions. But it has also hurt him. During his speech before the US Congress you could see that some of the members of Congress were listening to be entertained, not persuaded. They found his use of words enjoyable. But many had turned off their rational faculties. That happens when you've been warned the speaker is a 'smooth talker'. You prepare yourself not to be persuaded. 'Shields up, Captain Kirk! Red alert. Someone is talking at us!' That must be frustrating, to look out, see all those grinning faces and know that you are a side-show and not an opinion leader. But once you have the talent, it can be employed to advantage, as witnessed during the 2010 British elections, where there was a fear of Blair's abilities influencing enough votes to ensure a Labour victory. Like Bill Clinton, Blair's rhetorical skills are still formidable, still dangerous, because he knows what he is doing, even if the audience isn't open minded or isn't prepared to listen.

Blair has crafted an approach to public speaking that is very inventive and effective for those who still tune in. Given his long history in the public eye, and the reactions to the war in Iraq, perhaps not many people listen any more. But if they do, then Blair is an education.

I still find him fascinating. Here are some reasons why.

1. Good storytelling

This is an aspect of his style that now receives derision. But he is exceptionally good at telling stories within speeches, making the speech into a conversation about people we know. In a speech after 9/11, he spoke of meeting British families in New York City, attending church services with them and talking over tea and biscuits. In his speech before Congress, virtually out of the blue and away from his text, he spoke of a conversation between one of the Pankhurst sisters and Keir Hardie, and later spoke of a 'guy (out in Nevada or Idaho) getting on with his life'. In his speeches he likes to talk about conversations with constituents, with people touched by hardship or difficulties, with experts, with police or security officials, with immigrants and with people in all sorts of circumstances. He humanises his speeches with examples that provide powerful proof for his messages.

2. Vision

I've mentioned this in earlier chapters. In his 1997 speech at Brighton, he spoke of his vision for the United Kingdom and for Europe. He wrapped that vision up in British history and British values:

> My vision for post-Empire Britain is clear. It is to make this country pivotal, a leader in the world. With the US our

friend and ally. Within the Commonwealth. In the United Nations. In NATO. To use the superb reputation of our armed forces, not just for defence, but as an instrument of influence in a world of collective security and cooperation. And for Britain to lead in Europe again . . . For we have a vision of Europe. We want a people's Europe: free trade, industrial strength, high levels of employment and social justice, a democratic Europe.

Blair helps you imagine his vision. It is obtainable. It can be achieved. It is not simply idealistic. A concrete, yet principled, vision is the best kind to offer an audience. He does that.

3. Word economy
Part of having the intelligence behind the words is that Blair knows the power of individual words. He knows which words are most persuasive, and which ones have a forceful impact. So he is master of one-word sentences, or one-phrase sentences. In his 1994 'Modern Constitution' speech at Blackpool he started with this set: 'A belief in society. Working together. Solidarity. Cooperation. Partnership. These are our words. This is my socialism.' At the end, he said: 'Our Party: New Labour. Our mission: New Britain. New Labour. New Britain.' In his speech at Brighton in 1995, he spoke of 'decent people. Good people. Patriotic people. When I hear people urging us to fight for "our people", I want to say: "These are our people. They are the majority."' In his 1997 speech at Brighton he said: 'Creative. Compassionate. Outward-looking. Old British values, but a new British confidence.'

The words or phrases tell a deep story. There are profound and powerful mentions tied to those words. There are deeply-held values. The use of word economy allows Blair to make a more detailed and extensive case in less time than other speakers.

4. Vocal variety
Because he knows what to do with each word, Blair has a complex

use of various levels of volume and especially, rates of speed. Most speakers change rate and volume sentence to sentence. Blair does it word to word or phrase to phrase; he employs variety and strategic changes within sentences. If you were to chart his changes in rate, there would be remarkable variation within a speech, but, especially noticeably, within sentences. This keeps the sentences in the speech interesting and fresh, if done well. Most speakers risk losing an audience over time. Blair keeps their interest by working very hard to make the speech listenable.

5. Excellent emphasis

He knows what words to emphasise. For Blair, emphasis is not static. His changes in tone, rate and volume are one key to his use of important words. But he does more than that. He sometimes leans on a word, or makes it stand out with a gesture, or even looks out at the audience to telegraph an upcoming word. He will stop the left/right/left flow of his eye contact to look directly down at his loose-leaf manuscript to draw attention to a word or phrase. He will put his finger on the word on the manuscript. And he mixes all of this up. I'm sure some of it is just the passion and excitement of delivering a major speech, so some of it happens randomly. But he is too effective at this for mere luck or chance. He knows why the words are there. So he knows the important words the audience must hear. He emphasises those words in a variety of ways.

6. Natural, conversational style

All of this is happening with a voice that sounds conversational. Blair has elevated rhetoric that sounds natural. You don't think 'Oh, he has a written speech and he's reading it'. Rather, Blair makes the speech sound like a conversation, often complete with both sides of that conversation. He will give his opponent's view and then counter it with his own. Some of his speeches are really Platonic dialogues. In this self-initiated exchange of ideas, Blair is Socrates. His opponents are the well-meaning but mistaken figures out of *Euthyphro* or *Meno*. But the dialogue is a conversation, however well scripted. Both sides are usually fairly stated, which gives Blair's answers greater credibility. He also is able to frame his opponent's views in a way that allows him to occupy strong rhetorical ground without seeming to cheat or overtly disrespect his opponent. There is disagreement. But there is also civil acknowledgement of differing viewpoints, even if wrong.

Here is an example from his speech before the US Congress:

> And then reflect on this.
>
> How hollow would the charges of American imperialism be when these failed countries are and are seen to be transformed from states of terror to nations of prosperity; from governments of dictatorship to examples of democracy; from sources of instability to beacons of calm?
>
> And how risible would be the claims that these were wars on Muslims, if the world could see these Muslim nations still Muslim, but Muslims with some hope for the future, not shackled by brutal regimes whose principal victims were the very Muslims they pretended to protect?

Here is another example from his statement on the Hutton inquiry in 2004:

> Let me make it plain: it is absolutely right that people can question whether the intelligence received was right; and why we have not yet found WMD. There is an entirely legitimate argument about the wisdom of this conflict. I happen to believe now as I did in March that removing Saddam has made the world a safer and better place. But others are entirely entitled to disagree.

This Socratic dialogue method of speaking allows the community to remain united because it involves acceptance of disagreement without demonisation. It is also an example of what Aristotle called 'prudential thinking', because it tries to demonstrate a willingness to take the views and needs of all parties into account, working for the best outcome for all.

7. Excellent content

Blair's written words set up the effective delivery. His speeches have absorbing content, statements of value and principle, and policies based on principle. They give him a lot to work with. But they do more than that. His speeches grab considerable common ground. So Blair sounds reasonable, acting for the best interests of the country. Here is an example. In his 2001 Brighton speech, he talked about the need for 'economic competence' (good phrase). He said that British families relied on sound economic management. He mentioned the millions of families facing hardship because of the economic incompetence of his predecessors. Then he said: 'Economic competence is the pre-condition of social justice.' Fantastic line. Everyone wants some form of social justice. But who could defend economic incompetence?

Blair also uses inclusive language. In his 1997 speech, he said: 'We cannot buy our way to a safe society. We must work for it together.' That is a typical line from the speech. Explain a problem and then show how joint action is needed to solve it. Through this technique he is reaching out to the audience, building considerable common ground, finding a way to bring more people together. He justifies this move by explaining that inclusion is socialism, or, as he sometimes put it, 'social-ism'.

So Blair has persuasive, winning language that makes him sound good. The writing sets up the delivery.

Now we will turn to some case studies of great speechwriters. I have chosen three giants. Shakespeare may be the best. Winston Churchill needs no explanation: his words held a nation together. Ted Sorensen was the major speechwriter for John F. Kennedy. In my view, Sorensen was the best speechwriter of the twentieth century.

William Shakespeare

Good speakers are always looking to improve both the message and the performance. Here is a good source for practical tips: read Shakespeare. He was a master craftsman of speeches and understood the dynamics of public speaking.

In fact, Shakespeare would be well recognised from one speech alone: Marcus Antonius's funeral oration in *Julius Caesar*. The St Crispian's Day speech in *Henry V* is also a model. They are both works of awesome craft, with simple words, memorable phrases and lasting impact.

For example, consider the funeral speech by Marcus Antonius. Here is a reminder of the setting. Caesar has been assassinated. Constrained by a promise to Brutus that he will not speak against the conspirators, Antonius does something very cunning; his choice of words tells two tales, makes two diverse, contradictory points. On the surface, he 'praises' Brutus, speaking of Caesar's ambitions and his own friendship to Caesar. Underneath, he turns the attitude of the crowd from support for the conspiracy to anger against the murderers, making Caesar their hero and eventually leading them to decide Brutus and the others are traitors to Rome. It is shocking to see how the crowd slowly turns against the conspirators, with hatred and rage overwhelming all other emotions. Approved words are floating on the surface while underneath those same words tell the audience a more brutal, dismal tale of deceit, fear and cowardice by the murderous traitors. It has never, ever been equalled for its dark effectiveness.

I am not a Shakespeare scholar – far from it. But for a speechwriter, there is a lot to learn from Shakespeare. His speeches demonstrate traits that modern speechwriters strive to match.

1. He crafts a good beginning

The very start of the funeral oration is now a template for any political speech: 'Friends, Romans, countrymen, lend me your ears.' It is also a contrast with the earlier speech by Brutus: 'Romans,

countrymen and lovers [friends].' Antonius reorders the sequence
to encourage his commonality with the people, which he sees as
more important than emphasising country first. You can see why.
Try it yourself. Stand before a crowd and see the difference if you
begin with 'Friends' or 'Britons'. He has it right.

2. He uses the right words

Always strive for the right word, the best word for the message's
impact on the audience. Antonius speaks so the crowd will rise
up against the conspirators *precisely because he does indeed fulfil
his promise to Brutus*, finding words that transparently mean the
opposite of what he says, with acidic, corrosive effect, in much the
same way that Pope John Paul II's homilies in communist Poland
spoke of faith and God while making the audience think of freedom
and Poland. For example, Antonius's deadly, double-edged use
of the word 'honourable', mentioned again and again to describe
Brutus and the rest, does the job, showing they are anything but
that. When he mentions Caesar's 'ambitions', Antonius shows that
Caesar was a man of the people, not the power-hungry tyrant of
Brutus's earlier remarks. And Antonius does this long before he
reads the will that confirms Caesar's love and legacy for the Roman
citizens. As it unfolds, the speech is dazzling in its double meaning
and depth, and moving in its loyalty and tragedy. It is masterful in
its intent, construction, wording and execution. The speech is dark
and destructive, with lashing undercurrents of logic and feeling.
It runs counter to the view that a speech must utilise hope and
inspiration. Rather, it unites the audience in passionate rage.

3. He uses memorable phrases

Shakespeare seems to make it all seem so simple, tossing off
phrases that stick, condense the message and stay with you. And
these great phrases come fast and furious, just as Rachmaninov
suggests new melodies second by second, or Einstein new ideas
about a Newtonian world. Antonius has some unforgettable lines,
such as 'I come to bury Caesar, not to praise him'. He reminds the

crowd that 'the evil that men do, lives after them'. Looking at his dead friend, he says: 'My heart is in the coffin.' These are all phrases that outlive the circumstances of the speech.

4. He uses simple wording
Look again at the phrases in *Julius Caesar*. The words are simple. They are words that communicate well to the audience, showing the value and great strength of simplicity. The words may be used in new and stunning ways. But the words themselves are often one or two syllables, simple words that work well to share meaning.

There is another speech that illustrates the value of simplicity, found in *Henry V*. The St Crispian's Day speech is a brilliant example of the strength of simplicity: 'God's will! I pray thee, wish not one man more.' Look at the number of one-syllable words. Shakespeare understood that simple language is strong and best for communication, even of complex ideas.

5. He develops an inspiring message
Perhaps no speech is more inspiring than that on St Crispian's Day. This is a speech of positive unification. Outnumbered, against impossible odds, the King urges those unwilling to fight to leave, because 'we would not die in that man's company that fears his fellowship to die with us'. Henry would rather think about the small numbers of his followers: 'We few, we happy few, we band of brothers.' Great words. Eternal phrases. This speech has been copied, reworked and plagiarised perhaps more than any other speech. It is a strong speech of leadership, a model for creating strong unity and motivated results.

6. He unites with the audience
Henry's speech does this. There is none better. But Marcus Antonius's speech ends with a self-contracting, yet effective, unification of a different kind:

I come not friends, to steal away your hearts, I am no orator as Brutus is; but you all know me as a plain blunt man, that love my friend, and that they know full well, that gave me public leave to speak of him. For I have neither wit, nor words, nor worth, action or utterance, nor the power of speech, to stir men's blood. I only speak right on. I tell you that which you yourselves do know.

Antonius is one of them: 'plain' and 'blunt'. And he *has* stirred their blood. He used *exactly* the right words. He knows this only too well. Famously, after the crowd leaves to hunt for Brutus and the others, he says: 'Now let it work. Mischief thou art afoot, take thou what course thou wilt.'

7. He shows the process of attitude change

Time and again, Shakespeare dramatises a public speech, complete with audience, for our observation and study. We see the speaker deliver the message and we hear the stage audience's reactions. And we even react to the reaction of the stage audience. The speech has two audiences: the one we see on stage and the one in the stalls. We even hear the stage audience think out loud, talk among themselves and reveal their thoughts, during the progress of the speech in *Julius Caesar*. We listen to the slow, incremental and effective way Antonius brings about attitude change and compels the audience to action against the conspirators. The audience analysis and feedback aspects of this speech are extremely useful in showing how an audience comes to a point of collective agreement and unites behind a message.

Shakespeare understood that good speakers are very skilled at channelling the thinking of an audience. Often the audience is brought to a conclusion through the forceful logic and narrowing parameters of thinking in the speech. A speech should set parameters of thinking and then direct the audience, step by step, to a pre-determined conclusion. Antonius's speech shows how this happens.

8. *He uses subtle cadence*

The lines of these speeches are poetry too. Good speeches have cadence, a rhythm and a beat. I always look for the beat as reflected by both the words and the silence/spacing between the words.

There is all this and more in Shakespeare. So if you want to learn about good speeches, Shakespeare has much to say and show. And we should appreciate the imagination and craft necessary to make these speeches seem so real. Shakespeare's speeches are often so familiar and famous we forget they are creations of his mind, even if based on historical fact and intergenerational memory.

Shakespeare's speeches are part of the speechwriter's canon. These speeches are included because they are among the best ever written, masterpieces of speechwriting.

Winston Churchill

Time and again, Winston Churchill is viewed as a paradigm of public speaking. His recorded voice is still in demand. His collected speeches still sell. The content of his speeches held a nation together during extreme peril and mobilised it for years of sacrifice and danger. The British found courage and defiance in his phrases. His words helped define his time. The stirring language continues to inspire later generations. When anyone talks about the profound power of a speech, Churchill is probably mentioned more than any other speaker. Certainly, several of his speeches would be contenders among the greatest ever delivered.

The collection of Churchill speeches I favour is titled *Blood, Toil, Tears and Sweat*, edited by David Cannadine. One reason is the introduction, which takes the reader on a tour of greatness, both in writing and imagery. For Churchill was not a great speaker in the sense of having a melodious, engaging, supple voice, with great dexterity in emphasis, rate and volume. Indeed, his vocal delivery was actually poor, deprived of the conversational quality of a Franklin Roosevelt or Ronald Reagan, or a rapier-like display

of meaningful variety and pregnant pauses, like Tony Blair or
William Hague. Churchill's maiden speech, in 1901, was praised
for its accomplished argument and delivery. But one newspaper
mentioned his 'unfortunate lisp', and his delivery would remain
grainy, halting and often flat. Historian John Keegan called
Churchill's voice 'grating'. Cannadine mentions a stammer in
addition to the lisp, with a voice 'unattractive and unresonant . . .
which in his early years often made it painful to listen to him'.

But Churchill overcame those impediments and found greatness
in his rhetoric. He did this in several ways.

1. Hard work

Perhaps no one worked as hard as Churchill to become a good
speaker. Anytime anyone asks me to fix their speaking problems
I tell them about Churchill. He overcame problems much more
serious than those encountered by the vast majority of novice
speakers. Cannadine mentions the persistent and frantic efforts
to address his vocal difficulties. Churchill studied speeches very
carefully. He was a student of the craft. He memorised great
speeches. He spoke those great speeches out loud (a practice I
highly recommend). He visited voice specialists. He practised and
practised. In other words, he was honest with himself. He knew his
voice was weak. And he wrote to accommodate, even cover up, that
weakness by using unusual words, vivid imagery and good writing.

2. Personal style

Churchill created a unique oratorical style to mask some of his
difficulties. Cannadine calls it a 'personal style'. This style, argues
Cannadine, included stately sentences, resounding perorations,
invective, insult, detail, humour and deliberate commonplace. There
would be lofty oratory with inserts of conversational discussion,
even intimate details. There was imagery, colour and history.

3. Moving the words forward

Because of his speaking difficulties, Churchill quickly adjusted his speaking style to change the mix. The voice became less important; the words gained ascendency. He pushes the words forward, asking them in effect to take over. All he has to do is read the words with minimal vocal variety or emphasis. The words are so powerful that they do the work for him. Since he was an outstanding writer, this was a wise, fateful decision.

4. Literate language
There is a reason he received the Nobel Prize for Literature. He was a wonderful writer. Churchill loved words. He knew what to do with them. Words were his great strength.

5. Painting pictures
He loved to work in the details. He would transport the listener to the scene of battle or the corridors of power. He knew how to use words to let the listener's imagination take over. Here is a passage from 1919:

> With Russia on our hands in a state of utter ruin, with a greater part of Europe on the brink of famine, with bankruptcy, anarchy and revolution threatening the victorious as well as the vanquished, we cannot afford to drive over to the Bolshevist camp the orderly and stable forces which now exist in German democracy.

You can see the threatening forces of chaos and devastation pulling Germany towards doom. You can feel those forces at work.

6. Use of history
Churchill could conjure up the past. He could see the details of an event. He understood the human effort and cost in an enterprise. He had a long view, with an ability to look back at the present from the vantage point of decades in the future. He could see the present as an historian might, enabling him to see well beyond the moment. In a speech to Parliament in 1934, warning that Britain was vulnerable, he

spoke with intimate detail of European history, especially Prussian imperialism. And he could see history at work. In that speech he said: 'Wars come very suddenly. I have lived through a period when one looked forward, as we do now, with anxiety and uncertainty to what would happen in the future. Suddenly something did happen – tremendous, swift, overpowering, irresistible.' He then spoke of the beginning of the First World War. It provided an analogy of the rapid passage from peace to war, where the impossible becomes the inevitable. He was right.

7. Subtle cadence

It is a kind of poetry in prose, a way of making the language more compelling and punchy. It is also direct, simple and elevated, showing the great strength of the right kind of simple language. In his 1941 'Appeal to America', he said: 'We shall not fail or falter; we shall not weaken or tire. Neither the sudden shock of battle nor the long-drawn trials of vigilance and exertion will wear us down. Give us the tools and we will finish the job.'

Nice writing. Now, look at the rhythm of those lines, the way they flow, their movement when said out loud. There is a beat. . . 'We shall not fa-il or fal-ter.' You see, we can almost count out the beat. More to the point, the speech is written to provide such a beat. The verbs help: 'shall not fail or falter' and 'shall not weaken or tire'. Churchill liked action verbs. They help bring movement to a sentence.

Consider the famous passage from his remarks after Dunkirk in 1940, the 'Wars are not won by evacuations' speech. Here Churchill combines an underlying beat with Anglo-Saxon words and action verbs to help the British see exactly how they will respond to invasion. He paints a picture of resistance and defence. And please notice the seven uses of the verb 'fight'.

> We shall go on to the end, we shall fight in France, we shall fight on the seas and oceans, we shall fight with growing confidence and growing strength in the war, we shall

defend our island, whatever the cost may be, we shall fight on the beaches, we shall fight on the landing grounds, we shall fight in the fields and in the streets, we shall fight in the hills; we shall never surrender.

You can hear the beat, particularly when you factor in the pausing. And you can feel the steely commitment. The passage motivates and reinforces through the use of direct and simple language. There are no qualifiers, no weasel words, no use of 'maybe' or 'probabilities' or 'might be'. He means it: 'We shall never surrender.' I wonder if that line alone prevented an invasion, by both warning Hitler and emboldening the civilian population. In any event, the passages have a cadence that makes them more listenable and more powerful.

8. Remarkable detail
Churchill talks repeatedly of the state of military preparation, logistics of foreign armies and the state of preparedness of the civilian population. He doesn't just mention all of this. He seems to know a tremendous amount of the detail. He shares that detail in his speeches. The speeches in the Second World War are partially briefings to the British people. The citizens are asked to remain informed and to share in the sacrifices, as well as the decision-making. You get the sense that he isn't solely reliant on staff or experts, that he really knows. His leadership is based on having that knowledge, acquired tirelessly through meetings with the rank and file as well as the commanders, through first-hand inspection of destroyers, tanks and aircraft, which was true. He also had an extraordinary number of meetings with foreign leaders, most of whom relied on Churchill to come to them or to meet them somewhere outside the United Kingdom. His depth of knowledge would be noteworthy in any age. But it is simply remarkable in the circumstances of the Second World War. Contrast his movements and his knowledge with world leaders today in the war on terrorism. It is a different age, but Churchill would probably know more, have

seen more and travelled more, while maintaining closer contact with world leaders and offering more cogent and clear explanations of planning, execution and progress.

Churchill was a great speechwriter. He made the decision to be a master of the medium. When he was only twenty-two, he wrote an unpublished essay titled 'The Scaffolding of Rhetoric'. In that essay he observed: 'Of all the talents bestowed upon men, none is so precious as the gift of oratory. He who enjoys it wields a power more durable than that of a great king. He is an independent force in the world.' Churchill became an independent force that saved a nation and made his own history.

Ted Sorensen

Ted Sorensen was an aide, speechwriter and friend to John Kennedy for more than a decade, including Kennedy's three years as president. His background in law gave him a precision of mind that was invaluable in his writing. His love of words complemented and helped give voice to Kennedy's passionate interest in history, ideas and personalities. Sorensen's mind eventually melded with Kennedy's. As a result, Sorensen became an idea ghostwriter: thinking thoughts along the same lines as Kennedy, crafting the words Kennedy would have used if he had the time to devote himself fully to the writing of the text. Working with other powerful writers, including Harvard historian Arthur Schlesinger, Jr and Richard Goodwin, as well as an accomplished writer like Kennedy, Sorensen helped craft some of the greatest speeches of the last century.

Sorensen has written several books about Kennedy. But one of the most insightful is *Counselor*, an autobiography published in 2008. One chapter concerns the task of speechwriting. It contains a great amount of valuable insight into the process of producing effective, memorable speeches. Here is just a partial list of some of his thoughts on speechwriting.

1. Take the job seriously

Sorensen understood that every word would be under scrutiny. He didn't just throw words around or allow the President to 'wing it' with unscripted, spontaneous language. That would have been dangerous and unprofessional, perhaps stupid in some circumstances. Sorensen wrote: 'I approached my writing with special care, because I knew it would be heard and read all over the country, perhaps all over the world.'

2. Work directly with the speaker

Sorensen's work was reviewed directly by Kennedy. He did not write for a committee. He did not work through middlemen or layers of assistants and bureaucrats. That is the ideal way to craft a speech. The language remains fresh, the ideas unmediated. The speech usually is better as a result.

3. Love language

Sorensen said it was his 'chief qualification for speechwriting'. I think it is the best qualification for any speechwriter. Great speeches are a skilful employment of language. They can also be a celebration of it.

4. Speeches should be uplifting and unifying

Tone and direction are important. Sorensen and Kennedy thought that even political speeches should not be too partisan. They should rise above the battle and the moment. Sorensen's view is that 'its tone should be positive, inspirational, hopeful and forward-looking – not an endless litany of negative complaints about past misdeeds or the status quo'. That is why Kennedy's speeches have a powerful impact five decades later. They are timeless because they were written to transcend circumstance and context. Kennedy's speeches will be read hundreds of years from now, as are the speeches of Washington and Lincoln, because they concern ideas, human rights and the responsibilities of citizen and government. They aren't just about attacking opponents or pursuing political advantage. Substantive ideas are 'the most important part' of the speech.

5. Less is always better than more

Sorensen calls this one of the 'basic rules' of speechwriting. Speeches should be simple, direct and brief. For him, the Ten Commandments are a good example of ideal simplicity.

6. Choose each word as a precision tool

Words have jobs. 'Care and prudence' are necessary for selecting the proper word and the right sequence of words.

7. Organise the text to simplify, clarify, emphasise

Sorensen argues that a speech 'should flow from an outline in logical order'. And there should be a 'tightly organised, coherent and consistent theme'.

8. Use variety and literary devices to reinforce memorability

Kennedy's speeches used chiasmus, a technique for reversing words and ideas to make them more interesting and unforgettable, such as 'Let us never negotiate out of fear, but let us never fear to negotiate'.

9. Employ elevated language

That doesn't mean grandiose language. Far from it. The language must be simple, dignified and understood by everyone.

Sorensen understood the enormous power of words. The right speech in the hands of the right speaker 'can ignite a fire, change men's minds, open their eyes, alter their votes, bring hope to their lives and, in all these ways, change the world'.

Ronald Reagan in Berlin (Time & Life Pictures/Getty Images)

APPENDIX: SIX GREAT SPEECHES

In this section we will look at six great speeches. I have included them because I find them interesting, and I hope that you will discover in them something of value for your own rhetorical development. Each offers much that is different. I will begin each speech with a brief introduction. Then the text will follow. The six speeches we will consider are Pericles's Funeral Oration, Lincoln's Gettysburg Address, Kwame Nkrumah's 'I Speak for Freedom', Pope John Paul II's remarks at Vad Vashem, Margaret Thatcher's speech in Brighton after the IRA bombing of the conference hotel and Ronald Reagan's speech at the Berlin Wall.

Pericles

The first great speech may have been by Pericles. It was given sometime in the fifth century BC. The purpose of the speech was to remember the fallen in the first year of the Peloponnesian War. But the speech is more than a glorification of the dead. It is a statement of the importance of Athenian democracy. It is also a speech of empowerment, for those in a democracy decide its future. One could also argue it is a speech about good government, the glorification of culture and the lasting value of sacrifice. In the speech he talks about the dead receiving 'a praise that will never decay, a sepulchre that will also be most illustrious'. Such praise may also be given to the words of Pericles.

'Most of those who have spoken here before me have commended the lawgiver who added this oration to our other funeral customs. It seemed to them a worthy thing that such an honour should be given at their burial to the dead who have fallen on the field of battle. But I should have preferred that, when men's deeds have been brave, they should be honoured in deed only, and with such an honour as this public funeral, which you are now witnessing. Then the reputation of many would not have been imperilled on the eloquence or want of eloquence of one, and their virtues believed or not as he spoke well or ill. For it is difficult to say neither too little nor too much; and even moderation is apt not to give the impression of truthfulness. The friend of the dead who knows the facts is likely to think that the words of the speaker fall short of his knowledge and of his wishes; another who is not so well informed, when he hears of anything which surpasses his own powers, will be envious and will suspect exaggeration. Mankind are tolerant of the praises of others so long as each hearer thinks that he can do as well or nearly as well himself, but, when the speaker rises above him, jealousy is aroused and he begins to be incredulous. However, since our ancestors have set the seal of their approval upon the practice, I must obey, and to the utmost of my power shall endeavour to satisfy the wishes and beliefs of all who hear me.

'I will speak first of our ancestors, for it is right and seemly that now, when we are lamenting the dead, a tribute should be paid to their memory. There has never been a time when they did not inhabit this land, which by their valour they will have handed down from generation to generation, and we have received from them a free state. But if they were worthy of praise, still more were our fathers, who added to their inheritance, and after many a struggle transmitted to us their sons this great empire. And we ourselves assembled here today, who are still most of us in the vigour of life, have carried the work of improvement further, and have richly endowed our city with all things, so that she is sufficient for herself both in peace and war. Of the military exploits by which our various possessions were acquired, or of the energy with which we or our fathers drove back the tide of war, Hellenic or Barbarian, I will not speak; for the tale would be long and is familiar to you. But before I praise the dead, I should like to point out by what principles of action we rose to power, and under what institutions and through what manner of life our empire became great. For I conceive that such thoughts are not unsuited to the occasion, and that this numerous assembly of citizens and strangers may profitably listen to them.

'Our form of government does not enter into rivalry with the institutions of others. Our government does not copy our neighbours', but is an example to them. It is true that we are called a democracy, for the administration is in the hands of the many and not of the few. But while there exists equal justice to all and alike in their private disputes, the claim of excellence is also recognised; and when a citizen is in any way distinguished, he is preferred to the public service, not as a matter of privilege, but as the reward of merit. Neither is poverty an obstacle, but a man may benefit his country whatever the obscurity of his condition. There is no exclusiveness in our public life, and in our private business we are not suspicious of one another, nor angry with our neighbour if he does what he likes; we do not put on sour looks at him which, though harmless, are not pleasant. While we are thus unconstrained in our private business, a spirit of reverence pervades our public acts; we are prevented from doing wrong by respect for the authorities and for the laws, having a particular regard to those which are ordained for the protection of the injured as well as those unwritten laws which bring upon the transgressor of them the reprobation of the general sentiment.

'And we have not forgotten to provide for our weary spirits many

relaxations from toil; we have regular games and sacrifices throughout
the year; our homes are beautiful and elegant; and the delight which
we daily feel in all these things helps to banish sorrow. Because of the
greatness of our city the fruits of the whole earth flow in upon us; so that
we enjoy the goods of other countries as freely as our own.

'Then again, our military training is in many respects superior to that
of our adversaries. Our city is thrown open to the world, though, and we
never expel a foreigner and prevent him from seeing or learning anything
of which the secret if revealed to an enemy might profit him. We rely not
upon management or trickery, but upon our own hearts and hands. And
in the matter of education, whereas they from early youth are always
undergoing laborious exercises which are to make them brave, we live
at ease, and yet are equally ready to face the perils which they face. And
here is the proof: the Lacedaemonians come into Athenian territory not
by themselves, but with their whole confederacy following; we go alone
into a neighbour's country; and although our opponents are fighting for
their homes and we on a foreign soil, we have seldom any difficulty in
overcoming them. Our enemies have never yet felt our united strength,
the care of a navy divides our attention, and on land we are obliged to
send our own citizens everywhere. But they, if they meet and defeat a
part of our army, are as proud as if they had routed us all, and when
defeated they pretend to have been vanquished by us all.

'If then we prefer to meet danger with a light heart but without
laborious training, and with a courage which is gained by habit and not
enforced by law, are we not greatly the better for it? Since we do not
anticipate the pain, although, when the hour comes, we can be as brave
as those who never allow themselves to rest; thus our city is equally
admirable in peace and in war. For we are lovers of the beautiful in
our tastes and our strength lies, in our opinion, not in deliberation and
discussion, but that knowledge which is gained by discussion preparatory
to action. For we have a peculiar power of thinking before we act, and
of acting, too, whereas other men are courageous from ignorance but
hesitate upon reflection. And they are surely to be esteemed the bravest
spirits who, having the clearest sense both of the pains and pleasures of
life, do not on that account shrink from danger. In doing good, again, we

are unlike others; we make our friends by conferring, not by receiving, favours. Now he who confers a favour is the firmer friend, because he would rather by kindness keep alive the memory of an obligation; but the recipient is colder in his feelings, because he knows that in requiting another's generosity he will not be winning gratitude but only paying a debt. We alone do good to our neighbours not upon a calculation of interest, but in the confidence of freedom and in a frank and fearless spirit. To sum up: I say that Athens is the school of Hellas, and that the individual Athenian in his own person seems to have the power of adapting himself to the most varied forms of action with the utmost versatility and grace. This is no passing and idle word, but truth and fact; and the assertion is verified by the position to which these qualities have raised the state. For in the hour of trial Athens alone among her contemporaries is superior to the report of her. No enemy who comes against her is indignant at the reverses which he sustains at the hands of such a city; no subject complains that his masters are unworthy of him. And we shall assuredly not be without witnesses, there are mighty monuments of our power which will make us the wonder of this and of succeeding ages; we shall not need the praises of Homer or of any other panegyrist whose poetry may please for the moment, although his representation of the facts will not bear the light of day. For we have compelled every land and every sea to open a path for our valour, and have everywhere planted eternal memorials of our friendship and of our enmity. Such is the city for whose sake these men nobly fought and died; they could not bear the thought that she might be taken from them; and every one of us who survive should gladly toil on her behalf.

'I have dwelt upon the greatness of Athens because I want to show you that we are contending for a higher prize than those who enjoy none of these privileges, and to establish by manifest proof the merit of these men whom I am now commemorating. Their loftiest praise has been already spoken. For in magnifying the city I have magnified them, and men like them whose virtues made her glorious. And of how few Hellenes can it be said as of them, that their deeds when weighed in the balance have been found equal to their fame! I believe that a death such as theirs has been the true measure of a man's worth; it may be the first revelation of his virtues, but is at any rate their final seal. For even those who come short in other ways may justly plead the valour with which they have fought for their country; they have blotted out the evil with the good, and have benefited the state more by their public services than they have injured her by their private actions. None of these men were enervated by wealth or hesitated to resign the pleasures of life; none of them put off the evil day in the hope, natural to poverty, that a man, though poor, may one day become rich. But, deeming that the punishment of their enemies was sweeter than any of these things, and that they could fall in no nobler cause, they determined at the hazard of their lives to be honourably avenged, and to leave the rest. They resigned to hope their unknown chance of happiness; but in the face of death they resolved to rely upon themselves alone. And when the moment came they were minded to resist and suffer, rather than to fly and save their lives; they ran away from the word of dishonour, but on the battlefield their feet stood fast, and in an instant, at the height of their fortune, they passed away from the scene, not of their fear, but of their glory.

'Such was the end of these men; they were worthy of Athens, and the living need not desire to have a more heroic spirit, although they may pray for a less fatal issue. The value of such a spirit is not to be expressed in words. Anyone can discourse to you forever about the advantages of a brave defence, which you know already. But instead of listening to him I would have you day by day fix your eyes upon the greatness of Athens, until you become filled with the love of her; and when you are impressed by the spectacle of her glory, reflect that this empire has been acquired by men who knew their duty and had the courage to do it, who in the hour of conflict had the fear of dishonour always present to them, and who, if ever they failed in an enterprise, would not allow their virtues to be lost to their country, but freely gave their lives to her as the fairest offering which they could present at her feast. The sacrifice which they collectively made was individually repaid to them; for they received again each one for himself a praise which grows not old, and the noblest of all tombs, I speak not of that in which their remains are laid, but of that in which their glory survives, and is proclaimed always and on every fitting occasion both in word and deed. For the whole earth is the tomb of famous men; not only are they commemorated by columns and inscriptions in their own country, but in foreign lands there dwells also an unwritten memorial of them, graven not on stone but in the hearts of men. Make them your examples, and, esteeming courage to be freedom and freedom to be happiness, do not weigh too nicely the perils of war. The unfortunate who has no hope of a change for the better has less reason to throw away his life than the prosperous who, if he survive, is always liable to a change for the worse, and to whom any accidental fall makes the most serious difference. To a man of spirit, cowardice and disaster coming together are far more bitter than death striking him unperceived at a time when he is full of courage and animated by the general hope.

'Wherefore I do not now pity the parents of the dead who stand here; I would rather comfort them. You know that your dead have passed away amid manifold vicissitudes; and that they may be deemed fortunate who have gained their utmost honour, whether an honourable death like theirs, or an honourable sorrow like yours, and whose share of happiness has been so ordered that the term of their happiness is likewise the term of their life. I know how hard it is to make you feel this, when the good fortune of others will too often remind you of the gladness which once lightened your hearts. And sorrow is felt at the want of those blessings, not which a man never knew, but which were a part of his life before they were taken from him. Some of you are of an age at which they may hope to have other children, and they ought to bear their sorrow better; not only will the children who may hereafter be born make them forget their own lost ones, but the city will be doubly a gainer. She will not be left desolate, and she will be safer. For a man's counsel cannot have equal weight or worth, when he alone has no children to risk in the general danger. To those of you who have passed their prime, I say: "Congratulate yourselves that you have been happy during the greater part of your days; remember that your life of sorrow will not last long, and be comforted by the glory of those who are gone. For the love of honour alone is ever young, and not riches, as some say, but honour is the delight of men when they are old and useless."

'To you who are the sons and brothers of the departed, I see that the struggle to emulate them will be an arduous one. For all men praise the dead, and, however pre-eminent your virtue may be, I do not say even to approach them, and avoid living their rivals and detractors, but when a man is out of the way, the honour and goodwill which he receives is unalloyed. And, if I am to speak of womanly virtues to those of you who will henceforth be widows, let me sum them up in one short admonition: To a woman not to show more weakness than is natural to her sex is a great glory, and not to be talked about for good or for evil among men.

'I have paid the required tribute, in obedience to the law, making use of such fitting words as I had. The tribute of deeds has been paid in part; for the dead have them in deeds, and it remains only that their children should be maintained at the public charge until they are grown up: this is the solid prize with which, as with a garland, Athens crowns her sons living and dead, after a struggle like theirs. For where the rewards of virtue are greatest, there the noblest citizens are enlisted in the service of the state. And now, when you have duly lamented, everyone his own dead, you may depart.'

Abraham Lincoln

The Gettysburg Address is one of the most famous speeches ever given. Part of its greatness is its brevity. It is also a work of poetry, humble in language, sincere in its expression and touching in its humanity.

'Four score and seven years ago our fathers brought forth on this continent, a new nation, conceived in liberty, and dedicated to the proposition that all men are created equal.

'Now we are engaged in a great civil war, testing whether that nation, or any nation so conceived and so dedicated, can long endure. We are met on a great battlefield of that war. We have come to dedicate a portion of that field, as a final resting place for those who here gave their lives that that nation might live. It is altogether fitting and proper that we should do this.

'But in a larger sense, we cannot dedicate – we cannot consecrate – we cannot hallow – this ground. The brave men, living and dead, who struggled here, have consecrated it, far above our poor power to add or detract. The world will little note, nor long remember, what we say here, but it can never forget what they did here. It is for us the living, rather, to be dedicated here to the unfinished work which they who fought here have thus far so nobly advanced. It is rather for us to be here dedicated to the great task remaining before us – that from these honoured dead we take increased devotion to that cause for which they gave the last full measure of devotion – that we here highly resolve that these dead shall not have died in vain – that this nation, under God, shall have a new birth of freedom – and that government of the people, by the people, for the people, shall not perish from the earth.'

Kwame Nkrumah

Kwame Nkrumah led Ghana to independence and was one of the first modern spokespersons for Africa. In 1960 he gave a famous speech called 'I Speak for Freedom'. This was an inspirational speech for the post-colonial era, providing a remarkable set of symbols, words and emotions for generations of speeches in liberated countries. One could see this speech as a rhetorical model for countries emerging from colonial rule. Nkrumah was educated at Lincoln College in the United States, an historically black college. His classmates included future Supreme Court Justice Thurgood Marshall, the poet Langston Hughes and the bandleader Cab Calloway.

In 2009 Ghana celebrated fifty years of independence. So there has been recent renewed interest in this speech for its historical importance and its visionary idealism. It is certainly one of the few twentieth-century liberation speeches that have stood the test of time. It is often included in books of collected speeches.

'For centuries, Europeans dominated the African continent. The white man arrogated to himself the right to rule and to be obeyed by the non-white; his mission, he claimed, was to "civilise" Africa. Under this cloak, the Europeans robbed the continent of vast riches and inflicted unimaginable suffering on the African people.

'All this makes a sad story, but now we must be prepared to bury the past with its unpleasant memories and look to the future. All we ask of the former colonial powers is their goodwill and cooperation to remedy past mistakes and injustices and to grant independence to the colonies in Africa.

'It is clear that we must find an African solution to our problems, and that this can only be found in African unity. Divided we are weak; united, Africa could become one of the greatest forces for good in the world.

'Although most Africans are poor, our continent is potentially extremely rich. Our mineral resources, which are being exploited with foreign capital only to enrich foreign investors, range from gold and diamonds to uranium and petroleum. Our forests contain some of the finest woods to be grown anywhere. Our cash crops include cocoa, coffee, rubber, tobacco and cotton. As for power, which is an important factor in any economic development, Africa contains over 40 per cent of the potential water power of the world, as compared with about 10 per cent in Europe and 13 per cent in North America. Yet so far, less than 1 per cent has been developed. This is one of the reasons why we have in Africa the paradox of poverty in the midst of plenty, and scarcity in the midst of abundance.

'Never before have a people had within their grasp so great an opportunity for developing a continent endowed with so much wealth. Individually, the independent states of Africa, some of them potentially rich, others poor, can do little for their people. Together, by mutual help, they can achieve much. But the economic development of the continent must be planned and pursued as a whole. A loose confederation designed only for economic cooperation would not provide the necessary unity of purpose. Only a strong political union can bring about full and effective development of our natural resources for the benefit of our people.

'The political situation in Africa today is heartening and at the same time disturbing. It is heartening to see so many new flags hoisted in place of the old; it is disturbing to see so many countries of varying sizes and at different levels of development, weak and, in some cases, almost helpless. If this terrible state of fragmentation is allowed to continue it may well be disastrous for us all.

'There are at present some twenty-eight states in Africa, excluding the Union of South Africa and those countries not yet free. No less than nine of these states have a population of less than three million. Can we seriously believe that the colonial powers meant these countries to be independent, viable states? The example of South America, which has as much wealth, if not more, than North America, and yet remains weak and dependent on outside interests, is one which every African would do well to study.

'Critics of African unity often refer to the wide differences in culture, language and ideas in various parts of Africa. This is true, but the essential fact remains that we are all Africans, and have a common interest in the independence of Africa. The difficulties presented by questions of language, culture and different political systems are not insuperable. If the need for political union is agreed by us all, then the will to create it is born; and where there's a will there's a way.

'The present leaders of Africa have already shown a remarkable willingness to consult and seek advice among themselves. Africans have, indeed, begun to think continentally. They realise that they have much in common, both in their past history, in their present problems and in their future hopes. To suggest that the time is not yet ripe for considering a political union of Africa is to evade the facts and ignore realities in Africa today.

'The greatest contribution that Africa can make to the peace of the world is to avoid all the dangers inherent in disunity, by creating a political union which will also by its success stand as an example to a divided world. A union of African states will project more effectively the African personality. It will command respect from a world that has regard only for size and influence. The scant attention paid to African opposition to the French atomic tests in the Sahara, and the ignominious spectacle of the UN in the Congo quibbling about constitutional niceties while the republic was tottering into anarchy, are evidence of the callous disregard of African independence by the Great Powers.

'We have to prove that greatness is not to be measured in stockpiles of atom bombs. I believe strongly and sincerely that with the deep-rooted wisdom and dignity, the innate respect for human lives, the intense humanity that is our heritage, the African race, united under one federal government, will emerge not as just another world bloc to flaunt its wealth and strength, but as a Great Power whose greatness is indestructible because it is built not on fear, envy and suspicion, nor won at the expense of others, but founded on hope, trust, friendship and directed to the good of all mankind.

'The emergence of such a mighty stabilising force in this strife-worn world should be regarded not as the shadowy dream of a visionary, but as a practical proposition, which the peoples of Africa can, and should, translate into reality. There is a tide in the affairs of every people when the moment strikes for political action. Such was the moment in the history of the United States of America when the Founding Fathers saw beyond the petty wranglings of the separate states and created a Union. This is our chance. We must act now. Tomorrow may be too late and the opportunity will have passed, and with it the hope of free Africa's survival.'

Pope John Paul II

The Pope's speeches in Poland in 1983 were powerful religious and political messages, fracturing the foundation of the communist government's authority and enabling Poles to reject the legitimacy of that totalitarian regime. The speeches in Warsaw and in Częstochowa were landmark moments in the eventual liberation of Poland.

Those speeches were great in every possible sense of evaluation. There has been much written about those admirable and devastating words. So I have chosen another speech, one from the Pope's later years, given during a journey to Israel. In 2000, he spoke at Yad Vashem, the monument and memorial to the Holocaust. This speech shows a desire for unification between Catholics and Jews, as well as atonement for any role played by Catholics in the Holocaust. It is remarkable in its effort to reshape interfaith dialogue and establish common ground between two religions with such complex and destructive history. This is a speech of confession, reconciliation, redemption, cooperation and hope. The language offers a model for public speaking before hostile or sceptical audiences. It establishes common ground. It then works towards a careful conclusion of collective agreement and a fragile and respectful unification.

'The words of the ancient psalm rise from our hearts: "I have become like a broken vessel. I hear the whispering of many – terror on every side – as they scheme together against me, as they plot to take my life. But I trust in you, O Lord: I say, you are my God." [Psalms 31:13–15] In this place of memories, the mind and heart and soul feel an extreme need for silence. Silence in which to remember. Silence in which to try to make some sense of the memories which come flooding back. Silence because there are no words strong enough to deplore the terrible tragedy of the Shoah.

'My own personal memories are of all that happened when the Nazis occupied Poland during the war. I remember my Jewish friends and neighbours, some of whom perished, while others survived. I have come to Yad Vashem to pay homage to the millions of Jewish people who, stripped of everything, especially of human dignity, were murdered in the Holocaust. More than half a century has passed, but the memories remain.

'Here, as at Auschwitz and many other places in Europe, we are overcome by the echo of the heart-rending laments of so many. Men, women and children cry out to us from the depths of the horror that they knew. How can we fail to heed their cry? No one can forget or ignore what happened. No one can diminish its scale.

'We wish to remember. But we wish to remember for a purpose, namely to ensure that never again will evil prevail, as it did for the millions of innocent victims of Nazism.

'How could man have such utter contempt for man? Because he had reached the point of contempt for God. Only a godless ideology could plan and carry out the extermination of a whole people.

'The honour given to the "just Gentiles" by the state of Israel at Yad Vashem for having acted heroically to save Jews, sometimes to the point of giving their own lives, is a recognition that not even in the darkest hour is every light extinguished. That is why the Psalms and the entire Bible, though well aware of the human capacity for evil, also proclaim that evil will not have the last word.

'Out of the depths of pain and sorrow, the believer's heart cries out: "I trust in you, O Lord: I say, you are my God." Jews and Christians share an immense spiritual patrimony, flowing from God's self-revelation. Our religious teachings and our spiritual experience demand that we overcome evil with good. We remember, but not with any desire for vengeance or as an incentive to hatred. For us, to remember is to pray for peace and justice, and to commit ourselves to their cause. Only a world at peace, with justice for all, can avoid repeating the mistakes and terrible crimes of the past.

'As Bishop of Rome and successor of the Apostle Peter, I assure the Jewish people that the Catholic Church, motivated by the Gospel law of truth and love, and by no political considerations, is deeply saddened by the hatred, acts of persecution and displays of anti-Semitism directed against the Jews by Christians at any time and in any place. The Church rejects racism in any form as a denial of the image of the Creator inherent in every human being.

'In this place of solemn remembrance, I fervently pray that our sorrow for the tragedy which the Jewish people suffered in the twentieth century will lead to a new relationship between Christians and Jews. Let us build a new future in which there will be no more anti-Jewish feeling among Christians or anti-Christian feeling among Jews, but rather the mutual respect required of those who adore the one Creator and Lord, and look to Abraham as our common father in faith.

'The world must heed the warning that comes to us from the victims of the Holocaust, and from the testimony of the survivors.

'Here at Yad Vashem the memory lives on, and burns itself onto our souls. It makes us cry out: "I hear the whispering of many – terror on every side – but I trust in you, O Lord: I say, you are my God.'"

Margaret Thatcher

This is the speech Margaret Thatcher gave at the Conservative Party conference at Brighton in 1984. Earlier in the morning a bomb exploded in the Grand Hotel. It just missed killing the Prime Minister and her cabinet. Thatcher was advised not to give her speech. However, she was determined not to let terrorism disrupt the work of party or government. So this speech became famous for having been given at all. But the first paragraph showed a valiant determination not to give in to terrorists. The speech also has most of the major Thatcher themes: reducing government, privatisation, economic stabilisation through lower taxes and less government spending, strong defence, capital investment, defiance of the National Union of Mineworkers and others who want to take away the legitimate powers and authority of the government, and commitment to the rule of law and democracy. Thatcher may have given more memorable speeches, such as those during the Falklands War or her many speeches on Europe. But this speech is vintage Thatcher and has become a benchmark for language on the rule of law and opposition to terrorism. The ideas in this speech have become part of the political landscape, for better or worse.

The speech contains a very interesting, well-crafted argument. There is an attention to facts, details and events. There is a powerful sense of commitment to principle ('The Iron Lady'). There is a vision of a more prosperous Britain. But the affirmation of the rule of law and democratic process leaves an overriding impression of boldness, strength, courage and conviction.

'Mr President, my lords, ladies and gentlemen,

'The bomb attack on the Grand Hotel early this morning was first and foremost an inhuman, undiscriminating attempt to massacre innocent unsuspecting men and women staying in Brighton for our Conservative conference. Our first thoughts must at once be for those who died and for those who are now in hospital recovering from their injuries. But the bomb attack clearly signified more than this. It was an attempt not only to disrupt and terminate our conference; it was an attempt to cripple Her Majesty's democratically elected government. That is the scale of the outrage in which we have all shared, and the fact that we are gathered here now – shocked, but composed and determined – is a sign not only that this attack has failed, but that all attempts to destroy democracy by terrorism will fail.

'I should like to express our deep gratitude to the police, firemen, ambulancemen, nurses and doctors, to all the emergency services, and to the staff of the hotel; to our ministerial staff and the Conservative Party staff who stood with us and shared the danger. As Prime Minister and as leader of the party, I thank them all and send our heartfelt sympathy to all those who have suffered.

'And now it must be business as usual. We must go on to discuss the things we have talked about during this conference; one or two matters of foreign affairs; and after that, two subjects I have selected for special consideration – unemployment and the miners' strike.

'This Conservative conference, superbly chaired – and of course, our chairman came on this morning with very little sleep and carried on marvellously – and with excellent contributions from our members, has been an outstanding example of orderly assembly and free speech. We have debated the great national and international issues, as well as those which affect the daily lives of our people. We have seen at the rostrum miner and pensioner, nurse and manager, clergyman and student. In government, we have been fulfilling the promises contained in our election manifesto, which was put to the people in a national ballot.

'This government, Mr President, is reasserting Parliament's ultimate responsibility for controlling the total burden of taxation on our citizens, whether levied by central or local government, and in the coming session of Parliament we shall introduce legislation which will abolish the GLC and the metropolitan county councils.

'In the quest for sound local government, we rely on the help of Conservative councillors. Their task should never be underestimated and their virtues should not go unsung. They work hard and conscientiously in the true spirit of service and I pay special tribute to the splendid efforts of Conservative councils up and down the country in getting better value for money through greater efficiency and putting out work to competitive tender. This is privatisation at the local level and we need more of it.'

[section on privatisation omitted]

'Now, Mr President and Friends, this performance in the social services could never have been achieved without an efficient and competitive industry to create the wealth we need. Efficiency is not the enemy, but the ally, of compassion.

'In our discussions here, we have spoken of the need for enterprise, profits and the wider distribution of property among all the people. In the Conservative Party, we have no truck with outmoded Marxist doctrine about class warfare. For us, it is not who you are, who your family is or where you come from that matters. It is what you are and what you can do for our country that counts. That is our vision. It is a vision worth defending and we shall defend it. Indeed, this government will never put the defence of our country at risk.'

[section on defence and on European Union omitted]

'Now, Mr President, we had one of the most interesting debates of this conference on unemployment, which we all agree is the scourge of our times.

'To have over three million people unemployed in this country is bad enough, even though we share this tragic problem with other nations, but to suggest, as some of our opponents have, that we do not care about it is as deeply wounding as it is utterly false. Do they really think that we do not understand what it means for the family man who cannot find a job, to have to sit at home with a sense of failure and despair? Or that we do not understand how hopeless the world must seem to a young person who has not yet succeeded in getting his first job? Of course we know, of course we see, and of course we care. However could they say that we welcome unemployment as a political weapon? What better news could there be for any government than the news that unemployment is falling and the day cannot come too soon for me.

'Others, while not questioning our sincerity, argue that our policies will not achieve our objectives. They look back forty years to the post-war period, when we were paused to launch a brave new world; a time when we all thought we had the cure for unemployment. In that confident dawn it seemed that having won the war, we knew how to win the peace. Keynes had provided the diagnosis. It was all set out in the 1944 White Paper on Employment. I bought it then; I have it still. My name is on the top of it. Margaret H. Roberts. One of my staff took one look at it and said: "Good Heavens! I did not know it was as old as that!"

'Now, we all read that White Paper very carefully, but the truth was that politicians took some parts of the formula in it and conveniently ignored the rest. I reread it frequently. Those politicians overlooked the warning in that paper that government action must not weaken personal enterprise or exonerate the citizen from the duty of fending for himself. They disregarded the advice that wages must be related to productivity and, above all, they neglected the warning that without a rising standard of industrial efficiency, you cannot achieve a high level of employment combined with a rising standard of living.

'And having ignored so much of that and having ignored other parts of the formula for so much of the time, the result was that we ended up with high inflation and high unemployment.

'This government is heeding the warnings. It has acted on the basic truths that were set out all those years ago in that famous White Paper. If I had come out with all this today, some people would call it "Thatcherite" but, in fact, it was vintage Maynard Keynes. He had a horror of inflation, a fear of too much state control, and a belief in the market.

'We are heeding those warnings. We are taking the policy as a whole and not only in selected parts. We have already brought inflation down below 5 per cent; output has been rising steadily since 1981 and investment is up substantially. But if things are improving, why – you will ask – does unemployment not fall?

'And that was the question one could feel throughout that debate, even though people know there is always a time lag between getting the other things right and having a fall in unemployment.

'Why does unemployment not fall?

'May I try to answer that question? Well, first, more jobs are being created. As Tom King pointed out, over the last year more than a quarter of a million extra jobs have been created, but the population of working age is also rising very fast as the baby boom of the 1960s becomes the school leavers of the 1980s; so although the number of jobs are rising, the population of working age is also rising, and among the population of working age a larger proportion of married women are seeking work, and so you will see why we need more jobs just to stop unemployment rising and even more jobs to get it falling.

'Now, on top of that, new technology has caused redundancy in many factories, though it has also created whole new industries providing products and jobs that only a few years ago were undreamed of.

'So it has two effects: the first one redundancies, the second and slightly later, new jobs as new products become possible. This has happened in history before.'

[section on historical examples omitted]

'Mr. President, we cannot create jobs without the willing cooperation not only of employers but of trade unions and all of the workforce who work in industry and commerce as well.

'Yesterday, in the debate, we were urged to spend more money on capital investment. It looks a very attractive idea, but to spend more in one area means spending less in another or it means putting up taxes. Now, in government, we are constantly faced with these difficult choices. If we want more for investment, I have to ask my colleagues in cabinet: "What are you going to give up, or you, or you? Or you, or you?" Or should I perhaps ask them: "Whose pay claim are you going to cut, the doctors, the police, the nurses?" I do not find many takers, because we have honoured the reviews of pay for doctors, nurses and the police and others in full. And you would not have cheered me if we had not done so and quite right too, but I am bringing this to you because although people can say the way to solve unemployment is to give a higher capital allocation, I have to say: what are we going to give up? Or I have to turn to Nigel Lawson and ask him: which taxes would he put up? Income tax? The personal income tax is already too high. Value added tax? Well, I should get a pretty frosty reception from Nigel and I should get a pretty frosty reception from you. But I would be loath to ask him anyway.

'But you see, governments have to make these difficult choices, because as you know, whether your own households or whether your own businesses, there is a certain amount of income and you are soon in trouble if you do not live within it.

'But what I want to say to you is that we do consider these difficult choices in the public expenditure annual round and we are just coming up to it, and we have managed to allocate a very considerable sum to capital investment. Indeed, we have found the money for the best investment projects on offer and believe you me, it has been because of very good management in each and every department. It has been cutting out waste so we could make room for these things and be certain that we could say to you that we were getting value for money.

'Let me just give you a few examples of some of the investment projects for which we have found money, by careful budgeting.'

[examples omitted]

'So what is the conclusion that we are coming to? It is the spirit of enterprise that creates new jobs and it is government's task to create the right framework, the right financial framework, in which that can flourish and to cut the obstacles which sometimes handicap the birth of enterprise, and also to manage our own resources carefully and well.

'That is more or less what that Employment Policy White Paper in 1944 said, so let me just return to it, page 1. It is getting a bit old.

'"Employment cannot be created by Act of Parliament or by government action alone. The success of the policy outlined in this paper will ultimately depend on the understanding and support of the community as a whole and especially on the efforts of employers and workers in industry."

'It was true then, it is true now, and those are the policies that we are following and shall continue to follow, because those are the policies that we believe will ultimately create the genuine jobs for the future. In the meantime, it is our job to try to mitigate the painful effects of change and that we do, as you know, by generous redundancy payments and also by a Community Enterprise Scheme, which not only finds jobs for the long-term unemployed, but finds them in a way which brings great benefits to the communities. And then, of course, where there are redundancy schemes in steel and now in coal, the industries themselves set up enterprise agencies both to give help to those who are made redundant and to provide new training. All of this is a highly constructive policy both for the creation of jobs and a policy to cushion the effects of change.

'May I turn now to the coal industry?

'For a little over seven months we have been living through an agonising strike. Let me make it absolutely clear the miners' strike was not of this government's seeking nor of its making.

'We have heard in debates at this conference some of the aspects that have made this dispute so repugnant to so many people. We were reminded by a colliery manager that the NUM always used to accept that a pit should close when the losses were too great to keep it open, and that the miners set great store by investment in new pits and new seams, and under this government that new investment is happening in abundance. You can almost repeat the figures with me. £2 million in capital investment in the mines for every day this government has been in power, so no shortage of capital investment.

'We heard moving accounts from two working miners about just what they have to face as they try to make their way to work. The sheer bravery of those men and thousands like them who kept the mining industry alive is beyond praise. "Scabs" their former workmates call them. Scabs? They are lions! What a tragedy it is when striking miners attack their workmates. Not only are they members of the same union, but the working miner is saving both their futures, because it is the working miners, whether in Nottinghamshire, Derbyshire, Lancashire, Leicestershire, Staffordshire, Warwickshire, north Wales or Scotland, it is the working miners who have kept faith with those who buy our coal and without that custom thousands of jobs in the mining industry would be already lost.

'And then we heard – unforgettably – from the incomparable Mrs Irene McGibbon, who told us what it is like to be the wife of a working miner during this strike. She told us of the threats and intimidation suffered by herself and her family and even her eleven-year-old son, but what she endured only stiffened her resolve. To face the picket line day after day must take a very special kind of courage, but it takes as much – perhaps even more – to the housewife who has to stay at home alone. Men and women like that are what we are proud to call "the best of British" and our police who upheld the law with an independence and a restraint perhaps only to be found in this country are the admiration of the world.

'To be sure, the miners had a good deal and to try to prevent a strike the National Coal Board gave to the miners the best-ever pay offer, the highest-ever investment and for the first time the promise that no miner would lose his job against his will. We did this despite the fact that the bill for losses in the coal industry last year was bigger than the annual bill for all the doctors and dentists in all the National Health Service hospitals in the United Kingdom.

'Let me repeat it: the losses – the annual losses – in the coal industry are enormous. £1.3 billion last year. You have to find that money as taxpayers. It is equal to the sum we pay in salaries to all the doctors and dentists in the National Health Service.

'Mr President, this is a dispute about the right to go to work of those who have been denied the right to go to vote, and we must never forget that the overwhelming majority of trade unionists, including many striking miners, deeply regret what has been done in the name of trade unionism. When this strike is over – and one day it will be over – we must do everything we can to encourage moderate and responsible trade unionism so that it can once again take its respected and valuable place in our industrial life.

'Meanwhile, we are faced with the present executive of the National Union of Mineworkers. They know that what they are demanding has never been granted either to miners or to workers in any other industry.

Why then demand it? Why ask for what they know cannot be conceded? There can only be one explanation. They did not want a settlement; they wanted a strike. Otherwise, they would have balloted on the Coal Board's offer. Indeed, one-third of the miners did have a ballot and voted overwhelmingly to accept the offer.

'Mr President, what we have seen in this country is the emergence of an organised revolutionary minority who are prepared to exploit industrial disputes, but whose real aim is the breakdown of law and order and the destruction of democratic parliamentary government. We have seen the same sort of thugs and bullies at Grunwick, more recently against Eddie Shah in Stockport, and now organised into flying squads around the country. If their tactics were to be allowed to succeed, if they are not brought under the control of the law, we shall see them again at every industrial dispute organised by militant union leaders anywhere in the country.

'One of the speakers earlier in this conference realised this fact, realised that what they are saying is: "Give us what we want or we are prepared to go on with violence," and he referred to Danegeld. May I add to what that speaker said.

'"We never pay anyone Danegeld, no matter how trifling the cost, for the end of that gain is oppression and shame, and the nation that plays it is lost." Yes, Rudyard Kipling. Who could put it better?

'Democratic change there has always been in this, the home of democracy. But the sanction for change is the ballot box.

'It seems that there are some who are out to destroy any properly elected government. They are out to bring down the framework of law. That is what we have seen in this strike, and what is the law they seek to defy?

'It is the common law created by fearless judges and passed down across the centuries. It is legislation scrutinised and enacted by the parliament of a free people. It is legislation passed through a House of Commons, a Commons elected once every five years by secret ballot by one citizen, one vote. This is the way our law was fashioned and that is why British justice is renowned across the world.

'"No government owns the law. It is the law of the land, heritage of the people. No man is above the law and no man is below it. Nor do we ask any man's permission when we require him to obey it. Obedience to the law is demanded as a right, not asked as a favour." So said Theodore Roosevelt.

'Mr President, the battle to uphold the rule of law calls for the resolve and commitment of the British people. Our institutions of justice, the courts and the police require the unswerving support of every law-abiding citizen and I believe they will receive it.

'The nation faces what is probably the most testing crisis of our time, the battle between the extremists and the rest. We are fighting, as we have always fought, for the weak as well as for the strong. We are fighting for great and good causes. We are fighting to defend them against the power and might of those who rise up to challenge them. This government will not weaken. This nation will meet that challenge. Democracy will prevail.'

Reproduced with kind permission of the Margaret Thatcher Foundation

Ronald Reagan

Few speeches have been as provocative, dramatic and effective as the remarks delivered by Ronald Reagan on 12 June 1987. He demanded the destruction of the Berlin Wall. In November 1989 the almost unthinkable happened: the wall was breached, overwhelmed by Berliners on both sides, and then destroyed with an intuitive ferocity that has become iconic. Rarely do citizens personally get to demolish the means of their enslavement.

With East Berlin and the Brandenburg Gate as a backdrop, Reagan called for the end of a divided Berlin and of communism itself. The words he used have become part of our collective conscience: 'General Secretary Gorbachev, if you seek peace, if you seek prosperity for the Soviet Union and eastern Europe, if you seek liberalisation: come here to this gate! Mr Gorbachev, open this gate! Mr Gorbachev, tear down this wall!'

These words condense the message of the speech. They function as a powerful soundbite. They reach into the mind and have an explosive, and lasting, impact. This is speechwriting at its most effective.

That's one reason to include this speech in the book. It functions as an example of outstanding language in speechwriting. The argument is well stated. The audience is lead to a point of collective agreement. The solution is greeted with enthusiasm. The audience joins with the speaker. The speech makes international news; it makes history. This is what should happen in big-time speechwriting.

The stories behind the speech are important. The speechwriter, Peter Robinson, gives a fascinating account of its development. There was enormous opposition to the language, tone and intent of the original draft from within the administration. Some feared provoking Gorbachev. Others feared boxing him into a corner. Some worried that Reagan could not credibly back up the message, leaving him intertwined in his own rhetoric. Many of those previewing the speech in the White House and at the State Department wanted the remarks rewritten.

Reagan steadfastly remained committed to the direction, wording and intention of the original draft. So another reason for looking at this speech is its internal consistency and message development. That may be more important that the legendary soundbite. This is a paradigm speech for change, which is somewhat rare in foreign policy. Typically, in an address on foreign policy, the words of stasis are employed, smoothing over differences, finding common ground in order to enable cooperation. Language is vague, allowing diplomats room to move. In such a speech, when change is suggested, it is often fraternal and cautious. That is why most foreign policy speeches are not worth remembering. They really do say nothing, except, perhaps, to diplomats with trained ears, finding meaning in nuance.

In this speech, Reagan holds nothing back. He senses that the winds of change blow in his favour. The speech starts with

a reference to President Kennedy's remarks in Berlin. That is
an historical linkage that gives great weight to this speech. It
immediately recalls Kennedy's message of freedom and builds on
it, expanding it and working towards a forceful conclusion. Reagan
employs words as sledgehammers on the wall, and less than two
years later sledgehammers were tearing down the wall. This speech
is coherent and tightly constructed, which also is a rarity in foreign
policy speeches, which are often written by committee. Reagan's
argument about the bankruptcy of communism and the need
for freedom in eastern Europe remains electric and passionate
throughout the remarks. That is an amazing achievement in
any speech, even more so in one that presents a message to an
international audience.

Decades later, this speech continues its work. Democracy is
the best form of government. The walls of oppression, wherever
they might be, should come down. Reagan may have made better
speeches, such as his first inaugural address, the Pointe du Hoc
speech at Normandy or the remarks on the Challenger space
shuttle accident. Those speeches are masterpieces of imagination,
poetry and unification. But this speech shows what can be done if
the speaker has the courage, boldness and vision to use words to
their maximum effect.

'Chancellor Kohl, Governing Mayor Diepgen, ladies and gentlemen,

'Twenty-four years ago, President John F. Kennedy visited Berlin,
speaking to the people of this city and the world at the City Hall. Well,
since then two other Presidents have come, each in his turn, to Berlin.
And today I, myself, make my second visit to your city.

'We come to Berlin, we American Presidents, because it's our duty to
speak, in this place, of freedom. But I must confess, we're drawn here by
other things as well: by the feeling of history in this city, more than 500
years older than our own nation; by the beauty of the Grunewald and the
Tiergarten; most of all, by your courage and determination. Perhaps the
composer Paul Lincke understood something about American Presidents.
You see, like so many Presidents before me, I come here today because

wherever I go, whatever I do, *ich hab noch einen Koffer in Berlin* [I still have a suitcase in Berlin].

'Our gathering today is being broadcast throughout western Europe and North America. I understand that it is being seen and heard as well in the East. To those listening throughout eastern Europe, a special word: although I cannot be with you, I address my remarks to you just as surely as to those standing here before me. For I join you, as I join your fellow countrymen in the West, in this firm, this unalterable belief: *es gibt nur ein Berlin* [there is only one Berlin].

'Behind me stands a wall that encircles the free sectors of this city, part of a vast system of barriers that divides the entire continent of Europe. From the Baltic, south, those barriers cut across Germany in a gash of barbed wire, concrete, dog runs and guard towers. Farther south, there may be no visible, no obvious wall. But there remain armed guards and checkpoints all the same – still a restriction on the right to travel, still an instrument to impose upon ordinary men and women the will of a totalitarian state. Yet it is here in Berlin where the wall emerges most clearly; here, cutting across your city, where the news photo and the television screen have imprinted this brutal division of a continent upon the mind of the world. Standing before the Brandenburg Gate, every man is a German, separated from his fellow men. Every man is a Berliner, forced to look upon a scar.

'President von Weizsäcker has said: "The German question is open as long as the Brandenburg Gate is closed." Today I say: as long as the gate is closed, as long as this scar of a wall is permitted to stand, it is not the German question alone that remains open, but the question of freedom for all mankind. Yet I do not come here to lament. For I find in Berlin a message of hope, even in the shadow of this wall, a message of triumph.

'In this season of spring in 1945, the people of Berlin emerged from their air raid shelters to find devastation. Thousands of miles away, the people of the United States reached out to help. And in 1947 Secretary of State – as you've been told – George Marshall announced the creation of what would become known as the Marshall plan. Speaking precisely forty years ago this month, he said: "Our policy is directed not against any country or doctrine, but against hunger, poverty, desperation and chaos."

'In the Reichstag a few moments ago, I saw a display commemorating this fortieth anniversary of the Marshall plan. I was struck by the sign on a burnt-out, gutted structure that was being rebuilt. I understand that Berliners of my own generation can remember seeing signs like it dotted throughout the western sectors of the city. The sign read simply: "The Marshall plan is helping here to strengthen the free world." A strong, free world in the West, that dream became real. Japan rose from ruin to become an economic giant. Italy, France, Belgium – virtually every nation in western Europe saw political and economic rebirth; the European Community was founded.

'In West Germany and here in Berlin, there took place an economic miracle, the *Wirtschaftswunder*. Adenauer, Erhard, Reuter and other leaders understood the practical importance of liberty – that just as truth can flourish only when the journalist is given freedom of speech, so prosperity can come about only when the farmer and businessman enjoy economic freedom. The German leaders reduced tariffs, expanded free trade, lowered taxes. From 1950 to 1960 alone, the standard of living in West Germany and Berlin doubled.

'Where four decades ago there was rubble, today in West Berlin there is the greatest industrial output of any city in Germany – busy office blocks, fine homes and apartments, proud avenues and the spreading lawns of parkland. Where a city's culture seemed to have been destroyed, today there are two great universities, orchestras and an opera, countless theatres and museums. Where there was want, today there's abundance – food, clothing, automobiles – the wonderful goods of the Ku'damm. From devastation, from utter ruin, you Berliners have, in freedom, rebuilt a city that once again ranks as one of the greatest on earth. The Soviets may have had other plans. But my friends, there were a few things the Soviets didn't count on – *Berliner Herz, Berliner Humor, ja, und Berliner Schnauze* [Berliner heart, Berliner humour, yes, and the Berliner dialect].

'In the 1950s, Khrushchev predicted: "We will bury you." But in the West today, we see a free world that has achieved a level of prosperity and wellbeing unprecedented in all human history. In the communist world, we see failure, technological backwardness, declining standards of health, even want of the most basic kind – too little food. Even today, the

Soviet Union still cannot feed itself. After these four decades, then, there stands before the entire world one great and inescapable conclusion: freedom leads to prosperity. Freedom replaces the ancient hatreds among the nations with comity and peace. Freedom is the victor.

'And now the Soviets themselves may, in a limited way, be coming to understand the importance of freedom. We hear much from Moscow about a new policy of reform and openness. Some political prisoners have been released. Certain foreign news broadcasts are no longer being jammed. Some economic enterprises have been permitted to operate with greater freedom from state control.

'Are these the beginnings of profound changes in the Soviet state? Or are they token gestures, intended to raise false hopes in the West, or to strengthen the Soviet system without changing it? We welcome change and openness; for we believe that freedom and security go together, that the advance of human liberty can only strengthen the cause of world peace. There is one sign the Soviets can make that would be unmistakable, that would advance dramatically the cause of freedom and peace.

'General Secretary Gorbachev, if you seek peace, if you seek prosperity for the Soviet Union and eastern Europe, if you seek liberalisation, come here to this gate! Mr Gorbachev, open this gate! Mr Gorbachev, tear down this wall!

'I understand the fear of war and the pain of division that afflict this continent – and I pledge to you my country's efforts to help overcome these burdens. To be sure, we in the West must resist Soviet expansion. So we must maintain defences of unassailable strength. Yet we seek peace; so we must strive to reduce arms on both sides.

'Beginning ten years ago, the Soviets challenged the Western alliance with a grave new threat, hundreds of new and more deadly SS-20 nuclear missiles, capable of striking every capital in Europe. The Western alliance responded by committing itself to a counter-deployment unless the Soviets agreed to negotiate a better solution; namely, the elimination of such weapons on both sides. For many months, the Soviets refused to bargain in earnestness. As the alliance, in turn, prepared to go forward with its counter-deployment, there were difficult days – days of protests like those during my 1982 visit to this city – and the Soviets later walked away from the table.

'But through it all, the alliance held firm. And I invite those who protested then – I invite those who protest today – to mark this fact: because we remained strong, the Soviets came back to the table. And because we remained strong, today we have within reach the possibility, not merely of limiting the growth of arms, but of eliminating, for the first time, an entire class of nuclear weapons from the face of the earth.

'As I speak, NATO ministers are meeting in Iceland to review the progress of our proposals for eliminating these weapons. At the talks in Geneva, we have also proposed deep cuts in strategic offensive weapons. And the Western allies have likewise made far-reaching proposals to reduce the danger of conventional war and to place a total ban on chemical weapons.

'While we pursue these arms reductions, I pledge to you that we will maintain the capacity to deter Soviet aggression at any level at which it might occur. And in cooperation with many of our allies, the United States is pursuing the Strategic Defence Initiative – research to base deterrence not on the threat of offensive retaliation, but on defences that truly defend; on systems, in short, that will not target populations, but shield them. By these means we seek to increase the safety of Europe and all the world. But we must remember a crucial fact: East and West do not mistrust each other because we are armed; we are armed because we mistrust each other. And our differences are not about weapons but about liberty. When President Kennedy spoke at the city hall those twenty-four years ago, freedom was encircled, Berlin was under siege. And today, despite all the pressures upon this city, Berlin stands secure in its liberty. And freedom itself is transforming the globe.

'In the Philippines, in South and Central America, democracy has been given a rebirth. Throughout the Pacific, free markets are working miracle after miracle of economic growth. In the industrialised nations, a technological revolution is taking place – a revolution marked by rapid, dramatic advances in computers and telecommunications.

'In Europe, only one nation and those it controls refuse to join the community of freedom. Yet in this age of redoubled economic growth, of information and innovation, the Soviet Union faces a choice: it must make fundamental changes, or it will become obsolete.

'Today thus represents a moment of hope. We in the West stand ready to cooperate with the East to promote true openness, to break down barriers that separate people, to create a safe, freer world. And surely there is no better place than Berlin, the meeting place of East and West, to make a start. Free people of Berlin: today, as in the past, the United States stands for the strict observance and full implementation of all parts of the Four Power Agreement of 1971. Let us use this occasion, the 750th anniversary of this city, to usher in a new era, to seek a still fuller, richer life for the Berlin of the future. Together, let us maintain and develop the ties between the Federal Republic and the western sectors of Berlin, which is permitted by the 1971 agreement.

'And I invite Mr Gorbachev: let us work to bring the eastern and western parts of the city closer together, so that all the inhabitants of all Berlin can enjoy the benefits that come with life in one of the great cities of the world.

'To open Berlin still further to all Europe, east and west, let us expand the vital air access to this city, finding ways of making the commercial air service to Berlin more convenient, more comfortable and more economical. We look to the day when West Berlin can become one of the chief aviation hubs in all central Europe.

'With our French and British partners, the United States is prepared to help bring international meetings to Berlin. It would be only fitting for Berlin to serve as the site of United Nations meetings, or world conferences on human rights and arms control or other issues that call for international cooperation.

'There is no better way to establish hope for the future than to enlighten young minds, and we would be honoured to sponsor summer youth exchanges, cultural events and other programmes for young Berliners from the east. Our French and British friends, I'm certain, will do the same. And it's my hope that an authority can be found in East Berlin to sponsor visits from young people of the western sectors.

'One final proposal, one close to my heart: sport represents a source of enjoyment and ennoblement, and you may have noted that the

Republic of Korea – South Korea – has offered to permit certain events of the 1988 Olympics to take place in the North. International sports competitions of all kinds could take place in both parts of this city. And what better way to demonstrate to the world the openness of this city than to offer in some future year to hold the Olympic Games here in Berlin, East and West?

'In these four decades, as I have said, you Berliners have built a great city. You've done so in spite of threats – the Soviet attempts to impose the East-mark, the blockade. Today the city thrives in spite of the challenges implicit in the very presence of this wall. What keeps you here? Certainly there's a great deal to be said for your fortitude, for your defiant courage. But I believe there's something deeper, something that involves Berlin's whole look and feel and way of life – not mere sentiment. No one could live long in Berlin without being completely disabused of illusions. Something instead, that has seen the difficulties of life in Berlin but chose to accept them, that continues to build this good and proud city in contrast to a surrounding totalitarian presence that refuses to release human energies or aspirations. Something that speaks with a powerful voice of affirmation, that says yes to this city, yes to the future, yes to freedom. In a word, I would submit that what keeps you in Berlin is love – love both profound and abiding.

'Perhaps this gets to the root of the matter, to the most fundamental distinction of all between East and West. The totalitarian world produces backwardness because it does such violence to the spirit, thwarting the human impulse to create, to enjoy, to worship. The totalitarian world finds even symbols of love and of worship an affront. Years ago, before the East Germans began rebuilding their churches, they erected a secular structure: the television tower at Alexander Platz. Virtually ever since, the authorities have been working to correct what they view as the tower's one major flaw, treating the glass sphere at the top with paints and chemicals of every kind. Yet even today when the sun strikes that sphere – that sphere that towers over all Berlin – the light makes the sign of the cross. There in Berlin, like the city itself, symbols of love, symbols of worship, cannot be suppressed.

'As I looked out a moment ago from the Reichstag, that embodiment of German unity, I noticed words crudely spray-painted upon the wall, perhaps by a young Berliner: "This wall will fall. Beliefs become reality." Yes, across Europe, this wall will fall. For it cannot withstand faith; it cannot withstand truth. The wall cannot withstand freedom.

'And I would like, before I close, to say one word. I have read, and I have been questioned since I've been here, about certain demonstrations against my coming. And I would like to say just one thing, and to those who demonstrate so. I wonder if they have ever asked themselves that if they should have the kind of government they apparently seek, no one would ever be able to do what they're doing again.

'Thank you and God bless you all.'

BIBLIOGRAPHY

Aristotle. *Aristotle's Rhetoric and Poetics*, translated by W. Rhys Roberts (*Rhetoric*) and Ingram Bywater (*Poetics*). New York: Modern Library, 1954.

Aristotle. *The Ethics of Aristotle*, translated by J. A. K. Thomson. Harmondsworth: Penguin, 1953.

Axtell, Roger E. *Essential Do's and Taboos: The Complete Guide to International Business and Leisure Travel*. Hoboken, NJ: John Wiley, 2007.

Barnes, Jonathan. *Aristotle*. Oxford: Oxford University Press, 1982.

Bartlett, John. *Bartlett's Familiar Quotations*, 15th and 125th anniversary edition, revised and enlarged, edited by Emily Morison Beck. Boston: Little, Brown, 1980.

Bosrock, Mary Murray. *Asian Business Customs and Manners*. New York: Meadowbrook Press, 2007.

Boulton, Adam. *Tony's Ten Years: Memories of the Blair Administration*. London: Simon & Schuster, 2008.

Brown, Gordon. *Moving Britain Forward: Selected Speeches 1997–2006*, edited by Wilf Stevenson. London: Bloomsbury, 2006.

Buchan, John. *The King's Grace 1910–1935*. London: House of Stratus, [1935] 2001.

Buck, Philip W. (editor). *How Conservatives Think*. Harmondsworth: Penguin, 1975.

Buckley, William F., Jr. *Let Us Talk of Many Things: The Collected Speeches*. Roseville, CA: Forum, 2000.

Bunche, Ralph J. *Ralph Bunche: Selected Speeches & Writings*, edited by Charles P. Henry. Ann Arbor: University of Michigan Press, 1995.

Burnet, Andrew (editor). *Chambers Book of Speeches*. Edinburgh: Chambers, 2006.

Bush, George H. W. *Speaking of Freedom: The Collected Speeches*. New York: Scribner, 2009.

Bush, George W. *United We Stand: A Message for All Americans*. Ann Arbor, MI: Mundus, 2001.

Bush, George W. *We Will Prevail: President George W. Bush on War, Terrorism, and Freedom*. New York: Continuum, 2003.

Cambridge Editorial Partnership. *The Greatest American Speeches: The Stories and Transcripts of the Words That Changed Our History*. London: Quercus, 2006.

Cameron, David and Jones, Dylan. *Cameron on Cameron: Conversations with Dylan Jones*. London: Fourth Estate, 2008.

Campbell, Alastair. *The Blair Years: Extracts from the Alastair Campbell Diaries*. London: Hutchinson, 2007.

Campbell, Karlyn Kohrs and Jamieson, Kathleen Hall. *Deeds Done in Words: Presidential Rhetoric and the Genres of Governance*. Chicago: University of Chicago Press, 1990.

Chávez, César. *An Organizer's Tale: Speeches*, edited by Ilan Stavans. London: Penguin, 2008.

Churchill, Winston. *Blood, Toil, Tears and Sweat: The Great Speeches*, edited by David Cannadine. London: Penguin, [1989] 2002.

Churchill, Winston. *Never Give In! The Best of Winston Churchill's Speeches*, selected by his grandson, Winston S. Churchill. London: Pimlico, 2003.

Cicero. *De Oratore*, translated by E. W. Sutton and H. Rackham. London: William Heinemann, 1942.

Cicero. *Selected Political Speeches*, with revisions, translated by Michael Grant. London: Penguin, 1969.

Cmiel, Kenneth. *Democratic Eloquence: The Fight over Popular Speech in Nineteenth-Century America*. New York: William Morrow, 1990.

Cody, Edward. 'Mass honors Polish President: ash keeps many leaders away', *Washington Post*, 19 April 2010.

Connolly, Joy. *The State of Speech: Rhetoric & Political Thought in Ancient Rome*. Princeton, NJ: Princeton University Press, 2007.

Copeland, Lewis, Lamm, Lawrence W. and McKenna, Stephen J. *The World's Greatest Speeches: 229 Speeches from Pericles to Nelson Mandela*, 4th enlarged edition. Mineola, NY: Dover, 1999.

Cuomo, Mario. *More Than Words: The Speeches of Mario Cuomo*. New York: St Martin's Press, 1993.

Dale, Iain. *500 of the Most Witty, Acerbic and Erudite Things Ever Said about Politics*. Petersfield: Harriman House, 2007.

Dallek, Robert and Golway, Terry. *Let Every Nation Know: John F. Kennedy in His Own Words*. Naperville, IL: Sourcebooks MediaFusion, 2006.

Deaver, Michael K. *A Different Drummer: My Thirty Years with Ronald Reagan*. New York: HarperCollins, 2001.

Denby, David. *Snark: It's Mean, It's Personal, and It's Ruining our Conversation*. New York: Simon & Schuster, 2009.

Dimitrius, Jo-Ellen and Mazzarella, Mark. *Reading People: How to Understand People and Predict Their Behavior – Anytime, Anyplace*. New York: Random House, 1998.

Dobson, J. F. *The Greek Orators: The Beginnings of Oratory*. Chicago: Ares, 1918.

Edwards, Lee. *William F. Buckley Jr.: The Maker of a Movement*. Wilmington, DE: ISI, 2010.

Ehrlich, Henry. *Writing Effective Speeches: The Ultimate Guide to Making Every Word Count*, revised and updated edition. New York: Reed Business Press, 2004.

Esquire. *The Handbook of Style: A Man's Guide to Looking Good*. New York: Hearst, 2009.

Everitt, Anthony. *Cicero: A Turbulent Life*. London: John Murray, 2001.

Fast, Julius. *Body Language*, revised and updated edition. New York: MJF, 2002.

Flew, Antony. *Thinking about Social Thinking: The Philosophy of the Social Sciences*. Oxford: Basil Blackwell, 1985.

Flew, Antony. *Thinking Straight*. Buffalo, NY: Prometheus, 1977.

Garrison, Daniel H. *Who's Who in Wodehouse*, second revised edition. New York: International Polygonics, 1989.

Gelderman, Carol. *All the President's Words: The Bully Pulpit and the Creation of the Virtual Presidency*. New York: Walker, 1997.

Gilbert, Martin. *Churchill: A Life*. London: Heinemann, 1991.

Golway, Terry. *Together We Cannot Fail: FDR and the American Presidency in Years of Crisis*. Naperville, IL: Sourcebooks MediaFusion, 2009.

Golway, Terry. *Words That Ring through Time: From Moses and Pericles to Obama, Fifty-One of the Most Important Speeches in History and How They Changed Our World*. New York: Overlook Press, 2009.

Goodrich, Chauncey A. *Select British Eloquence: Embracing the Best Speeches Entire of the Most Eminent Orators of Great Britain for the Last Two Centuries*. Indianapolis: Bobbs-Merrill, [1832] 1963.

Gottheimer, Josh (editor). *Ripples of Hope: Great American Civil Rights Speeches*. New York: Basic Civitas, 2003.

Grant, Tony (editor). *From Our Own Correspondent: A Celebration of Fifty Years of the BBC Radio Programme*. London: Profile, 2005.

Greer, Shane (editor). *So You Want to Be a Politician*. London: Biteback, 2010.

Grice, Andrew. 'PM's tactics puzzling as rebel MPs plot against him', *The Independent*, 10 January 2004.

Hansen, Drew D. *The Dream: Martin Luther King, Jr. and the Speech That Inspired a Nation*. New York: Ecco, 2003.

Harré, Rom. *Personal Being: A Theory for Individual Psychology*. Cambridge, MA: Harvard University Press, 1984.

Hawthorne, Julian (editor). *Orations of American Orators*, volumes I and II. New York: Collier, 1900.

Hawthorne, Julian (editor). *Orations of British Orators*, volumes I and II. New York: Collier, 1900.

Heald, Tim (editor). *The Best After-Dinner Stories*. London: Folio Society, 2003.

Heffer, Simon (editor). *Great British Speeches: A Stirring Anthology of Speeches from Every Period of British History*. London: Quercus, 2007.

Henderson, Jeanette and Henderson, Roy. *There's No Such Thing as Public Speaking: Make any Presentation or Speech as Persuasive as a One-on-One Conversation*. New York: Prentice Hall, 2007.

Hitchens, Christopher. *Why Orwell Matters*. New York: Basic, 2003.

Holdforth, Lucinda. *Why Manners Matter: The Case for Civilized Behavior in a Barbarous World*. New York: G. P. Putnam's Sons, 2009.

Holmes, Richard. *In the Footsteps of Churchill*. London: BBC, 2005.

Holzer, Harold. *Lincoln at Cooper Union: The Speech That Made Abraham Lincoln President*. New York: Simon & Schuster, 2004.

Hughes, Dominic and Phillips, Benedict. *The Oxford Union Guide to Speaking in Public*. London: Virgin, 2000.

Humes, James C. *Speak like Churchill, Stand like Lincoln: 21 Powerful Secrets of History's Greatest Speakers*. Roseville, CA: Prima, 2002.

Humes, James C. *Speaker's Treasury of Anecdotes about the Famous*. New York: Harper & Row, 1978.

Huxley, Aldous. *Eyeless in Gaza*. London: Chatto & Windus, 1936.

Jamieson, Kathleen Hall. *Eloquence in an Electronic Age: The Transformation of Political Speechmaking*. New York: Oxford University Press, 1988.

Jamieson, Kathleen Hall. *Packaging the Presidency: A History and Criticism of Presidential Campaign Advertising*. New York: Oxford University Press, 1984.

Jamieson, Kathleen Hall and Birdsell, David S. *Presidential Debates: The Challenge of Creating an Informed Electorate*. New York: University Oxford Press, 1988.

Jenkins, Roy. *Churchill*. London: Macmillan, 2001.

Johnson, Paul. *Churchill*. New York: Viking, 2009.

Jones, Nicholas. *Soundbites and Spin Doctors: How Politicians Manipulate the Media – and Vice Versa*. London: Cassell, 1995.

Jones, Susan. *Speechmaking: The Easy Guide to Writing and Giving Speeches*, new edition. London: Politico's, 2004.

Jordan, Barbara. *Speaking the Truth with Eloquent Thunder*, edited by Max Sherman. Austin: University of Texas Press, 2007.

Keegan, John. *Winston Churchill: A Life*. New York: Penguin, 2002.

Kemp, Rod and Stanton, Marion (editors). *Speaking for Australia: Parliamentary Speeches That Shaped Our Nation*. Crows Nest, NSW: Allen & Unwin, 2004.

Kenin, Richard and Wintle, Justin (editors). *The Dictionary of Biographical Quotation of British and American Subjects*. New York: Knopf, 1978.

Kennedy, George A. *The Art of Persuasion in Greece*. Princeton, NJ: Princeton University Press, 1963.

Kennedy, George A. *Classical Rhetoric and Its Christian and Secular Tradition: From Ancient to Modern Times*. Chapel Hill: University of North Carolina Press, 1980.

Kennedy, George A. *A New History of Classical Rhetoric*. Princeton, NJ: Princeton University Press, 1994.

Kennedy, John F. *Let the Word Go Forth: The Speeches, Statements, and Writings of John F. Kennedy 1947–1963*, selected by Theodore C. Sorensen. New York: Delacorte Press, 1988.

King, Martin Luther, Jr. *A Testament of Hope: The Essential Writings and Speeches of Martin Luther King, Jr.*, edited by James M. Washington. San Francisco: Harper & Row, 1986.

Koch, Edward I. *The Koch Papers: My Fight against Anti-Semitism*. New York: Palgrave Macmillan, 2008.

Lincoln, Abraham. *The Language of Liberty: The Political Speeches and Writings of Abraham Lincoln*, edited by Joseph R. Fornieri. Washington, DC: Regnery, 2009.

Lucas, Stephen E. *The Art of Public Speaking*, 9th edition. Boston: McGraw Hill, 2007.

Lukacs, John. *Blood, Toil, Tears and Sweat: The Dire Warning – Churchill's First Speech as Prime Minister*. New York, Basic, 2008.

MacAfee, Norman (editor). *The Gospel According to RFK: Why It Matters Now*. Boulder, CO: Westview Press, 2004.

MacArthur, Brian (editor). *The Penguin Book of Historic Speeches*. London: Viking, 1996.

MacArthur, Brian (editor). *The Penguin Book of Twentieth Century Speeches*, fully revised and updated edition. London: Penguin, 1999.

Mandela, Nelson. *Nelson Mandela: In His Own Words*, edited by Kader Asmal, David Chidester and James Wilmot. New York: Little, Brown, 2003.

Martin, Judith and Nakayama, Thomas. *Experiencing Intercultural Communication: An Introduction*, 3rd edition. Boston: McGraw Hill, 2008.

Mays, Benjamin E. *Born to Rebel: An Autobiography*. New York: Scribner, 1971.

Metcalf, Allan. *Presidential Voices: Speaking Styles from George Washington to George W. Bush*. Boston: Houghton Mifflin, 2004.

Minow, Newton N. and Lamay, Craig L. *Inside the Presidential Debates: Their Improbable Past and Promising Future*. Chicago: University of Chicago Press, 2008.

Molloy, John T. *Dress for Success*. New York: P. H. Wyden, 1975.

Morgan, Nick. *Give Your Speech, Change the World: How to Move Your Audience to Action*. Boston: Harvard Business School Press, 2003.

Morrison, Terri and Conaway, Wayne A. *Kiss, Bow or Shake Hands: The Bestselling Guide to Doing Business in More Than 60 Countries*, 2nd edition. Avon, MA: Adams Media, 2006.

Murphy, James J. *Rhetoric in the Middle Ages: A History of Rhetorical Theory from St Augustine to the Renaissance*. Berkeley: University of California Press, 1974.

Nabokov, Vladimir. *Speak, Memory: An Autobiography Revisited*. New York: Putnam, 1966.

Noonan, Peggy. *John Paul the Great: Remembering a Spiritual Father*. New York: Viking, 2005.

Noonan, Peggy. *On Speaking Well: How to Give a Speech with Style, Substance, and Clarity*. New York: Regan, 1999.

Noonan, Peggy. *What I Saw at the Revolution: A Political Life in the Reagan Era*. New York: Random House, 1990.

Noonan, Peggy. *When Character Was King: A Story of Ronald Reagan*. New York: Viking, 2001.

Obama, Barack. *The Inaugural Address 2009*. London: Penguin, 2009.

Olive, David. *An American Story: The Speeches of Barack Obama*. Toronto: ECW Press, 2008.

Orwell, George. 'Politics and the English Language', in *George Orwell: A Collection of Essays*. San Diego: Harcourt Brace, 1981.

Pease, Allan and Pease, Barbara. *The Definitive Book of Body Language*. New York: Bantam, 2006.

Peter, Laurence J. *Peter's Quotations: Ideas for Our Time*. New York: William Morrow, 1977.

Pindar, Ian. *The Folio Book of Historic Speeches*. London: Folio Society, 2007.

Poole, Steven. *Unspeak: How Words Become Weapons, How Weapons Become a Message, and How That Message Becomes Reality*. New York: Grove Press, 2006.

'Program provides stability for families on the brink: Faith-based organization in Tarrant County offers housing for up to 2 years', *Fort Worth Star Telegram*, 20 September 2008.

Puellella, Philip. 'Pope meets with 8 who were abused by priests', *Washington Post*, 19 April 2010.

Quintilian. *The Institutio Oratoria of Quintilian*, translated by H. E. Butler, 4 vols. London: William Heinemann, 1920.

Reagan, Ronald. *Speaking My Mind: Selected Speeches*. New York: Simon & Schuster, 1989.

Reed, Thomas B. (editor). *Modern Eloquence*, 15 vols. New York: American Law Book, 1903.

Reiman, Tonya. *The Power of Body Language: How to Succeed in Every Business and Social Encounter*. New York: Pocket, 2007.

Remini, Robert V. and Golway, Terry (editors). *Fellow Citizens: The*

Penguin Book of US Presidential Inaugural Addresses. New York: Penguin, 2008.

Rhoades, Geri. *The Warrior and the Little Girl: Create Power and Joy in Your Work Life*. Newton, MA: Tanzanite Press, 2005.

Richards, Paul (editor). *Tony Blair: In His Own Words*. London: Politico's, 2004.

Robinson, Peter. *How Ronald Reagan Changed My Life*. New York: Regan, 2003.

Roloff, Michael E. and Miller, Gerald. *Persuasion: New Directions in Theory and Research*. Beverly Hills, CA: Sage, 1980.

Rorty, Amélie Oksenberg (editor). *Essays on Aristotle's Rhetoric*. Berkeley: University of California Press, 1996.

Rose, Norman. *Churchill: An Unruly Life*. London: Taurus Parke Paperbacks, [1994] 2009.

Ross, Raymond. *Speech Communication: Fundamentals and Practice*, 4th edition. Englewood Cliffs, NJ: Prentice Hall, 1977.

Russell, Henry (editor). *The Politics of Hope: The Words of Barack Obama*. London: New Holland, 2009.

Safire, William (editor). *Lend Me Your Ears: Great Speeches in History*, updated and expanded edition. New York: W. W. Norton, 2004.

Seldes, George. *The Great Thoughts*. New York: Ballantine, 1985.

Sharpley-Whiting, T. Denean. *The Speech: Race and Barack Obama's 'A More Perfect Union'*. New York: Bloomsbury, 2009.

Shirley, Craig. *Rendezvous with Destiny: Ronald Reagan and the Campaign That Changed America*. Wilmington, DE: ISI, 2009.

Sorensen, Ted. *Counselor: A Life at the Edge of History*. New York: HarperCollins, 2008.

Stephens, Philip. *Tony Blair: The Making of a World Leader*. New York: Viking, 2004.

Stevenson, Charles L. *Ethics and Language*. New Haven, CT: Yale University Press, 1944.

Strunk, William, Jr. and White, E. B. *The Elements of Style*, 2nd edition with revisions, an introduction, and a chapter on writing. New York: Macmillan, 1972.

Suriano, Gregory R. *Great American Speeches*. New York: Gramercy, 1993.

Thatcher, Margaret. *The Collected Speeches*, edited by Robin Harris. London: HarperCollins, 1997.

Usborne, Richard. *The Penguin Wodehouse Companion*. Harmondsworth: Penguin, 1988.

Waldman, Michael. *POTUS Speaks: Finding the Words That Defined the Clinton Presidency*. New York: Simon & Schuster, 2000.

White, Ronald C. Jr. *The Eloquent President: A Portrait of Lincoln through His Words*. New York: Random House, 2005.

Widmer, Ted. *American Speeches: Political Oratory from Abraham Lincoln to Bill Clinton*. New York: Library of America, 2006.

Wirthlin, Dick, with Hall, Wynton C. *The Greatest Communicator: What Ronald Reagan Taught Me about Politics, Leadership, and Life*. Hoboken, NJ: John Wiley, 2004.

Worek, Michael. *My Fellow Americans: Presidents Speak to the People in Troubled Times*. Buffalo, NY: Firefly, 2009.

INDEX